Evidence and explanation in social science

Evidence and explanation in social science

An interdisciplinary approach

Gerald Studdert-Kennedy
Faculty of Commerce and Social Science
University of Birmingham

Routledge & Kegan Paul
London and Boston

First published in 1975
by Routledge & Kegan Paul Ltd
Broadway House, 68-74 Carter Lane,
London EC4V 5EL and
9 Park Street,
Boston, Mass. 02108, USA

Printed in Great Britain by
Unwin Brothers Limited
The Gresham Press, Old Woking, Surrey
A member of the Staples Printing Group

© *Gerald Studdert-Kennedy 1975*

ISBN 0 7100 8157 X

Contents

Figures

Acknowledgments

It is possible that a few of my former students will look at this book, whether out of nostalgia or a less sentimental curiosity. They will recognize some material and some preoccupations. But if, as I hope, they also find something less depressing than a disinterred course, much of the credit is theirs. They were patient with earlier approaches to what I attempt here, and they argued me out of several unrewarding enthusiasms. A number of colleagues read parts of the manuscript at various stages and drew my attention to inadequacies. I am particularly grateful to David Coates, Dick Degerman, Joe Kaufert and Adrian Leftwich.

It was to have been written in collaboration with T. V. Sathyamurthy, Since that idea was dropped, he has given me the best of the bargain, relentless criticism, relentless encouragement and apt suggestions in greater numbers than I would dream of advertising. Most of them have been incorporated in one way or another, though what has become of them is my responsibility alone. I have accepted these gifts in the spirit of what the anthropologist Marshall Sahlins calls generalized reciprocity, in which 'the counter is not stipulated by time, quantity or quality', thereby acknowledging both the value I place on our personal and working relationship and the inadequacy of my contribution to it.

My wife Judith introduced me to important and relevant discussions among biologists. She has also been patient, but not too patient, with work in progress. I am deeply grateful to her.

I am grateful for permission to reproduce the following material: Figures 1 and 2 from E. Evans-Pritchard, The Nuer, Oxford University Press, 1940; Figure 3 from Marshall Sahlins, 'The segmentary lineage: an organisation of predatory expansion', American Anthropologist, 63, no. 2, 1961; Figure 4 from David Butler and Donald Stokes, Political Change in Britain, Macmillan, London and Basingstoke, and St Martin's Press, New York, 1969; Figure 7 from Keith Hope, Elementary Statistics, Pergamon Press, 1967; Figure 8 from Robert Putnam, 'Toward explaining military intervention in Latin American politics',

Acknowledgments

World Politics, 20, no. 1 (copyright © 1967 by Princeton University Press).

Finally, I would like to thank Jenny Jones and Jenny Saxby for their generous help with the typescript.

CHAPTER ONE

Equilibrium and historical change

I

This book attempts to explore some of the difficulties and
ambiguities that lie behind a familiar set of distinctions, between fact and theory or, to be more cautious, evidence and
explanation. It is written from a point of view—that of the social
scientist particularly interested in politics—which is sometimes
credited with a coherence and consistency for which there is in
fact very little basis indeed. The most cursory survey of a
voluminous literature reveals a variety of approaches to the
analysis of political phenomena, both within and between related
disciplines. These reflect different assumptions, which are
sometimes incompatible, about the nature of theory or explanation, and they therefore turn to confront the 'facts' or the
evidence on different terms. One might begin to account for
this copious variety of approaches by pointing out that different
disciplines are concerned with different aspects of social experience, that they ask different kinds of question and in consequence develop their own appropriate forms of explanation.
They each make a contribution to a comprehensive understanding of a process that is phenomenally complex. This is obviously
true. University departments with distinguishable, if overlapping, interests have proliferated as scholars have elaborated
and sophisticated their different modes of inquiry. There may
be other less acceptable reasons for increasing compartment-
alization in the social sciences. It may have undesirable
consequences which need to be offset by promoting interdisciplinary research and encouraging students to study for
joint degrees. But it is inevitable that different kinds of inquiry
should develop distinctive methodologies and conceptual frameworks, and these are unlikely to achieve rigour or sophistication
unless they are refined intensively by specialists.

However, the student of politics is perhaps peculiarly aware of
being planted at a crossroads where several more specialized
kinds of inquiry are bound to intersect and where very different

kinds of demand are being made on what he thinks of as his
subject matter. If he is often tempted to be something of an
historian, he is also required to pursue elaborate ethical and
philosophical questions and project these into an analysis of
complex events. Psychologists and social psychologists demand
his attention as they open up many aspects of the dynamics of
group behaviour. Demographers and economists insist that
whatever the relevance of the factors these specialists examine,
they have effects only within the context of broadly determining
processes, and that these must be analysed in terms of their
own dynamics. The list could be extended. Above all there is
the insistent demand to be 'scientific', whatever that may mean,
which introduces a medley of objectives and criteria which are
often less well established in the disciplines that bred them than
social scientists have always realized.

It is an uncomfortable situation, and it is out of the question to
be casually eclectic. Different disciplines may, broadly speaking,
be concerned with different kinds of questions and they may have
devised different and appropriate ways out of their respective
difficulties. But where the questions cluster around the preoccupations of the student of politics, we have to ask if the
various forms of explanation are congruent or incongruous.
Our inquiry is bound to be interdisciplinary, but we cannot
simply assume that the fragmentary insights will inevitably add
up into some kind of whole. We cannot take the methodologies of
other disciplines for granted. Indeed, we cannot think of distinguishing the methods of handling evidence from all the other
aspects of an explanation, the form in which problems are posed,
the assumptions that are made about the nature of reality. In
short, in order to decide if the oblique light thrown on our problems by alternative perspectives illuminates or misleads, we
have to come to terms with the epistemological problems these
alternative perspectives raise. And this, to complicate life
further, involves more than becoming some kind of jack-of-all-
trades, because many of our most interesting problems involve
a hybrid situation in which a mode or form of explanation that
is standard in one area has been translated into another in
order to deal with very different, but yet in some sense analogous evidence.[1] We have to recognize the fact that the interdisciplinary approach, which is increasingly referred to as the
inevitable next phase of development in the social sciences, involves very much more than a broad-minded accumulation of
complementary perspectives. It is essential to evade the restrictions of institutional boundaries and to poach on other
people's preserves when the problems seem to demand it, but

any advance will have to be earned by spending what may seem to be an inordinate amount of time questioning the whole basis of what we are doing at any given point.[2] Barry concludes his recent critique of what he sees as the dominant types of approach to explanation and theory with bleak pessimism.[3]

> The most striking fact, to me at least, is how primitive is the stage things are still in.... When I say that this is an under-developed area I am not primarily referring to the fact that books are thin on the ground, but to the distance still to go to the goal of verified theories and general propositions.

He is measuring this elementary state of confusion against certain assumptions about what kind of an animal a theory might or should be, but it is hard to disagree with his broad judgment. Another sceptic, who was also concerned with other general approaches to the study of politics, is quite as blunt. 'The fact is that the language of contemporary political science and its representation of social phenomena are inadequate, and nothing short of a fundamental rethinking and reformulation of the epistemological foundations of the discipline is sufficient.'[4] Cross-fertilization from other disciplines has undeniably stimulated the study of politics, but it is also, and increasingly, exposing its confusions and difficulties.

We can only begin to come to terms with these conclusions by trying to explore them in detail. No fundamental reformulation will emerge from these pages; but a discussion that deals with the difficulties experienced in a number of related attempts to marshal evidence into persuasive patterns and explanations should at least raise some of the significant issues and indicate where some productive opportunities lie. A consideration of the analysis of stability and change, which continues as the main theme of the book, serves as an introduction to the kind of critical analysis which the inadequacies of the language of political science oblige us, at this stage, to engage in. At this point it might be as well to proceed to an example without further prefatory generalization.

II

Almost exactly in the centre of Africa, wedged in between the Congo and Uganda, lies Rwanda, the northern segment of the former trust territory of Rwanda-Urundi. The original inhabitants of the area, now in a small minority of about 5 per cent of the population, are physically small, somewhat larger than true pygmies. They hunt and make pottery. For centuries they have formed the quite insignificant lower caste in the society. They are known as Twa, and for our present purposes we can forget about them. Another small minority, about 10 per cent of the population, was for some centuries in undisturbed occupation of the top layer of the social system. These were the latest arrivals on the scene. They were warriors, tall, light-skinned, the owners of cattle and the guardians and beneficiaries of the dominant pastoral values of the society. They are known as Tutsi. A German visitor, writing in 1916, says:[5]

> The longer one has travelled in negro countries, and the better one has got acquainted with the negro character, the more one is impressed with the proud reserve of the Tutsi. There is no restless curiosity, no noise, partly fearful, partly goodhearted welcome, as with most other negroes. The tall fellows stand still and relaxed, leaning over their spears while watching the Europeans pass or approach, as if this unusual sight did not impress them in the least.

The Tutsi had a literature that celebrated the virtues of their longhorned cattle and quite explicitly advanced the ideological premise of the fundamental inequality of man. The Premise of Inequality is in fact the title of an analysis of this society by the French anthropologist J. J. Maquet,[6] which provides a starting point for our discussion. A characteristic moment of inspiration in Tutsi oral poetry is the following: 'You cow, who save me the shame and fatigue of the hoe'. A critical fact, which a Marxist would seize on instantly as basic to the analysis of this society, was that all the cows in Rwanda were owned by Tutsi. It was not the versatility of this breed of cattle that saved their owners from the shame and labour of digging, but the fact that the system of property ownership involving cattle was the means by which they controlled the rest of the population. This 85 per cent remaining of the population were dark-skinned and of normal build. They had previously dominated the Twa, but had been defeated in Tutsi invasions. They were known as Hutu. Their access to cattle was through a complicated system of personal clientship, binding individual Hutu to individual Tutsi. In return for the staples provided by cattle and for physical protection from their patrons, who were the soldiers as well as the aristocrats of the society, they formed the labour force and produced the surplus that maintained the military and administrative élite. In 1960 only 3 out of 604 chiefs or sub-chiefs were Hutu.

Some early observers have claimed that this structure of subordination, the premise of inequality, was maintained by straightforward physical coercion on the part of the Tutsi. If this were the case, the complexities of this supposedly primitive political system would be of no particular interest to us. But Maquet proposes a much less straightforward explanation of the extraordinary stability of the system. The relationship was originally established by force, but force is a very expensive sanction to use in order to maintain a complex division of labour in a society, with its attendant inequalities of opportunity and obligation. The threat of mere coercion may well be relevant to an explanation of the 'success' of the system, but Maquet looks to other evidence as well. The facts he selects as relevant, the questions and preoccupations he has on his mind and the explanation he offers are determined by a very specific perspective, which is considered here as an example of a strong tradition in social anthropology.

Maquet describes the society in terms of a stable system of relations. Generally, a system consists of a set of interdependent parts or processes, such that variations at one point in the system necessarily stimulate repercussions and reactions elsewhere in the system, and such that there is a tendency for the structure of the system of relations to remain relatively stable. If there are new or unfamiliar stimuli impinging on the system from its outside environment, it will attempt to adapt, but it will attempt to do so as an integrated and as it were organic whole, without radically altering the structure of relationships it has evolved to cope with the problem of survival. Maquet sees the kingdom of Rwanda as a system of functionally interrelated parts, of purposive structures and adaptive processes.

In one form, the idea of a political system is as old as the study of politics. Aristotle classified the Greek city states with reference to their dominant institutional characteristics. The notion of a system of institutional checks and balances that are designed to disperse power and provide a contrivance for controlling the resolution of conflict and for making decisions is perfectly familiar to the student of political institutions. But Maquet is looking outside the formal institutional structures to a complex of beliefs, acknowledged obligations and expectations which define for people the nature of the society to which they belong. He expects to find a system of beliefs and values or perhaps interlocking, reciprocal systems of beliefs and values which motivate people to continue behaving in certain ways and as it were define the range of possible forms of behaviour that seem to people practicable and conceivable. Of course, beliefs, informal rules of conduct, attitudes towards the symbols and guardians of power and authority and so on are not 'facts' of the kind for which we can ever secure unequivocal evidence. We may choose to infer the existence of certain psychological states from the behaviour we observe, from statements and actions. The behaviour we observe may be sufficiently regular and emphatic to encourage confident in-ferences, but clearly we encounter a major problem here for any analytical approach whatsoever. By what kind of imagina-tive projection are we to identify how someone, quite possibly in a very alien situation, experiences life, and how can we determine the relationships between his perceptions and his behaviour?

In any event, the system Maquet identifies has to be described simultaneously in terms of an ingenious institutionalized struc-ture and of what we may refer to loosely as an ideology, a set of shared beliefs about the nature of social relationships. For example, the institution of clientship—the mutual expectations entertained by patron and client—was governed by elaborate norms which had the effect of reducing or providing outlets for potentially destructive tensions and hostilities. The Tutsi patron could always recover his cows if his Hutu clients failed to deliver the agreed quantities of produce. However, if the patron chose to go beyond the accepted norms governing the exploitation of clients, his Hutu dependant could move to another patron, after performing some simple ritual gesture of sever-ance. The effectiveness of the right to do this was guaranteed by rivalries among the ruling class. The more clients you could recommend, the more distinguished a figure you cut, so you naturally tried to avoid losing clients, and you might even try attracting new ones.

There were elaborations on this basic hierarchical relationship which helped ensure the stability of the system. Certain con-ventions preserved its integrity. Like Plato's guardians, with whom, by all accounts, they would readily have identified them-selves, the Tutsi aristocrats were given a special education. Tutsi who fell on hard times would be leased cattle, in return for non-menial services, by richer members of the caste. These would be subleased to Hutu, thereby protecting the social standing of indigent gentry.

The centralized authority structure of Rwanda threw a complex latticework over these basic ethnic relations. All members of the society were involved in three separate authority structures.

Territorial chiefs ran a system of tax collection, on a local basis. But dues for military services of the Tutsi were separately collected. Finally, there was an overall network of loyalty relations, culminating in the mwami or king, who was seen by Hutu and Tutsi alike as a divine and paternal figure representing the whole society.

Some of the other integrative factors represent a considerable political achievement and it would be wrong to think of them as emerging with a kind of organic inevitability out of the situation in which these oddly assorted groups found themselves. The country itself is exceedingly difficult to administer in a centralized way. It lies along a mountainous spine between the basins of the Congo and the Nile. Communications are very difficult and administrative delegation is inevitable. The nature of the terrain would seem to encourage the development of independent bailiwicks and very local loyalties. However, the royal court presided over a series of hierarchies of chiefs, each one controlling different aspects of the subject's obligations. There were even two chiefs with the same territorial jurisdiction, one of whom was concerned only with food revenues, the other with taxes on livestock. So jealousy and mistrust among the chiefs were maintained. Coalitions against a strong mwami were difficult to organize. The system as a whole profited from these horizontal tensions, in the sense that they were part of a stable equilibrium of checks and balances.

One would expect the main tensions to be the vertical or hierarchical ones, between Tutsi and Hutu, since the former gained quite disproportionately from the situation. But the Hutu, it is apparent from the evidence, also believed in the premise of inequality. What we might describe, in Gramsci's term, as a hegemonic ideology,[7] constituted their experience of the nature of things. The authority of the Sovereign, the ruling caste, was maintained in the last resort by Hobbes's primary sanction of fear. But it was also maintained by custom, habit and belief. There had evolved an agreed set of values which established the legitimacy, in the eyes of the subjects, of the existing distribution of property and authority, and of the system of customary law that defined rights and obligations, to the advantage of Tutsi, the disadvantage of Hutu. That does not mean that the Hutu actually liked being dominated or that they did not resent the arrogance of their betters. It does mean that, as long as the system was permitted to continue largely un-affected by the strong external pressures of the colonial powers, there was no sort of collective feeling that anything about the structure of political and social relations was properly open to

significant change or modification. The Tutsi had conquered
some 400 years back, and things had gone on long enough for
the nature of the society to be regarded as primordially established.

The persuasiveness of Maquet's explanation of the stability of
this society lies in the implications he reads into the networks
of economic, political and ritual relationships which he was able
to observe. His observations accumulate, not simply as a series
of ethnographic details, but into a description of a distinctive
set of checks and balances, a social contrivance of legitimate
sanctions, customary laws and the distribution through inheritance of the activities requisite to maintain internal order and
external security. There is an implicit analogy with some kind
of organic system; the regular performance of particular activities and the repetition of established patterns of interaction is
both dependent on and in turn sustains the general stability of
the system. Society itself is a seamless web and the past, like
the Cartesian deity, becomes relevant only in the general and
remote sense of representing whatever force set the mechanism
in motion.[8] The explanatory problem for Maquet was to identify
the components of the equilibrium. He avoids the objection that
he is presenting a formal and mechanical picture, by locating
the most fundamental coherence of the society in what Leach
has described as an 'ideal system',[9] an agreed idea of how the
society ought to be ordered. It was ideal in the sense that the
society only approximated to it—individual Tutsi might lack the
social or physical characteristics of the true aristocrat, or the
individual mwami might fail to live up to the expectations of
his role—but the ideal system provided a coherent set of criteria which made sense of life for the individual and committed
him to the expected forms of behaviour without an overt invocation of sanctions. We need not suppose that an overall social
and political stability was the conscious objective of any individuals within the system, but this was, according to Maquet,
for a long time the result of their consensus.

This system no longer exists. It disappeared finally in a series
of appalling massacres of Tutsi by Hutu. A CMS missionary,
writing after the first in 1959 said:[10]

> Very many [Hutu] were compelled by terrorist tactics to
> join the bands (indeed these were the majority). Many we
> saw were stunned and ashamed that such things could be.
> Many were resentful but dared not show their resentment.
> They called the war muyaga—the wind, something that comes
> you know not whence, and goes you know not whither.

We have a detailed historical account of the two kingdoms[11] and there is space for no more than a cursory outline here. Very shortly after independence there was a popular uprising against a Tutsi clique which had attempted to install a new mwami and, after the elections, large numbers of Tutsi fled to Burundi, as it is now called. Some of them established a terrorist organization, known as Inyenzi or the Cockroaches, with the intention of recovering the Tutsi heritage by force. For about eighteen months there was relative peace; the old feudal contracts were abrogated and the Hutu former clients took over two-thirds of their patrons' cattle, but not more, whilst Tutsi continued in Rwanda as essential trained personnel. The later massacres of 1963 were a spontaneous reaction to three unsuccessful invasions of Rwanda by Tutsi attempting to return to their former homes. The invasions seemed to threaten the Hutu with a return to their former subordinate status, in a reunited Rwanda-Urundi. The massacres demonstrated that the system had gone, and with it the system of beliefs and values that had given coherence to the lives of its members.

Even a cursory historical account can point to some obvious explanatory factors. The stability of the system had for some time been more apparent than real. The distribution of power it embodied had been maintained by the colonial presence in the interests of administrative convenience, first by the Germans from 1890 under the agreement reached at the Berlin Conference of 1884, and then by the Belgians under League of Nations mandate and United Nations trusteeship. The European powers introduced new factors which were bound in the long run to undermine the old coherence of organization and ideology. Arabica coffee had been introduced and was being successfully farmed by the Hutu, with important consequences for their former economic dependence. Missionaries had been active, challenging by the style of their personal relations with Africans the apparently 'natural' hierarchy of genetic endowment. It had become normal for numbers of Hutu to emigrate temporarily to Uganda (and in particular to Buganda) to work, where they were introduced to new ideas. Lemarchand attempts to assess the contribution of such general developments and of particular occurrences and personalities to the course of recent events.

We naturally look for an historical account of what happened, but how does this demand affect our willingness to accept the contrasting explanations implicit in Maquet's description of the defunctive social system? By organizing his description in

terms of an implicit analogy with an organic system, he may
have accepted the impossibility of writing a real history of a
non-literate African community, and in this he represents a
distinctive strand in the discipline of social anthropology. The
idea of writing a history of such a society had generally been
taken to be rather pointless.[12] There is, for a start, no written
evidence of any consequence, and oral traditions require very
special treatment if they are to be used to reconstruct an actual
historical past, as opposed to a past that contemporaries for
one reason or another find it necessary or convenient to believe
in.[13] Even if some historical account were feasible, it might
have little more value than a chronology of Old Testament
worthies or a chronicle of the fortunes of medieval kings. But
anthropologist and historian start, at least, by raising different
questions. The concern of the anthropologist is the behaviour
he himself observes, the interconnectedness of things in the
society that interests him. Where the evidence itself is sparse
and suspect and where the problem of explaining manifest
changes does not force an historical dimension on him, it is
hardly surprising that he should turn to the subsisting conditions and look there for an explanation of the enduring stability
of the social system. The central question does not appear to
be posed in historical terms, so another form of explanation can
be developed that dispenses with or modifies the historian's
focus on processual change, causes and consequences. The
broad general rubric which identifies such an explanation is
that of the 'functional' or systemic theory or explanation. If not
exactly anti-historical, it is at least ahistorical. As a preface
to an historical account, Maquet's analysis must strike one as
oddly disconnected from the dramatic and bloody sequel.

Obviously, a problem of evidence rises in many different forms
and the historian of non-literate societies is not its only victim.
It is always necessary to consider how the availability of some
forms of evidence and the absence of others in any given instance help to shape the conduct of an analysis and at times to
determine the nature of the conclusions and the implications of
an explanation.

But an explanation reflecting this organic analogy may also
have the effect of ensuring that there will be certain kinds of
subsequent events which will escape the frame of reference.
A synchronic analysis of a social system that, as it were, chops
a thin slice out of historical time, inevitably merges structure
and process. An inventory of the relationships observed over
a short period of time, and assumed to be stable and persistent
regularities, establishes the essential 'facts', the structure that

maintains the social and political process. But what if these patterns of 'facts' dispose themselves rather differently if they are observed at a different point in time? Is there anything in the first functional explanation that makes sense of the intervening modifications? The concepts of equilibrium or stability (which are not equivalents, as we shall see) that are implicit in this kind of functional explanation can accommodate marginal adjustments in response to pressures from outside the system. But how substantial do these adjustments have to be before we are forced to concede that the system as it was originally described has been fundamentally changed? And if we do make this concession, what possibilities are open to us? Must we start de novo to describe a new system, fall back on narrative, or look to some other form of explanation?

Such questions about the missing historical dimensions also lead us to wonder about the nature of the elements or 'parts' that are integrated in such an anthropologist's model of a specific and stable system. Professor Radcliffe-Brown is generally regarded as the most outstanding representative of the British (and subsequently the Chicago) school of social anthropology, and is therefore regularly pressed into service, despite his disclaimers, by critics in need of a straw man. He provides us with a condensed general answer.[14]

> direct observation does reveal to us that these human beings are connected by a complex network of social relations. I use the term 'social structure' to denote this network of actually existing relations. It is this that I regard it as my business to study if I am working, not as an enthnologist or psychologist, but as a social anthropologist. I do not mean that the study of social structure is the whole of social anthropology, but I do regard it as being in a very important sense the most fundamental part of the science.

But, to confront Maquet's system of social relations with the later history of the 'actually existing' relations he explored is to raise the awkward question of what it is exactly that we understand by a relationship. A relationship, as opposed to a random encounter, is presumably a recurrent or continuing interaction of some kind between individuals which is invested by them with some kind of meaning. The manifestations of a relationship may persist, though one or more of those involved may be shifting his subjective interpretation of them and evaluating them in a new way. In Rwanda, cattle taxes continued to be paid till the revolution, but no doubt with a surly acquiescence that would have quite different implications from those of the uncritical resignation that may have been associated with this part of the social process in former times.

A structure of relationships is no more stable than the values that interpret them for the participants over time, and anthropologists are in fact well aware of the dangers of synchronic studies in this respect. They expect to discover, from second and third field trips, not only that forms have changed, but also that persisting institutions seem to occupy new positions in the system because the values they previously organized have changed. A synchronic analysis raises this problem particularly clearly, but it should be pointed out at once that this, too, is very far from being a private occupational disorder of the social anthropologist. As we shall see, it is a major problem for any social scientist, even where he is explicitly concerned with the time dimension. It is, for example, a fundamental problem in the analysis of political participation, voting behaviour and political parties.

Finally, Maquet creates a fundamental difficulty in the use of the concept of change itself. The strength of the latent organic analogy is such that his model of the social system seems to deny the society any potential of its own for generating an historical and transformative process. Evidently the virus must be introduced from outside. There are the missionaries, the coffee beans, the hesitant Belgian administrators who, in Lemarchand's account, suddenly swing their backing from Tutsi to Hutu at the time of Independence. Within the frame of reference of the analysis, the virus is a random infliction. And yet, all these factors, though they have been distinguished from the system that is subjected to change, are integrally involved in the historical development of Rwanda.

By fastening on this particular account of this particular kingdom, we are bound to fall upon a stark contrast between two broadly different kinds of explanation. In what follows we can examine and considerably qualify this contrast, both by considering a number of other 'functional' or systemic explanations and by distinguishing different levels of historical explanation. But, whatever the qualifications to come, the contrast is real enough. We have one picture of a political kingdom, during its long, stable and, in a curious sense, timeless phase, in terms of interconnections, reciprocities, checks and balances, regularities of behaviour; we have another that suddenly erupts out of the former, violent, confused, unpredictable, whose events cannot be explained as the dependable results of regular systemic features, but rather in the form of a breathless historical narrative that tries, as best it can, to piece together a unique and unrepeatable story. We could simply leave it at that, keeping the two categories of explanation in separate compartments, as it were for different purposes, one for the analysis of stability, and the other to account in some measure for change. But that would shelve some important questions.

The general form of explanation reflected in Maquet's analysis developed in anthropology to a great extent as a reaction to an earlier historical type of explanation. This contained some naïve evolutionary assumptions. It is hardly a caricature to say that the central idea was that nineteenth-century European society represented the spearhead, or at least the bridgehead, of social evolution, and that societies of a different kind were undergoing a more primitive phase of development. Primitive societies were a providential reminder of how far European man had come. This assumption, which organized the interpretation of a mass of ethnographic data in Sir James Frazer's Golden Bough, [15] has long been discredited among anthropologists; however, it is worth pointing out in passing that a good deal of recent literature by sociologists and political scientists on change in the so-called underdeveloped countries makes remarkably similar assumptions—that democratic and pluralistic social and political systems, such as those of some highly industrialized countries, are the inevitable, necessary and desirable products of certain stages of economic and technological development.

But the functionalist form of explanation has very important roots in earlier political theory as well, that is to say that it has affinities with a mode of analysis that is explicit about its speculative and normative import. The political theorists in the European tradition that conventionally begins with Plato and Aristotle have argued simultaneously about the manifest or observable, and the potential nature of men and of societies. They can all be said to have attempted to persuade their readers to accept their assumptions about the true nature of man and then to be convinced by the speculative conclusions they constructed upon them. To varying degrees they have attempted to explain specific historical actualities, but their concern has invariably been to construct abstract systems of relations, relations between concepts that seem to identify and summarize, but above all to evaluate the essential features of individual and collective relationships. To the extent that any form of analysis, historical or 'systemic', is involved in passing judgments and evaluating the alternatives open to societies and political actors, it is part of and incorporates the terms of

reference of this philosophical tradition. Attempts at systematic and scientific analysis and explanation in the social
sciences and in history are frequently evasive and inexplicit
about their connections with the normative aspects of their
procedures. Very often, behind competing explanatory theories
and perspectives there lie differences that are anterior to the
choice of specific problems, the nature of relevant evidence, or
the appropriateness of a particular methodology. These differences emerge from contrasting assumptions about the nature
of explanation and our understanding of social behaviour. A
closer examination of the apparent polarity between functional
or systemic, and historical forms of explanation uncovers a
whole series of ways in which the evidence can be constituted
into relevant 'fact', classified and assimilated to the conceptual
structure of an explanation. These are not convenient alternatives to apply variously to appropriately matched problems, so
much as perspectives stemming from alternative epistemological assumptions. Such assumptions constitute more or less
explicit definitions of the nature of social reality rather than
propositions that can be directly subjected to test. It may be
possible to identify their roots, in a descriptive or philosophical
tradition, or in the dynamics of a conflict precipitated by the
psychological development of an exceptional individual. But that
in itself provides no criterion of their validity.

In the case of Maquet and the functional anthropologists we can
go to one venerable source in political theory, at a point where
the analysis of Radcliffe-Brown's 'actually existing relations'
began to assume importance in a distinctively modern way, but
where the focus of concern was a philosophical debate, in this
instance mainly with Thomas Hobbes.

'Mankind', wrote Montesquieu, in a passage that is frequently
quoted, 'are influenced by various causes; by the climate, by the
religion, by the laws, by the maxims of government, by precedents, morals and customs; whence is formed the general spirit
of nations.'[16] The range of variation between possible com-
pounds that different proportions of these elements may create
in different societies is, as he recognized, enormous, and it is
the object of his monumental work to reduce this range to a
manageable number of types, to make it possible to compare
complex entities and to generalize about the similarities and
differences between the various categories. His intention is
analogous to that of the contemporary economist or psychologist who uses the statistical techniques of factor or cluster
analysis to organize otherwise unmanageably complex information by subjecting it, through the good offices of a computer, to

what are, in effect, mathematically sophisticated forms of
averaging. At a later stage we shall have to consider the role
of quantitative analysis in comparative studies, as well as its
uses for social anthropologists, political scientists and others.
But for the most part, the anthropologist, like Montesquieu,
cannot readily put numbers on things to simplify either his
problems of comparison or the problem of deciding what the
relative weight of different factors should be in his explanation.

For Montesquieu, the complex compound which he seeks to
identify is the 'general spirit' of any given society, and this,
Aron points out, 'is not a partial cause comparable to the others,
but a product of that totality of physical, social and moral
causes. But it is a product which enables us to understand what
constitutes the originality and unity of a given collectivity.'[17]
However, as Montesquieu himself points out, 'This subject is
very extensive. In that crowd of ideas which presents itself to
my mind, I shall be more attentive to the order of things than
to the things themselves. I shall be obliged to wander to the
right and to the left, that I may investigate and discover the
truth.'[18] Anthropologists have always wandered in directions
indicated by Montesquieu—no serious monograph fails to begin
by setting its community's social relationships in their ecological milieu, for example—but the analysis of a 'totality of
causes' is a pretty grand ambition. As Hugh Stretton has
recently pointed out, we tend to think in terms of the 'two dear
old-fashioned figures of speech used to express the complexities of social change; "endless chains of cause and effect", and
"the seamless web of history" '.[19] To the problem of identifying
chains of cause and effect we must return, but Montesquieu did
not underestimate the problems of tracing out the totality of
causes or, as the anthropologist would more reticently put it,
the interconnectedness of things. How does one begin to unravel
a seamless web? The problem, he pointed out, was the 'surfeit
of facts', the endless recession of interconnections. Only the
crudest doctrinaire is content with sociological or political
analysis that is not, in contemporary jargon, multifactorial and
trying to be comprehensive, but some factors are going to seem
more important than others. In some senses, the question of
the relative importance of different factors, the threads that one
should pursue in an analysis, cannot be decided by observation
and testing, because the choice is implicated in an epistemology,
in the prior evaluations and assumptions through which a
problem is formulated and confronted. So an analysis that pur-
ports to present a totality, an explanation of a complete or
comprehensive system or process, must in fact be highly selec-

tive, an abstraction from the confused surfeit of facts, of those interconnections between those factors that are critical to the mind of the analyst. This is not to say that the selection of factors is random or arbitrary, or that it should not be challenged by evidence or alternative conceptual formulations, on the contrary. But the selection of facts, and the nature of the abstract system or pattern of cause and effect that is suggested, reflect the outcome of a highly complicated psychological process. It involves an interplay between the observation of evidence and those patterns of selective perception that have been encouraged by a particular discipline of inquiry or derive from more general ideological preferences. An evaluation of the product involves an assessment of this process.

Maquet, in this particular analysis, was clearly much less interested in chains of cause and effect than in a regular recurrence of reciprocal causes and effects, interconnections that combined to sustain a remarkably stable social structure and organization.[20] His emphasis is on the values or ideology which established the consensus on the 'ideal system'. This is given greater emphasis than the coercive features of the system. It would be unfair to say that he is predicting eternal stability for his system, but the potential agents and vehicles of change are, as it were, extraneous to the structure of interrelations he has abstracted from the surfeit of facts. His emphasis on the pattern of forces maintaining a particular stability has a blind side to it, which we can see as a sleeping legacy of the tradition in theory that was shaped by Montesquieu. Behind such a perspective is a sense, and even a reverence, for the organic nature of a society, its complexity, its 'natural' process of slow and integrated adaptation. Indeed social anthropologists have frequently echoed Montesquieu's condemnation of meddlesome social engineering which is based on a fragmentary understanding of the functional interdependencies of the system. Clearly, in the general form of such an analytical perspective, there is a cautious and conservative bias. And there are, of course, famous attempts to transpose a similar search for functional relationships and systemic totalities to highly differentiated societies, for example by the American sociologists Parsons and Merton, where similar criticisms are reinforced by the suspicion that any transformative process that might develop in the society would be characterized as undesirable in a normative sense because it disrupted the existing state of 'equilibrium'.

However, there is no simple and necessary connection between the use of a particular model of the social system and such broadly conditioning philosophical assumptions. Maquet cannot fairly be criticized with those who have made a heavy ideological investment in the analytical categories of consensus and integration. As he points out elsewhere,[21] he sees the synchronic model as a snapshot, as it were, that freezes and allows us to contemplate the interacting components of a social system in a period of relative equilibrium. When the equilibrium goes, the model must be discarded. In his particular example, it seems reasonable to suppose that the society had been in a state of structural equilibrium for very many years. His model abstracts certain recurrent relationships, of power, of authority and of mutual obligation, and describes the stability of the social totality in terms of a hypothesis about the mutually integrating effect of these relationships. The injection of some fresh factor may, quickly or over time, undermine the internal adjustment of the system.

But there are objections to accepting even the more modest claims of a synchronic functional model. If factors precipitating change are introduced into the system, the model ceases to be valid. But at what point? The difficulty is that such factors become part of the system of relationships, generally take time to realize their potential and then have uneven consequences. In some respects, in the formal structure and presumably in the beliefs of the Tutsi élite, and at least of some others, the features isolated in the synchronic model continued well into the colonial period. The model defines these as the system, and factors introducing change as exogenous to it. However, these exogenous factors had infiltrated the system and shifted the nature of social relations from early on in the colonial period. The frozen gestures of the snapshot make no allusion to these as maturing components of the social system. At least we can object that the scope claimed for a theory explaining structural continuity has not been made clear. We might also wonder about the hypothesis on which the theory is based. The integrity of the system depended, according to the model, on the functional integration of a structure of belief and various economic and political organizing principles. But if, during the most interesting period of Rwandan history, the model has no means of qualifying the notion of integration by taking account of the historical variation affecting different components of the system, we are left with an excessively indeterminate picture of whatever combination of interacting elements constitutes or has constituted the social totality.

Maquet's analysis has obviously been chosen as an extreme example of an explanation based on the hypothetical integration

of certain general regularities. The model is something of a
straitjacket. It reifies a particular pattern of observations and
classifies others inflexibly as external to the theoretical system.
At the same time, the problem raised by the uneven nature of
social change suggests that the focus and contrast of the snapshot are not sharp enough to support the necessary assumptions
about the nature of social integration. There are many other
anthropological studies, some of which will be considered in the
following chapter, which are more self-consciously oriented
towards capturing the essential dimensions of social and
political change and more sensitive to the reproach that the
methodology of the social anthropologist represents a formal
denial of the relevance of history. However, before turning to
these and to the light they throw on some very basic concepts,
such as structure, stability and equilibrium, we should briefly
consider two points which will become important later.

III

The first point has to do with the differences between an account
of change that emerges from a general interpretation of regularities of behaviour in a society, and an historical account
which is constructed round a chronology.

Maquet's functional analysis fits plausibly with what is known
about the pre-colonial kingdom of Rwanda. Thereafter its
theoretical validity becomes increasingly dubious and it does
not claim to offer insights into the shape and direction of relatively recent events. Generalization so diffuse is hard to
challenge and consequently unrewarding to pursue back into the
evidence. One might reasonably argue, shrugging off this contribution from social science, that the only possible kind of
explanation for the drastic and bloody changes that overtook the
kingdom of Rwanda around the time of its independence would
emerge from a very detailed historical account. So much
happened in such a short space of time, and so many tactical
decisions were taken by the participants on the basis of uncertain information, that the development of events was constantly and significantly affected by occurrences that were not
in any specific sense predictable or part of a regular process
of any kind. Certainly, the historian would note facts that were
the unique products of an unrepeatable combination of cross-
currents in time and space. Such unique contingencies are of

course an embarrassment in the pursuit of laws or generalizations about social and political change, and where they follow thick and fast they may be totally frustrating.

In the political theory of Machiavelli, the contingent events of history fall into the residual category of chance or <u>fortuna</u>, the determinants of which cannot be either foreseen or controlled. The traditional figure of the bitch goddess does not appear in the pantheon of the contemporary theorist, but he still requires, in his generalizing explanations, a residual category of chance or random events.[22] He need not assume that such events are totally arbitrary or malicious, or lack causes which can in principle be located. But he thinks of them as random in a special sense. His interest in generalization of one kind or another directs his attention, naturally enough, to those factors that seem to him most generally, and most powerfully, determinative of the type of development or state he is interested in explaining. If he is successful, his generalizations will hold for whole categories or classes of events. Their precision will depend on the impact of other factors, and it is these he thinks of as introducing random variations into the broad patterns his generalizations identify. But, clearly, where stable and structured patterns of behaviour are undergoing extreme and rapid change, these 'random' events may be highly determinative and of great interest to the historian. The most rewarding type of explanation in this case may be an explanation in terms of specific antecedent or efficient causes through a meticulous reappraisal of unique events. Other types of explanation may be defeated by the nature of the evidence, or may simply be inappropriate.[23]

However, this contrast between the generality of the social scientist and the concrete particularity of the historian is a contrast between extremes. The contrast is sometimes referred to as a starting point for discussion of the differences between the two general modes of explanation. But historians constantly make generalizations, even generalizations about structures and beliefs that are essentially similar to those made in our illustration from the anthropological literature. Likewise, one's objection to Maquet's analysis may not be that it consists of a structure of generalizations, so much as that his generalizations needed to be more highly differentiated, elaborating differences between subgroups, regional variations and so on. The result would have been a less elegant picture of the whole, but it might have got closer to the relevant tensions and pressures. This may seem an obvious point, but discussions that fail to get beyond it are quite common.

The second point concerns the level of abstraction of the categories of an explanation. The questions that can be asked about
any particular sequence of events can be framed to resolve very
different kinds of uncertainty. For the purposes of some questions, the relevant 'facts' may be there in the particular events
of terrorism, invasion and massacre that characterized relations between the Tutsi and the Hutu in the early sixties. Other
explanations may refer to these same facts, but in much more
abstract terms. The particular events find themselves absorbed,
as it were, into the terms of a discussion that seeks to reduce
the complexity of events by a process of abstraction into a set
of interrelated and compendious concepts, such as 'class' or
'caste' or 'colonialism'. As we shall see, every identification
of the 'facts' in political and historical explanation is an act of
abstraction; our problems have to do with the implications of
these different degrees of abstraction and with their validity.
However, it would be quite mistaken to confuse this point, that
interesting questions may be asked about the course of political
events at very different levels of abstraction, with differences
between the types of explanation pursued by the various disciplines. Many historians have identified patterns and features of
historical change that could only be described in a vocabulary
of broad abstractions, however meticulous their sifting of
specific sources and materials. We shall see that there is no
essential difference between the problem of evaluating these
abstractions as they are advanced by historians or by other
kinds of social scientist. An explanation of social and political
changes in Rwanda cries out for the introduction of concepts
such as 'class' or 'caste', at least on the face of it, and an
historian might well turn to them. But their utility and validity
can only be assessed, as has been suggested here, by exploring
the latent assumptions that tie them together or distinguish
them in the mind of the analyst, and by seeing what factors,
relationships, patterns, they identify in the surfeit of facts and
which they single out as critical.

CHAPTER TWO

Versions of structure

I

The contrast between the synchronic and the historical explanation, which is also, by implication, a contrast between stability
and change, is too stark and simplistic to survive much further
discussion. Certainly, it would be unfair to suggest that Maquet
is indifferent to the dynamics of social change or supposes that
an understanding of structural regularities can only account for
continuities of form and organization. But in this account he
does take a representative stance that has deep roots in the
discipline of social anthropology. His explanation makes strong
assumptions about the structural components of the social
system and their functional integration. It is also presented in
such a way as to raise unanswerable questions about the nature
of that integration at any given point in time. It is not easy,
therefore, to say exactly what it is that the explanation accounts
for, but neither does it seem reasonable to treat his model of
the Rwandan social system as a merely arbitrary abstraction
from the available data. He invokes a complex of factors, and
places them in relation to each other in a system of relationships that would at least seem arguable to his colleagues. The
specific emphases of his study seem to press a contrast between
quite distinct kinds of explanation, but there seems to be no
reason for regarding these as logically incompatible.

The discussion in this chapter attempts to explore the possibilities of a type of explanation that concerns itself with systemic
regularities, and with the functional interdependence of the
components of a social totality. It does so from within the
tradition of the social anthropologists, and in a highly selective
manner. The examples that are compared here develop different
aspects of the theoretical core of the discipline, though they are
not necessarily the obvious landmarks in an intellectual history,
and there is no solid consensus among social anthropologists as
to their relative importance.[1]

There are a number of advantages in attempting to consider

general conceptual and methodological problems as they are
refracted through this particular body of material. To an
observer leaning over the fence from an adjacent discipline, the
social anthropologist seems to have the advantage of working
within a field that is in some respects unusually coherent and
integrated. The coherence does not, to be sure, reflect any
easily achieved agreement among individual anthropologists. On
the contrary, one very soon comes to think of major names in
the field as points round which intellectual hostilities polarize
with a clarity that is at least partly a function of strong differences of personality and temperament.[2] The sense of coherence
has more to do with the nature of the arguments and the scope
of the explanations that are being attempted. A strong ethnographic tradition, a focus on careful observation and the rigorous
compilation of data, is bonded to a level of theoretical discussion
that is explicitly oriented towards articulating a comprehensive
analysis. Theoretical categories identify the major interlocking
processes of a totality of relationships within a specific and
theoretically circumscribed social environment, and, whatever
the disagreements about them (kinship, age-set, ritual and so on)
or about their hypothetical interconnections, they have to be
identified in operational terms. As a matter of professional
skill, this appears to be done with an eye for systematic method
at least as sharp as is to be found among political scientists in
general.[3] It is within a context sensitive both to an empirical
method, with its limitations, and to the theoretical reconstruction of complex social configurations that the disagreements
take place.[4] This integration of theory and evidence may be
more apparent than real, but the field does offer the possibility
of considering the relationship between the two within a common
arena. The political scientist has a more confused time of it.
His discipline survives in eclectic pluralism, where an unreliable mutual tolerance substitutes for integration. Departmental
arrangements tend to recognize and institutionalize a gulf
between theory and method, theory and institutions, theory and
process. This is reflected, for example, in characteristically
indecisive assertions of the 'relevance' of theorists such as
Hobbes, Burke and Mill to the meticulous siftings of the better
electoral studies. These are the great achievements of the
positivist strand in modern political science, but the ambivalence of their findings in the context of a generalized theory
of democracy is by now notorious. The generalizations of
political theory are both complex and abstract, and relate to
behavioural patterns that cannot be compactly identified in the
pluralist structures of a complex society.[5] Even substantial
accumulations of 'hard' evidence tend to relate to the level of

theoretical discussion as fragments, with the result that there is considerable uncertainty about the best point of leverage for a critical assessment.[6] It may simply be illuminating to begin a discussion of problems that are of general importance in the social sciences within a less obviously fractured discipline.

It may also be very naïve to do so, as an outsider who has not even passed through the anthropologist's rite de passage of a period of fieldwork; but the justification for a certain kind of naïvety in interdisciplinary understandings has already been argued by a distinguished anthropologist.[7] So without hoping to disarm criticism, we can at least see how far these studies take us into the question of explanation in the social sciences.

There are other and more particular advantages in this strategic choice of material. In an obvious sense, the accelerating contemporary transformation of the human environment is driving the anthropologist, or at least his most familiar stereotype, out of business. Quite simply, there is an increasing and irreversible shortage of relatively unmodified 'traditional' societies to study. It has not taken much wit to point out that the collective response of the anthropologists has been an eminently functional one. They have simply redefined the boundaries of their discipline. This adaptation has not been simply expedient, a bid for academic survival. It is a logical development that has brought the anthropologist much closer to the historian in the diachronic analysis of structural change. It has brought him closer to the political theorist and the economist in a concern with the material concomitants of change and its implications for the quality of life within particular societies and communities.[8] He is alongside the sociologist in that the craft and theory of fieldwork are being used to explore social and political processes in societies that are generally taken to be modern and developed.[9]

These are general justifications for discussing a particular body of studies. The examples fill out the contours of conceptual and methodological questions that cannot be left as a matter of naïve concern by any social scientist.

This chapter takes one stage further a consideration of the theoretical categories of structure, stability and equilibrium, which clearly organize Maquet's ethnographic data. We should come to see that, ubiquitous though these concepts are in the social sciences, they cannot be given a comprehensive glossary definition, because each of them straddles a basic dilemma, namely the question of the relationship between the theory or interpretations of the observer and the social reality or interpretations of those he observes. What is structure a structure of? Is it a relation among independent observed entities, or an interpretation, a patterning of perceptions that somehow satisfies the intellectual requirements of the observer? On what grounds can social behaviour be described as being in a state of stability or equilibrium? We can only ask such questions of specific studies that make use of these categories in their explanations. When we do so, it is common to come upon studies that confuse what is relevant and meaningful to the analyst with what may be relevant and meaningful to those he claims to be studying. The difficulties the anthropologist normally encounters in the field over language and idiom dramatize this problem, and must at least make him sensitive to the tentative nature of his reconstruction of orientations within an alien society. For social scientists working within their own cultures the problem may be masked by the 'common sense' assumptions in the light of which they interpret their data.[10]

This tension between the analyst's use of theoretical categories and the social reality he claims to interpret does not evaporate when it is discovered. Different interpretations of similar data may reflect incompatible positions on fundamental epistemological issues, and therefore form part of the inconclusive debate over what Sheldon Wolin describes as alternative 'visions' of the nature and possibilities of man in society.[11] Essentially similar data may be transposed from an ebullient major to a tragic minor key in a fundamentally different interpretation. It may be impossible to resolve such a conflict of understandings by any further resort to evidence; the mood of the interpretation is in some sense an independent decision. But it is also the case that we can negotiate fresh understanding by trying to come to terms with other formulations of the questions that may be asked. The studies we are concerned with in what follows represent an intellectual tradition in this sense: that we can see fundamental epistemological shifts emerging out of a common frame of reference. But we also see interpretations being less drastically modified in response to finer adjustments of focus.

It is convenient to begin with the general notion of a social system as an organically integrated whole.

II

The use of some kind of organic analogy in the analysis of

social structure and organization is well established in Western
social theory. The metaphor may at times be little more than a
literary convenience.[12] It has frequently been exploited as part
of a vivid political rhetoric.[13] But it may be present as a latent
and powerful image, organizing a perspective on social reality
and structuring analysis. The organicist concepts of the health
and sickness of a society orient Durkheim's analysis, for
example. And he is an important link between Montesquieu, on
whom he wrote early in his career, and later social anthropologists.[14] In social anthropology the image is pervasive. We are
concerned with research programmes that are committed to the
vision of societies as complex totalities. The idea of a scientifically valid dissection of an integrated social physiology
expresses the analytical ideal. Systematic practice is embedded
in pre-scientific assumptions about the nature of society. What
has to be assessed in each case is the relationship between the
method that probes the dimensions of a social reality, and the
explicit and inexplicit assumptions of the general orientation.
Thus, Radcliffe-Brown is explicitly committed to the assumption
that any significant pattern of behaviour that could be observed
in the empirical world of groups and institutionalized relationships would find a place on analysis as a functional unit in a
network of reciprocities. An explanation of the whole would
consist of a description of all these significant regularities, an
exposition of how the energies of the parts combine to sustain
the whole and ensure its survival and orderly adaptation. But, he
insists, only an intensely controlled method can hope to establish
these reciprocities. Montesquieu's work had been crowded with
'functional explanations', in which apparently remote features
of a society were interrelated, and these interactions made to
explain yet other characteristics by means of ad hoc hypotheses
engagingly disguised as factual assertions. For example, he
establishes quite breathtaking connections between the cold
climate of Europe, the tendency of European men to drink
immoderately, the relative equality of women, and the success of
Christianity.[15] Radcliffe-Brown regards such conjectural
explanations, common enough in the ethnographic literature from
which he departed, with bleak disfavour, because they consist of
hypotheses that cannot be verified—imaginative and plausible
perhaps, but outside the reach of falsification. He is positive
that no explanation of an observed relationship should be taken
seriously by a social scientist unless it is framed in a way that
acknowledges the possibility that it can, in principle, be confronted with contradictory evidence and ruled out of court.[16]

As he sees it, the answer to the problem of a scientific method is to be found in three systematic activities. The first consists in making certain abstractions from the surfeit of available and observable 'facts' about a society. The second consists in subjecting these patterns of abstracted characteristics to a process of classification. The third is to make logical comparisons between the groups and subgroups that have emerged. Together, these steps are the basis for explanations that will ideally take the form of general laws, or at least of very powerful generalizations about classes and types of situation, relationship or event. These will be comprehensive and presumably capable of yielding predictions. The task of the observer, in sum, is to categorize, to classify, to compare and, finally, to generalize without falsifying the particular.

The remainder of this chapter is for the most part concerned with the first of these analytical activities—the selection of particular patterns of observations and their presentation as factual evidence by means of a set of abstract categories. Chapter 3 will begin to explore some problems of classification and comparison.

The following examples serve to show how particular facts come to be invested with significance by being absorbed into the categories of a general explanation. Each explanation within the common tradition of inquiry seeks to justify itself by an implicit definition of comprehensiveness, which is met in its ability to accommodate a range of often surprisingly disparate evidence. But in each case there is leverage for critical objection. It may seem reasonable to argue that a critical dimension has been avoided, historical time, for example. The implications of a particular use of concepts, such as structure or system, may be restrictive or meet epistemological objections.

III

In his discussion of the analysis of kinship systems, Radcliffe-Brown classifies an odd assortment of tribes into two groups.[17] One includes the Omaha Indians, other Sioux and Algonquin Indians, such as Osage, Winnebago and Fox, the Miwok of California, the Nandi and Bathonga of East Africa, some tribes among the Lhota Nagas of Assam and some New Guinea tribes. The second group includes the Choctaw Indians, other south-eastern tribes such as the Cherokee, the Crow and Hidatsa of the Plains, the Hopi, groups in the Banks Islands in Melanesia

and one community in West Africa. His assertion of important
similarities within these groups is entailed in the significance
he sees in kinship. In each case observations uncovered
anomalies, as we would tend to see them, in the ways individuals
habitually described their relatives. Apparently self-evident
genetical relationships, with cousins, uncles, nieces and so on,
were systematically 'misdescribed', so that, for example, an
individual would describe a cousin on his father's side by using
the same term as he applied to his father himself, whilst he
would apply to a cousin on his mother's side the term appropriate to a son. Speculative explanations had been put forward for
this kind of capriciousness, but Radcliffe-Brown's is more
comprehensive and more satisfying. That is to say, he has an
integrating and explicit core assumption, about the critical
importance of kinship in the kind of society he was concerned
with, as the idiom in which relations of property, obligation and
authority are expressed. Asymmetries in kinship terminology
are therefore not curiosities in need of explanation, but clues to
an institutionalized patterning of behaviour which specifies the
content appropriate to different relationships, the reciprocities
of right and obligation. To the extent that the assumption is
valid for particular societies, kinship is the skeletal structure
of the totality in a sense that gives the organic allusion particular force. Other 'facts' that might be observed—economic
exchanges, violence, even conventions about humour and
ridicule—take on a kind of coherence and intelligibility as the
regularities they manifest are seen as an extension of the
fundamental structural properties of the social system extracted in terms of the idiom of kinship.[18] That is to say that
evidence is selected as relevant by an observer on the basis of
a prior category which directs the line of inquiry, in effect by
presenting a leading question: 'How do these people construe
relations of blood and marriage?' The assumption is that the
structural integration of a social system is such that subsequent
questions, searching out the logical implications of the kinship
system, will indicate a tissue of subtle functional links between
superficially disparate observations. Thus, one observer has
recorded the existence of a form of conventionally licensed
abuse between a man and his maternal kin among the Dogon of
the former French Sudan. The Dogon themselves 'explain' this
social institution in terms of their own physiological and thera-
peutic theories—a good shouting-match purges the liver of
poison. But it may also make sense to an observer if it is seen
as a mechanism for expressing and controlling certain relationships within a particular type of kinship structure. A theoretic-
ally-oriented analysis will prefer the latter explanation, because

it is less partial and conjectural, and because it is consistent
with other manifestations of a similar kind in many other
societies.[19]

The analysis of kinship is a highly technical matter. It is taxing,
for example, in the understanding it demands of nuances of
terminology in a given language, and in the shifting use of terms
during an individual's life cycle.[20] There is ample room for
controversial reconstructions. It also generates the kind of
aggregate data that lends itself to abstract, even mathematical,
representation and analysis. The possibilities in the rigorous
technical exploitation of such data can loom disproportionately
large beside more elusive problems, and in this respect there are
interesting parallels with other areas of esoteric methodological
sophistication, such as electoral analysis in political science.
These can be considered in a later chapter, but it is the self-
evident structural importance of the category of relationships
that is of interest here. The issue is of a general theoretical
importance. Radcliffe-Brown is making very strong assumptions, and we are a long way from Montesquieu's loose and
speculative functionalism. On what basis is this theoretical
primacy of kinship categories established? Is it possible that
the prior category assumption was overconfident, or even based
on a misunderstanding of the kind of explanation that social
action is open to? It is not clear that the existence of observable
regularities of some demonstrable significance can be taken as
evidence that the variable in question is uniformly significant in
a given type of society, or that it does in fact manifest regularities of the kind demanded by a generalizing science. How do
we know that formally similar observations taken at different
times or places are indeed similar and comparable in their
implications?

Radcliffe-Brown's claim is that the problem of selecting
relevant evidence can be resolved systematically, that it is
possible to identify certain categories as of fundamental importance and to pursue the interconnections that weave about them
in such a way as to identify the essential structural properties
of the social totality. In principle, the importance of a category
of relationships is first advanced as an hypothesis. This is
tested by an exploration of the internal logic of the finite
number of forms which the category of relationships can take.
The basis for such an exploration is a comparative study that
demonstrates consistent implications for other sets of relationships—of power and authority, for example, or economic transactions. The outcome of such an inquiry necessarily takes the
form of a series of generalizations which describe how a given

pattern of social facts necessarily entail others in determinate array.

The process of analysis begins, naturally enough, with the observation that in certain societies people refer to their kinship relations in many different connections. It proceeds through various stages of abstraction. A 'kinship system' is an abstraction, of course, that in one sense exists only in the mind of an analytically disposed observer. The 'facts' which it reduces to some kind of pattern consist of an accumulation of observations indicating that individuals who are known to be connected in specific ways biologically or through marriage tend, with a high degree of regularity, to refer to each other in certain ways, and treat each other in certain ways. It is a system of meaning for the people who are part of it, though they may see no point in generalizing about it as a whole. So it is also in a sense an empirical system, a specific social institution operating according to norms and understandings that could be codified and related contextually to others. The point is rather an elusive one, but Radcliffe-Brown certainly thought in terms of the existence of systemic relations as an empirical process analogous to that of an organism. The analytical system is therefore something like a map, the details of which correspond directly and specifically with certain recurrent details of social behaviour.

We frequently refer to discussions at 'different levels of abstraction', though we have no conventional unit of measurement that distinguishes between one level of abstraction and another. If we had, perhaps we would avoid some of the arguments that never seem to make contact with each other, though they are ostensibly about the same thing. But, clearly, any shift in the level of conceptual abstraction introduces new implications. In the case of the two groups of tribes referred to above, Radcliffe-Brown is committed by his assumptions and expectations to look for as powerful and inclusive an explanation as he can find. He achieves this, to his own satisfaction at least, by collapsing the two groups into one. In terms of a formal description of kinship terminology there are significant differences between the two. For example, in the group that includes the Choctaw, individuals are respectful towards the ('Father') cousins on the paternal side. In the group that includes the Omaha, this kind of deference would go towards the ('Mother') cousins on the maternal side. But taken to another level of abstraction these are not differences at all, since the complex of asymmetries in one group are a mirror image of those in the other. Conceived as architectural structures, they are the balanced wings of a single analytical construction.

This analytical move is very significant in the context of Radcliffe-Brown's inquiry. It is precisely this 'structure' that he is after; this abstract 'fact' is the essential clue to the un-ravelling of all the other functional interconnections of which the society is constituted. A preliminary process of abstraction provides him with two groups. At a further remove they are both members of the same species, and the assumption is that the more general structural specifications are also the more fundamental and essential. Such structural facts, it is suggested, represent a set of constraints that will operate in a similar sense in all societies in which they are to be found in similar form. Beneath a wealth of variation, the ultimately significant determinants can be located; and their logical consequences can be expressed as general principles or laws. The end-products of the analysis are general statements about whole classes and types of social totality. These emerge from propositions that achieve their scientific generality by expressing the patterns within specified sets of observations at a high level of abstrac-tion. Valid explanations of particular forms of social action are, as it were, corollaries of these more universal theorems.

The pressure to achieve this kind of theoretical generality decisively predetermines the kind of structural analysis that is going to emerge from comparative observation. This becomes clear as soon as we ask when the evidence on kinship designa-tions was first collected. All at once, or over a long period of time, or some of it at one time and some at another? This seems a very elementary methodological question, but we could redirect it to the theoretical constructs themselves. How long does it take to identify the structural regularities you are looking for? How regular do regularities have to be before they qualify as appropriate evidence for a scientific and comparative analysis? The scarcity and equivocal nature of historical evidence in pre-literate societies has already been referred to, but this is not even identified as a problem in this functionalist orientation, which sees the question of how a system is function-ing now as quite distinct from any question about how it came to be functioning in this way and not some other. Within such an analysis of structures, time is not an important variable. The functional model is an abstraction in more senses than one. Its components are distilled from the medium within which we can recognize the acceleration and decay of social processes, or describe the experience of individuals. Social structure has been consolidated into a concrete reality, and the analysis of

contingent historical change has been discarded along with the
vague speculations of the evolutionary theories Radcliffe-Brown
despised. In order to aggregate the evidence that is needed,
duration is taken as a constant and not a theoretically interesting variable. The units out of which the model is constructed
represent averaged and aggregated social experience, a
synchronic abstract.

However, if the temporal sequence of events, however regularly
structured, is not to be taken for granted, and if problems of
social order, balance and conflict are to be identified in terms
of individuals and groups confronting novel situations within
complex constraints that can only be described in terms of
durations, cycles, periods, then the theoretical claims of such a
functional approach need drastic qualification. But this is not
to pronounce a verdict of analytical failure. The attempt to
establish a comparative theory of structures in such societies
was very productive. We can illustrate two further stages in
this development. The first is in a classic study of the political
institutions of the Nuer by Evans-Pritchard, a pupil of Radcliffe-Brown's. Kinship relations provide the skeleton of
Evans-Pritchard's theoretical reconstruction of Nuer society,
but a significant shift has taken place in the general orienting
assumptions about the objectives of a systematic empirical
inquiry and the kind of explanation it can produce. Sahlins
offers a secondary analysis of this book, not by challenging its
data or the interpretations, as far as they go, but by widening the
angle of vision and reconsidering the internal structure of Nuer
society within a frame of reference that includes adjacent
communities.[21]

IV

The Nuer occupy an area that straddles a network of rivers
above the confluence of the Blue and the White Nile. They are
pastoral and mobile, aggressive to their neighbours, poor, but as
disdainful of aliens as the Tutsi, though, unlike them, passionately
egalitarian amongst themselves. The unfortunate anthropologist,
as Evans-Pritchard's wry introduction makes clear, can expect
to be ignored, or, almost worse, to be vexed and teased beyond
endurance in the course of his inquiries. Mary Douglas has
written a compact summary of the predicament of an alien
observer.[22]

The political organization of the Nuer is totally unformulated.
They have no explicit institutions of government or administration. Such fluid and intangible political structure as they
exhibit is a spontaneous, shifting expression of their conflicting loyalties. The only principle of any firmness which
gives form to their tribal life is the principle of genealogy.
By thinking of their territorial units as if they represented
segments of a single genealogical structure, they impose
some order on their political groupings. The Nuer afford a
natural illustration of how people can create and maintain a
social structure in the realm of ideas and not primarily, or
at all, in the external, physical realm of ceremonial, palaces
or courts of Justice.

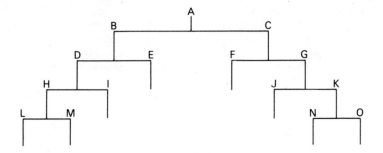

Figure 1   Genealogical segmentation of a Nuer clan

Note: The letters represent persons from whom the clan and its segments claim descent. A complete tree would indicate the balancing
of segments at different levels of inclusiveness.

There is little here of the sharp, concrete kinship structure of
the previous type of analysis. The (partly fictitious) genealogical structure can be discovered, with patience, and represented
in a dendrogram which shows how residential units come to be
related to each other in a series of balanced segments of
different degrees of inclusiveness. (See Fig. 1.) But this is a
schematic picture of an evidently fluid social experience,
notable for scrapping and feuding at every level. Far from
being institutionalized, the different kinship links of the segmentary system are selectively invoked by individuals in need
of temporary support. The first problem for the observer is to
discover the principles which make sense for the participants
of a baffling alignment and realignment of groups round an
accumulation of quarrels, some settled swiftly, some smoulder-

ing on indefinitely to be reactivated as occasion offers. His second problem is to make use of this evidence to develop an explanation that will account for the survival and continuity of the society in this form, and for any significant changes that can emerge from such a social organization. Such an explanation is likely to start with an analysis of kinship as the basic principle of organization, but its comprehensiveness will depend on how this comes to be articulated to the other aspects of social behaviour which an anthropologist usually considers, such as ritual and myth, and also to ecological factors.

Evans-Pritchard found that among the Nuer the residential unit is identified with a primary unit of a particular lineage, though not everyone there will in fact belong to that lineage. Obviously, it is within this unit that the individual will develop his closest associations, and, by the same token, at this level disputes are likely to be more frequent. At the same time they will be subject to stronger controlling sanctions, since they are potentially highly disruptive. But above this level it is not possible to identify segments as constant categories or groups. The Nuer simply do not think of them in such terms. The segments only exist at all with reference to some specific issue—feud or marriage, for example—and they only exist with reference to each other. The nature of the issue defines the scope of the conflict, and the means by which it must be expressed or reconciled: fighting with spiked bracelets, clubs or spears, payment in blood-cattle and so on. Thus when z^1 and z^2 fight, no one

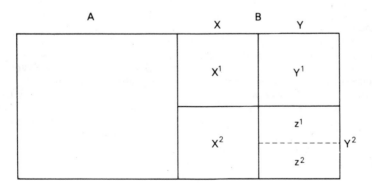

Figure 2   Organization of conflict between Nuer segments

Note: The letters, $z \ldots A$, represent segments at increasing levels of inclusiveness. A and B would fuse as Nuer to fight Dinka or other neighbours.

else is involved. But if someone in z^2 starts something with someone in Y^1, then the whole of Y^2 is necessarily involved. Conflict extends on a similar pattern when anyone in Y is in serious conflict with anyone in X, or anyone in B with anyone in A. This neat abstract was distilled from actual conditions of malingering confusion. (See Fig. 2.)

What Evans-Pritchard sees through this is a dynamic system with certain properties. The confusions of feuding can be described as a layered series of conflicts and alignments, which he describes as a process of fission and fusion. The anarchy is structured, in the sense that its patterns have a degree of predictability. The exigencies of a subsistence livelihood provide ample occasion for disputes, particularly over grazing. An analysis of the history of such disputes, in conjunction with an analysis of the segmentary structure of loyalties which locates each individual Nuer in relation to all other members of his society, to the dead and to the supernatural, uncovers the morphological characteristics of an endemic state of conflict.

Furthermore, other aspects of the consciousness of the Nuer, which can be inferred from the norms and formulae for arbitration, their ritual practices and their myths, throw light on and support the structural analysis. The interpretation of such evidence is obviously peculiarly difficult. Earlier ethnographers had tended to regard the religious beliefs they examined as pre-scientific and irrational. In this case, they are studied sympathetically and in great detail in the belief that together they form a collective expression of intersubjective understandings of the different, seasonally regulated relationships within the society.[23] Theoretical presuppositions about the functional integration of different aspects of the social structure, and the nature of non-rational beliefs in a collective awareness, provide a frame of reference within which the beliefs are interpreted. The beliefs are taken to explain, dramatize and justify certain forms of behaviour and to define the limits of social activity. In this kind of analysis, the anthropologist is in a similar position to the sensitive literary critic; he runs the risk of reading more into the text, as it were, than he can actually demonstrate is there, particularly as he is prepared to see functional consequences in aspects of such behaviour which he knows are not part of the conscious intentions of the participants. But the plausibility of his accumulation of hypotheses depends on their overall coherence, in the light of his analysis of fissions and fusions, into which the analysis of kinship structure leads him.

It is not possible to do justice here to these ramifications of the analysis. A brief comment on the nature of political leadership may give some indication of how quite distinct aspects of the social process can be brought into focus in such an organized search for interdependencies. The structural characteristics of the system entail substantial constraints even for the exceptional individual seeking to emerge as a leader with a personal following. Given a combination of luck and enterprise, a man may emerge as gat twot, or 'bull of the camp'.[24]

> Lineage, age, seniority in the family, many children, marriage alliances, wealth in cattle, prowess as a warrior, oratorical skill, character and often ritual powers of some kind, all combine in producing an outstanding social personality who is regarded as head of a joint family and of a cluster of cognatic kinsmen and affines, as a leader in village and camp, and a person of importance in the rather vague social sphere we call a district.

Outside his village, however, he is simply well known and respected, but lacks any political status. The intermittent possibilities of leadership in war cannot be consolidated in the subsequent fragmentation. In order to achieve the necessary independence an individual will somehow have to be placed outside the inclusive structure of the segmentary system. In fact the structure allows for this. A marginal figure known as the 'leopard-skin chief', who is invested with certain ritual powers, can act as an arbitrator in disputes, in cases where both parties are interested in settling, if they can do so without losing face. Evans-Pritchard stresses that this figure as such never acquired any great authority, but his existence represents a structural possibility for modifications in social organization in response to new pressures. Early in this century a former leopard-skin chief was able to develop a reputation as a prophet, taken to be possessed by one of the sky-spirits. His son, Gwek, continued the role, by invoking a myth of spiritual succession. Gwek's political significance is indicated by his death at the hands of government forces in 1928. There were other prophets, but under the colonial circumstances they could hardly be successful. However, an analysis of their relation to the segmentary structure and to the shared categories of ritual and cosmology shows how they could become the focus for an altered sense of Nuer identity.

The theoretical developments of this study seriously undermine some of the Radcliffe-Brownian assumptions, and modify our sense of the significance of the detailed observations that can be organized into evidence. The fluidity of the notion of kinship among the Nuer raises doubts about the analytical significance of this category as a central unit of analysis, not with respect to Nuer society specifically, but generally with respect to the comparative analysis of formally similar features of kinship or lineage structure. Mere segmentation in a lineage system manifestly includes a very wide variation of structural forms. The problem for a comparative analysis is to discriminate between them and place them in groups with essential structural characteristics in common. As we have seen, this may involve identifying at a more inclusive level structural similarities that are veiled by manifest differences. It may also involve moving in the opposite direction. Subgroups may be differentiated as other structural characteristics—varying within groups that are similar in more general respects—emerge as significant determinants of distinctive totalities. But once we are forced, as we seem to be by the social values of the Nuer, to consider kinship and lineage relations in terms of the meaning these have for specific groups of people at different points in time, we are bound to develop doubts about the self-evident priority of certain aspects of the kinship structure. Our confidence in the fundamental nature of structural principles that have been several degrees abstracted from the perceptions and values of the individuals in a society must weaken when we discover that behaviour and the significance attached to that behaviour varies as the contextual significance of relationships changes over time, and in response to the normal incidents of social life. The static and severely ahistorical orientation of the earlier kind of analysis has necessarily become here more fluid, more clearly a function of a series of durations, seasonal and generational in particular, over which the structure projects its form, as a harmonic sequence does in music. These must strike us as highly specific to a particular ecological context and technology. Attention has to focus round the evaluation by Nuer of the conditions they find themselves in, and only secondarily on the formal structural characteristics the ethnographer routinely uncovers.

Evans-Pritchard's indifference to the kind of comparative generalization demanded by his predecessor, his preference for generalizing about a particular society, entail assumptions about the medium in which his evidence is suspended which are in an important sense different from those which lie behind the earlier comparative studies. As Pocock has pointed out, Malinowski's injunction to social anthropologists to attach great importance to learning the language of their subjects is given a new dimension here. The language of the Nuer is not regarded simply as a more or less intractable idiom through which information about kinship designations, ritual, myth and the rest are to be collected. It is not simply a social record, but actually shapes and constitutes the system of meanings within which the Nuer live. The problems raised by this general assumption about the nature of language and its relationships to consciousness and rationality have been extensively developed since this study was written.[25] They are recognized here as being at the root of the more optimistic attempts at structural comparison. 'The fact that the analysis is conducted in the realization that the words used and the things or behaviour to which they refer are to be understood in their relatedness as constituting meaningful systems—this is what marks the originality of The Nuer.'[26] Such meaningful systems are by definition particular.

The analytical shift began in fact in an earlier work in which there is an implicit comparison between systems of belief that are to all appearances radically different, between Zande beliefs in magic and witchcraft and our own assumptions about belief, causality and moral order.[27] A more constricted functionalism would have searched Azande society for direct connections between different institutions, in terms of their reciprocal functions in sustaining an integrated society. Establishing these links would have constituted a sufficient explanation. But here Evans-Pritchard is more tentative and exploratory. Beliefs are explored in relation to behaviour in an attempt to identify logical connections between them, however strange the individual beliefs. This complex of meaning and behaviour is placed in relation to the formal structure of the system. We are offered a rich basis for comparisons, but 'neither from the facts adduced nor from the manner in which they are explained would it be possible to extract anything resembling a law of human society or even a scientific statement about witchcraft in general.' Montesquieu's preoccupation with totalities survives in a modification of Radcliffe-Brown's functional analysis.[28]

It is important to note that by this stage the individual institution—in this case, witchcraft—is only the point of entry to the perception of sets of relations. In short one can begin to speak of the structural analysis of social life as opposed to the functional analysis of social structures.

However, with The Nuer one fundamental assumption of the structuralist approach is not relaxed. For all its fluidity, we are still emerging from the analysis with a perception of a

totality. The overall strategy of exploring the particular in the
pursuit of general laws of broad validity is relaxed and this
means that there is far less explicit reference to general
patterns of cause and effect or reciprocal causation between
and within typical institutional structures. Connections are
certainly indicated in causal terms but in a sense that is closer
to Montesquieu's own usage, 'thus the law which permits only
one wife is physically conformable to the climate of Europe.'[29]
Conditions are sufficient rather than necessary. But institutions, beliefs, behaviour are represented as 'conformable' to
each other: the totality is functionally integrated. Is this an
assumption that forecloses any alternative interpretation of the
evidence, or is it just a fact that has been accurately recorded?
It is perfectly possible that Evans-Pritchard by design or good
fortune landed on an exceptional kind of society, whose empirical characteristics happened to be perfectly vulnerable to a
particular set of theoretical assumptions. But even if this is
the case we are still left with a question about the general
validity of the assumptions. There are references in the book
to forces that were beginning to modify Nuer society, but these
were external, the Arabs and the British. As appeared to be
true of Maquet's Rwanda, the complex of institutions served to
maintain the internal stability and coherence of the society,
blending fissiparous and integrating forces in a simple but
effectively articulated fabric. Is there any possibility of trans-
posing the evidence in order to cast a critical light on the
explanation that has been put forward? Sahlins's reappraisal is
a provocative attempt to do just this.

V

Change and time as an historical dimension are somewhat
ambivalently introduced in The Nuer. For Sahlins they constitute
the central problem in analysis. His leading question might be
'How does structure shape the historical process?' The purpose
of a structural understanding of a society is to be able to make
sense of historical events. Synchronic analysis must throw
light on process, which can only be understood diachronically.
From this point of view it is methodologically mistaken to
isolate the society from its international context and the history
of its relations with its neighbours. No radical theoretical shift
is involved here. On the contrary, Sahlins is simply picking out
an aspect of the organic analogy that is frequently underplayed.

Societies, like organisms, have to survive in specific environ-
ments, inhabited by other competitive societies or organisms.
In fact this competitive situation provides the context in which
climate and geographical resources take on their importance.
Its central significance, not recognized by Evans-Pritchard, is
indicated by the map (see Fig. 3) which shows Nuerland as an
amoebic shape inserted between two receding segments
occupied by the Dinka and pressing on an area occupied by the
Anuak. Nuer expansion has been in a west—east direction as
adjacent segments have leap-frogged over each other in the dry
season for grazing for their all-important cattle. The Nuer
have expanded at the expense of their neighbours, even though
their technology and general culture are very similar, particularly in the case of the Dinka.

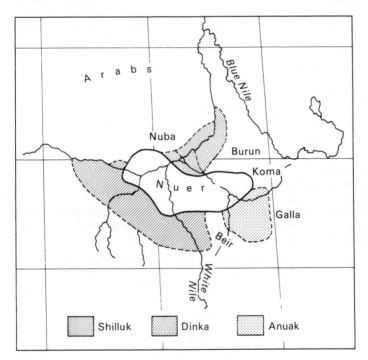

Figure 3   Tribal map of Nuer, Shilluk, Dinka and Anuak

The structural analysis had confined itself to asking how a
particular set of behavioural patterns maintained Nuer society
in equilibrium internally and in a variable relationship with
existing resources. But the historical fact of Nuer success, an

incursion and redistribution of territory at their neighbours'
expense, suggests a reformulation of the structural problem.
In what sense is the internal equilibrium a function of expansion
into already occupied territory? The question is not, clearly, in
competition with the problem confronted by Evans-Pritchard.
It is more inclusive, and a plausible answer to it may subsume
a structural explanation of the internal equilibrium of the
system. It entails thinking about structure in a way that is less
abstract, precisely because it is not concerned to exclude the
factor of time in an attempt to specify regularities. In the process it explores ambiguities in the concepts of structure and
equilibrium, which are critical to the development of this
analytical tradition.

Sahlins's hypothesis is based on a more critical consideration
than the principle of segmentation, discussed earlier, has
always been given. In doing so he is working against the grain
of the Radcliffe-Brownian assumptions about classification and
comparison. Instead of seeking the more fundamental principle
in the more general and inclusive structural feature, he is
insisting that the relevant property for a powerful structural
explanation consists of a group of characteristics that are to be
found in the case of the Nuer (and also of the Tiv in central
Nigeria), but not in many other societies that have been loosely
described as segmentary lineage systems. Mere segmentation
is an overinclusive category with a limited explanatory bite.

But a specific subtype of segmentation, represented by these
societies, and few others, can organize an attractive explanation
for the regional history of interethnic relations. The explanation
that emerges is a satisfying one for two complementary reasons:
it seems to make sense of a specific historical process, and it
takes account of crucial aspects of the process.[30]

> Nuer expansion is perhaps an outstanding instance of the Law
> of Cultural Dominance, the principle that the cultural system
> most effective in a particular environment will spread there
> at the expense of thermodynamically less effective systems.
> In any event it is clear that the Nuer have been able to expel
> the Dinka because of the superior military potential of the
> Nuer segmentary lineage system. While the Nuer and Dinka
> are alike in culture, there are differences in social organiza-
> tion. On the Dinka side these differences amount to the tragic
> flaw that has condemned them to a history of withdrawal.

The analysis applies the logic of the complementary massing of
lineage segments, according to the scope of the issue at stake,
to external conflict as well as conflict within the system. As the

segments disperse in the pursuit of grazing they get involved in conflicts with other societies at the territorial margins in which they can combine as Nuer, whilst their opponents have no complementary principle for organizing their resistance. The internal logic of Dinka structure leads them to break down into groups of decreasing size. They have no 'ideal system' or set of appropriate cues capable of fusing disparate units at the appropriate time. For the particular purpose, the particular circumstance, their structure lacks any principle capable of mobilizing them as a totality in more than a loose cultural sense. The only possibility of avoiding Nuer attentions, which was realized by the Ngok Dinka and the riverain Anuak, was to be engaged in modes of production that were irrelevant to the demands of the Nuer pastoralists.

An elaborated definition of the segmentary lineage system, which provides a set of structural specifications for a very limited range of societies, makes sense of the historical 'predatory expansion' of the Tiv and the Nuer in terms of a combination or functional complex of variables. Sahlins distinguishes six, of different degrees of significance. Most important is the relative and contingent nature of segments, which has been referred to.[31]

> They are not permanent, absolute entities, but relative ones. Called into being by external circumstances, the level of organization achieved is in direct proportion to the social order of the opposition, and the lineage segment ceases to function as such when opposition is in abeyance.

This aspect of social organization exists in a context of shared norms, specific genealogical ties, and norms regulating the conduct of dispute. Above all, the combination of characteristics is a possibility for tribal societies at a particular stage of development which happen to be faced with the problem of having to move into an 'ecological niche' that is already occupied. To survive at all they must displace others. Their simplified principles of social action enable them to identify with a substantial collectivity when the occasion demands it. The same principles of self-identification in terms of an unambiguous and unified lineage structure, which patterns relations between residential units, provides a sufficient political mechanism for managing the disputes that normally arise internally. The structure is a flexible vehicle for forcing a specific historical tendency. Seen from this perspective, other regular features of the society, such as the nature of individual leadership, fall into place in a context that is extended in scope rather than altered.

A summary runs, at this point, the risk of oversimplification, since Sahlins's analysis presupposes The Nuer and only needs to recapitulate part of its argument. The fresh focus on the segmentary structure identifies a necessary condition for the successful expansion of the Nuer, but this habit of organization, an unquestionable social fact for the Nuer themselves, is obviously in a complex relationship with other aspects of their awareness of the nature of things. Thus, extending the scope of the segmentary principle does not imply that internal conflicts were regarded in the same light as those with neighbours or other groups. Internal fighting was regarded as a much more serious affair, requiring real courage and combative skill; pillaging the Dinka, by contrast, was a highly rewarding form of field training. And yet, Dinka and Nuer cultures had a great deal in common, including, evidently, a myth explaining their respective roles as robbers and warriors.[32] There is an osmotic structural relationship between Nuer and Dinka groups at the territorial margins, and Dinka captives find themselves incorporated into the lineages of their captors and treated without discrimination as Nuer.[33] But the cultural parallels are lodged in an unbalanced structural relationship between the two peoples. The Dinka have a theology of their own, in clan divinities and their emblems, through which they can in principle transcend the divisions and oppositions between clansmen.[34] They even have prophets who have used this common theology to form political combinations among traditionally divided Dinka.[35] However, both myth and historical memory are un-ambiguous about their competitive status with the Nuer. The complexities of these self-sustaining perceptions, on both sides, can be very plausibly related to the critical structural differ-ence which Sahlins reconsiders. It may be that by concentrating on the ecological problem faced by the Nuer as late arrivals on a, by then, crowded scene, he has oversimplified the impulse behind the demographic changes that have taken place. The different forms of collective awareness, the practice and traditions of military skills, sheer confidence, would presumably come to play an independent and complementary function. But the structural analysis does relate the patterns of internal and external behaviour. The anarchic equilibrium of the internal political system can be seen as a function of structured relat-ions in a wider political system, which would ultimately, after the military operations of the 1920s, include Anglo-Egyptian and other external powers.

Echoes of the organic analogy can be detected in Sahlins's hypothesis, but taken together the two studies move us some way from an organicist caricature of a functional analysis. The synchronic analysis forms an abstract conceptualization of what seem to be the fundamental structural properties of social organization among the Nuer; and what can be described as a behavioural equilibrium, emerging from modulated forms of violence, is identified as the particular state of such a structure—under certain historically contingent conditions set by local ecology and by the internal structure, organization and beliefs of adjacent societies. The entities that are brought into functional relation with each other are abstractions, concepts that provide condensed characterizations of relationships between individuals. Unfolded, they would, presumably, make sense to the Nuer or the Dinka, but in themselves they do not correspond to categories they habitually use. For the observer, however, they represent an intelligible summary of systematic relationships that can be identified locally and knitted into more inclusive patterns of ever-increasing complexity.

At the same time, a difficulty of the greatest importance has emerged for the assumptions that are to be made about comparative evidence. The Radcliffe-Brownian quest for the grail of generality tended to assume that these observable components that were isolated as key elements of structure and fed into systematic comparative analyses are constants that have the properties of the constants that one supposes physicists, chemists and others to be concerned with. Sahlins, pursuing an understanding of particular totalities, Tiv and Nuer, questions this kind of abstractive analysis. The nature of a particular structure or a small group of comparable structures, is to be found in its distinctive complex of characteristics, in this case variants and specializations of the segmentary principle of organization.[36] The parts which the observer can distinguish may have, in different combinations, very different kinds of significance, different consequences, different meanings for the individuals whose social reality is constituted by them. In other words, particular elements abstracted from different social totalities may be very far from comparable. Different social wholes may call for different analytical strategies if their structural principles are to be systematically uncovered. It may be that this complexity invalidates any attempt at what Radcliffe-Brown would have recognized as systematic analysis, as opposed to the essentially artistic evocation, as he saw it, of the historian.

On this basis we appear to be left with a severely modified functionalist approach. The possibility of a rigorous and scientific theoretical development, to which Radcliffe-Brown had optimistically pointed, seems to dissolve, or at least recede indefinitely, as subsequent work complicates his assumptions. A narrow functionalism assumed that all things connect to form integrated social totalities and that the problem was to identify the types of totality and the dynamic principles of each type. Subsequent studies are uneasy about, or indifferent to, these systematic possibilities. They raise doubts about the assumption of functional integration. However, they are within the same tradition of inquiry in their attempts to abstract from the surfeit of particular facts essential structural principles. They continue to experiment with the implications of the concept of equilibrium, the idea of identifying a pattern of regularities at an appropriate level of abstraction that will in some sense satisfy the demand for an explanation of the life of 'the social whole'. Sahlins's secondary analysis illustrates one, relatively manageable, complication, which came from projecting the structural explanation onto an historical process. But the evidence on the Nuer appears to have a manifest coherence. More intractable and demanding fields of evidence force the anthropologist into making further demands on his conceptual vocabulary, whilst hanging on to such guidelines as his discipline provides to the articulation of the surfeit of facts. A final example illustrates this.

VI

An analysis of kinship and lineage structures carries Turner a long way in his study of the Ndembu.[37] But his professionalism here calls into question some of the assumptions in his own tradition. The point, of course, about identifying the kinship structure is that it is presumed to indicate the outlines of a particular social dynamic, distributing a distinctive network of relationships of dependence, obligation and authority across the entire society. The analytical units of this structure, patriliny, matriliny and so forth, were taken to entail certain invariant consequences. Turner finds a society in which matrilineal descent counts in the fundamental matters of inheritance and succession. In other words, the structure emphasizes the relationship between mother and children, powerfully supporting this basic family unit with an institutionalized significance which, by implication, undermines other possible connections. The connection between father and children is the obvious one. The anthropologist looks to find other familiar institutions that will have the effect of modifying the concentration round this family unit and integrating it into a broader collectivity. In many societies some form of age-set system serves this purpose, and among the Ndembu, youngsters at a certain age have to live with their age mates. This horizontal bonding of the age-set is emphasized by ritual hostility between adjacent age-sets. Since these are one generation deep, the effect is to create broad groups between which conventional tensions exist, though the alliance between alternate generations is a means of integrating the residential unit.

However, there are also other cross-cutting structural principles, and Turner's analysis revolves round the suggestion that these, far from combining to form an integrated totality, have the effect of creating and cultivating disruptive tensions which cannot be satisfactorily resolved by political means. A fundamental contradiction is introduced by the principle of virilocal marriage; a woman marries outside her village and goes to live with her husband. The significance here of this principle of social organization can only emerge from seeing it in the economic and cultural context of Ndembu society. These people survive, marginally, on hunting and cassava cultivation. The survival of a village settlement depends critically on the resources of manpower it can attract and retain. In the natal village, a man's marriage is everyone's gain, but a woman's is everyone's loss, despite the compensation of bride price. The consequences for a stable structure of relationships are very serious.[38]

> A system of patrilineages, if it is to be the 'skeleton of the social structure' requires virilocal marriage; a system of matrilineages requires uxorilocal marriage. The patricentric family in the former is what Professor Fortes calls the 'growing tip' of the lineage system, and like the lineage is attached to a locality. In matrilineal uxorilocal societies the local matricentric family is such a growing tip. If female members of a matrilineage remain in one settlement and import their spouses, each woman becomes the source and nucleus of a local lineage which may attain considerable depth in a society where settlement is anchored to limited resources.

But this is precisely what does not happen among the Ndembu, and the structure fails to accommodate the contradiction. Once a women is married, she is always vulnerable to the magnet of her natal village, where she is welcome on certain terms, and particularly if she has children, should she become dissatisfied with her husband. The ritual sanctions that keep men to hunting and women to cassava cultivation provide her with a functional economic independence which facilitates divorce and mobility. Under the circumstances, it is hardly surprising that marriage and divorce become the focus for political activity in a constant series of disputes which tend to disintegrate residential units. In fact, with the Ndembu, kinship is the idiom in which the society expresses its failure to develop significant political institutions, even of the subliminal kind developed by the Nuer.[39]

> It would seem almost to be the consistent idiom of Ndembu social structure that certain basic sets of ties which tend to be interwoven so as to reinforce one another in many small-scale societies, should here be separated from one another; further, the cohesion of the total society in some measure depends not on the juxtaposition and correlative operation of the ties, but on their disjunction, and even on their opposition. Thus maternal descent groups have no local centre, and vicinages are made up of villages most of which are unrelated by lineal descent. Descent and post-marital residence are not congruent. Spatial and social mobility throw territorial, kinship and political affiliations out of alignment. A few fixed points exist in the social structure to provide a measure of stability within the general flux.

Turner pursues with great sensitivity the consequences of the stresses generated by the structure of what he refers to as this 'community of suffering'. In the process he consolidates a structural analysis that is not consonant with Radcliffe-Brownian expectation. Where existing studies of ritual, among the Tallensi or the Swazi for example, lead one to expect that ritual will reflect and embody the structure of social action, he is forced by observation and his own participation in ritual occasions to account for the function of ritual in other ways, which include an important psychological component. In structural terms, he sees ritual as a rather desperate expedient for patching up, intermittently, a politically unstable society. The fund of shared beliefs and practices provides an assortment of expressive collective modes which can be invoked to bring to the surface all sorts of suppressed conflicts between individuals and groups. The therapy is a temporary and cathartic one, in the sense attached by Aristotle to the experience of watching a dramatic imitation of tragic events, or of listening to music.[40] And it is significant that such modes of expression come into play, particularly, after some apparently inexplicable natural disaster, such as a plague, has struck the community. Because the natural order is believed to be responsive to the moral order of society, there is powerful supernatural sanction for ritually exploring society's hidden disorders.

So a concept of structure, if it can be used to accommodate contradiction as well as functional integration, is essential to the analysis, and the prior category assumptions of kinship and lineage are not necessarily tautological and analytically inert, as Leach argues they too frequently become.[41] But what happens, in all of this, to the functionalist notion of equilibrium? Conflicts are interpreted and played out according to the norms and beliefs that have come to be associated with kinship. They have a familiar and repetitious shape to them and follow a regular course each phase of which evokes predictable patterns of behaviour. Observing these 'social dramas' Turner distinguishes four recurrent phases, from the public breach of a norm—frequently because of incompatible structural demands on the individual—through a phase of mounting crisis, to the invocation of various formal and informal adjustive mechanisms, to a final stage of temporary reintegration, or breach and the division of the village. There are relatively stable and shared interpretations of discord, and it is this context of shared meanings and patterns of behaviour through which conflicts are enacted which gives the society such cohesion as it has. Analytically we can identify an equilibrium in these cycles of barely satisfactory readjustments, achieved through the medium of a complex of values and beliefs. However, the implications of the concept have been altered here more manifestly than they had been in Sahlins's diachronic analysis of the expansionist equilibrium of the Tiv and the Nuer. In those cases structural equilibrium over time had been a sympton of a successful integration of elements of organization in the context of a system of beliefs and meanings. These were coherent in the broad sense that they identified a set of collective priorities. The priorities were unambiguous and the means for realizing them were there in the principles of social action. Harmony there was not, but beliefs and patterns of behaviour were highly integrated. In the overriding sense determined by narrowly defined economic priorities, social organization was highly effective. Turner makes use of the idea of equilibrium, but in an increasingly elusive sense which will have to be considered in greater detail in the following chapter. The idea is now much less of a reflex of functionalist assumptions about the tendency of social totalities to maintain their interrelated units, of persons and groups, in some kind of balance, than an analytical device for providing an accurate characterization of the shape taken by a process over time in a particular situation. The shift

in significance means that the concept serves a different purpose in the explanation. Identifying the components of a structure in dynamic equilibrium is no longer the same kind of end-
point in an analysis. Where the assumption had been that
disturbance of relations within the social totality would be
followed by readjustive responses of a defensive and adaptive
kind, preserving the integrity of the organism, it had seemed
sufficient to identify the integrating components of the structure.
Equilibrium was the dynamic aspect of structure. But here the
social system is seen to contain contradictions and discontinui-
ties. There are also, independently, possibilities for decay as
well as for successful structural maturation. So it becomes
necessary to develop means for analysing the constraints
within which a range of possibilities evolves through space and
time. In combination with other factors, ecological or economic
for instance, the structure, even in the fractured sense given the
term in this analysis, creates a limited range of options for
members of the society. Within this range of options competing
interests will seek to manipulate the possibilities to their own
advantage. This process may lead to a cyclical reversion to the
status quo, but 'The new equilibrium is seldom a replica of the
old. The interests of certain persons and groups may have
gained at the expense of those of others.' There are continuities,
broadly repetitive processes taking place at different levels and
over different spans of time. But if, at a broad level of abstraction, these can be seen as projecting some degree of structural
coherence over time, this must be subject to an awareness of
the changes that are taking place, possibly masked by apparent
continuities of form. The abstract equilibrium model provides
a frame of reference for the identification and analysis of substantive changes. It is an analytical convenience rather than an
assumption about the properties of any empirical social totality.

VII

Even a descriptive résumé of a handful of studies cannot avoid
expressing preferences and passing judgments. These are
intended, but the purpose here is to explore a theme which could
be illustrated with a much wider spread of instances. In addition
to the perspectives on the notion of social structure that have
been touched on, we could consider studies that take social
structure to 'consist of a set of ideas about the distribution of
power between persons and groups of persons'[42] or others

that think in terms of models of social reality (Lévi-Strauss), of interpersonal relations developed through status positions (Eggan), of an abstraction of the constant features of patterns of organization of social relations (Fortes), of groups, associations and institutions (Ginsberg), or, rather tentatively, of relations that seem to be of critical importance (Firth), or even, rather comprehensively, of 'social reality' itself (Nadel).[43] In each case we have an intermediate theoretical term, undoubtedly one of central and pervasive importance in the analysis of a totality of social processes, since it designates the features and properties of the skeleton or basic morphology of that totality. But there are shifts of emphasis and perspective. In some cases, and it is suggested that this would be true of the studies by Evans-Pritchard, Sahlins and Turner, the shifts of perspective reflected in different definitions are not fundamentally incompatible. They identify different aspects of a situation seen essentially in the same terms, or they reflect substantively different patterns of social experience in the societies that are being analysed.

In other cases the differences reflect incompatible theoretical claims at a number of levels. There are quite different assumptions about the nature of the relationship between the categories of the observer and the experiences of the observed. Abstract categories combine to constitute mutually exclusive descriptions of the nature of social reality. Thus, a definition of political action turns out to be the reciprocal, to use a mathematical analogy, of an associated definition of social structure. Radcliffe-Brown identifies as social structure the institutionally defined and regulated arrangements of people in relationships. Learning the critical idiom of kinship of course involves absorbing the categories employed by the people concerned, however bizarre these might seem. But his comparative, 'scientific' method moves him rapidly away from the surface differences between societies towards a series of limited but comprehensive generalizations. The social structure is identified via the social facts of institutionalized relationships, and the jump in abstraction is then justified by the consistency with which the more general model of a functional complex seems to accommodate other aspects of observable behaviour. Evans-Pritchard's perspective, however, is fundamentally different in that he defines social structure in terms of the relations between social groups. Again, the idiom is kinship, but the implications are different. Groups in Nuerland can only be described as social institutions in a qualified sense: their existence is contingent on specific situations. Different conceptions

of political action are entailed in these different senses of
'social structure'. The institutional core to Radcliffe-Brown's
perception presents political action very much as a matter of
organization. The 'political' identifies and abstracts that aspect
of the total society which is concerned with the control and
regulation of coercive force, whilst the political in Evans-
Pritchard's glossary of terms is present in the structural relations between groups.[44] Whatever the empirical turmoil of Nuer
life, there is a pattern over time, and the abstract structural
principle of 'fission and fusion' makes sense of it. We are presented with a context for historical choice, rather than a pattern
of functional necessities.

The contrast between these two theorists reflects a standard
debate in the social sciences. The contrast between Turner
and Maquet is more elusive, and is centred less on differences
over comparative analysis in general, than on assumptions about
the functional and normative integration of societies and the
dimensions of social experience that are relevant to these
issues. Both conceive social structure in terms of parameters
internal to the societies themselves, probably with less justification in Maquet's case than in Turner's. There is an implicit
theory behind Maquet's analytical programme that lends itself
to summary paraphrase in terms of organic imagery. Turner,
on the other hand, finds himself observing signs of a general
failure of neat social evolution and adaptation. He suggests that
among the Ndembu the social process works itself out systematically through principles of organization which interact
and over time define a situation of endemic conflict. The social
structure consists of these patterned and dynamically interacting relationships. His assumptions cannot be assimilated to
the organic metaphor. Maquet frames his problem in such a
way that he is led to identify an ingeniously articulated system
of political and social organization, and a broad consensus about
the nature of social relations sustained and dramatized by unequivocal ritual and ideology. The analysis fails to generate any
urgent questions about the nature and quality of the beliefs and
values of different groups of individuals. It sees collective
behaviour as broadly consistent with the general expressions of
belief and ideology. But the stresses of social organization are
problematic for Turner, and he therefore requires evidence of
the most inaccessible kind on the collective anxieties, adjustments and interpretations which constitute the existential
significance of his abstracted 'social structure'. These are
expressed in the idioms of ritual, myth and dreams. They are
obscure to the participants, full of stress and often unmanage-

able, but the observer must attempt to locate an inner logic and coherence in their confusions by decoding them. The key is provided by an analysis of the social arrangements that have been roughly outlined, but that, as Pocock observed of the Azande study, is only a point of entry into the whole. The interrelations of the social totality are manifold, but for Turner, by virtue of his implicit definition of the nature of that totality, they are also obscure and must lead him in the direction of submerged subjective processes.

The contrasts between these two studies suggest that we have reason to regret that anthropologists working in Africa were not subject to the compulsory transfers that kept district commissioners from getting too attached to a particular community. To oblige Turner to investigate the social structure of Rwanda, and Maquet to do the same for the Ndembu would be a nice refinement of comparative method.

CHAPTER THREE

Scientific inquiry

I

The illustrations of the last chapter have at least redefined the schematic contrast between an historical explanation of change and a structural explanation of a state of social stability. In different hands we can see that an equilibrium model is not a synchronic snapshot in any simple sense. It is a hypothesis about a complex of interrelations which are realized over time, not a single segment of time, because different subsystems will have what Gluckman calls different structural durations, [1] but a series of encapsulations which intermesh and intervene on each other. It is not necessarily committed to an assumption of functional integration in an organic sense. The empirical reality referred to may be full of conflict, but the model would then claim to identify the recurrent structural contradictions that determine such conflict. Whether it refers to systematically sustained social stability or not, it claims to identify the configuration in terms of which any change or transformation will have to be defined. Gluckman notes that both Marx and Durkheim, in their analyses of emergent dominant principles of change over a much more extended time span, necessarily start from a structural analysis of an equilibrium period.

Critics have pointed out that any equilibrium model is a severe abstraction which ignores important aspects of the social reality of the society under observation and elides others. Velsen, for example, has charged Evans-Pritchard with tidying up messy confusions that are central and not marginal to relations among Nuer. [2] Gluckman himself has argued that the feud is misunderstood in the same study because no explanation is offered of how Nuer reconcile two frequently conflicting sets of kinship ties, those deriving from the organizing principle of patrilineal descent and those based on normal human affection and connections with the maternal side. [3] This is not the place for a discussion of the substantive merits of these criticisms, but they underline a dilemma for a theoretical social

science. In order to make sense of any social behaviour the
observer needs some image of a coherent process, which will
be expressed in an interrelated set of abstract theoretical categories. Necessarily, these are selective with respect to any
observation he may make, and there are a great many possible
reasons for differences between one set of theoretical abstractions and another. The evidence itself may be opaque or fragmentary. The observer will have an epistemological position,
however inexplicit or confused. He will have come to an understanding of what the content and form of an illuminating explanation should be. Thus, he may look for hypotheses and generalizations about substantial numbers of comparable instances
(Radcliffe-Brown), about recurrent events in a particular but in
some sense representative situation (Evans-Pritchard), about
a limited subset of cases (Sahlins and Barnes), about a particular
situation in which frequently encountered types of relationship
are found, linked to certain stressful and limiting consequences
(Turner). Each of these orientations, and there are others,
entails a distinctive synthesis of abstractions from the particular, and generalization about events over time.

But how can we compare these theoretical alternatives? Can we
test them individually, or use them to test each other? Do we
erode them through piecemeal confrontation with items of
evidence they overlook? How do they justify themselves in
relation to the evidence? This chapter and the next consider
some of the activities these questions suggest in the light of
an idea already invoked by Radcliffe-Brown, the idea of a
'scientific' analysis of social behaviour. We will be obliged to
recognize that the idea means different things to different
people, even different things to natural scientists in different
fields. We will also have to recognize that social scientists
who emphasize their scientific aspirations are often far from
clear about the epistemological and methodological foundations
of the natural sciences. Perhaps they may be forgiven, since
natural scientists themselves tend to turn over their epistemological problems to philosophers of science, who are mainly
read by other philosophers—and by questing social scientists.
That the temptations are hot is indicated by the vogue of
Thomas Kuhn's stimulating and readable book on theoretical
revolutions in the natural sciences.[4] Social scientists, particularly some sociologists and political scientists (Marxists
included), have found fresh dignity and comfort in rephrasing
his thesis to apply to the irresolute and confused state of theory
in their own subjects. But they have done so for the most part
in a loosely philosophical manner, and without recognizing the

highly contentious nature of his arguments even as they apply
to the natural sciences themselves.[5] We should discuss later
these presumed parallels between the ways particular theories
succeed each other in the natural and social sciences. But
since these chapters are concerned more with the form any
given theoretical explanation should take, it is worth referring
to the uncertain grasp of parallels at another level as well.
It is often suggested, with some justification, that (non-Marxist)
social scientists have looked to physics for an ideal formal
model for a theoretical explanation. They see it in the predic-
tively powerful hypothetico-deductive theory that is presumed
to be the staple above all of physical explanations. But some
fields in physics are by no means theoretically orderly, and
indeed twentieth-century developments give rise to grave
doubts about the nature of scientific logic and the concept of
causality itself.[6] Whilst for biologists the classical deductive
ideal is a literally meaningless one that 'reduces to pulp ecology,
animal geography, evolution theory, ethology, developmental
physiology and others'.[7] Indeed, most historians, even those who
have been urging a more self-consciously 'theoretical' orientation on their colleagues,[8] would find in a general description
of biological explanation a not inaccurate sketch of their own
activities. Such theoretical explanations depend on an adequate
specification of the general context, whilst the deductive explanation attempts to exclude or hold constant extraneous variables.
Interwoven with a biological explanation there will usually be
unstated generalities, often trivial in themselves and permitting
exceptions, which have to be used with the professional judgment
that only immersion in a discipline can provide.

At this level, scientific analysis subsumes a range of theoretical
forms which themselves reflect a variable series of relationships between the observer and different fields of evidence.
Theoretical formulations may specify causal connections or
complex systemic interactions. Their implications for prediction and empirical control will vary. Their different degrees of
elegance and pungency are a function of the possibilities of
experimentation and of measurement of discrete interacting
elements.

The preoccupation with scientific method in the social sciences
has tended to reflect a belief in a hierarchy of explanatory
modes, presided over by the classical deductive model and
descending by degrees through the less developed sciences.
The result has been obeisance to an unattainable ideal and a
preference for explanations that seem to prefigure it in embry-

onic form. Methodological developments which are standard lower down in this hierarchy are also emulated, techniques of classification and measurement and, in some disciplines, even experiment, but these are often regarded as the foundations of a developed science and incomplete in themselves.

In one sense, this idealization of different levels of explanatory power in the natural sciences is simply naïve. Thus one characteristic of a successful theory in physics is 'parsimony'; it is a compact formalization that identifies in a very comprehensive manner variations in observed behaviour. But parsimony, or elegance, is not some kind of independent aesthetic criterion in the light of which any theory may be assessed. Social scientists, on occasion, seek its endorsement as if it were. Clearly, a compact and comprehensive theoretical explanation improves on one that is diffuse and partial, but only so long as its abstract categories really bind together observations of the phenomena with which it is concerned. It is absurd to hunt for simulacra of the theorems of experimental physics, if such research, given certain types of evidence, can in the nature of things produce little more than contingent generalities.

But at the same time, such naïvety is only an extreme reflection of assumptions that have pervaded the social sciences. These assumptions, loosely characterized as positivist, thread back through intricate networks in Western thought. [9] They seem to lead naturally in the direction of a methodology that has had its supreme successes in classical physics, but they have been of fundamental importance throughout the natural sciences. One argument which is critical of the notion of a unitary scientific method has it that such assumptions are in place in the natural sciences but not in any science of human behaviour. In the natural world facts are facts in an unequivocal and 'inexorable' sense. [10] The facts of social behaviour, on the other hand, are indefinitely variable, the values, beliefs, fears, choices, visions, persuasibilities and the rest, of human beings. To subject these to a positivist methodology is to make a serious philosophical error. The very idea of a social science is therefore a contradiction in terms. But this distinction between the natural and the social is too easy. Philosophical objections can be made to certain positivistic assumptions about the nature of fact and reality, whether or not we are concerned with natural phenomena. To press such philosophical objections successfully is, obviously, not to dismiss as invalid the methods, achievements and conclusions of science. The connections between philosophical assumptions, analytical methods, and conclusions or discoveries are subtler than that.

By the same token, we cannot in the case of work by social scientists read backwards in a direct or simple sense from the formal shape of an explanation, or from the techniques of measurement and classification employed, to their epistemological assumptions. It may be a reasonable suspicion that a social scientist making an energetic attempt at an explanation in a deductive mould is accepting a certain picture of science and its subject matter, but the suspicion may be disarmed by a particular characterization of the evidence and a particular use of the theory.

The argument of this chapter is that there are important parallels in analytical method between the natural and the social sciences, and that we are not concerned with two orders of reality and two types of understanding that are distinct in quite the sense that is commonly invoked. On the other hand, it is clear that there are differences which are not simply differences of degree. A triangular relationship between the orienting assumptions of the observer, the perceptions and choices of the observed, and an analytical method, is unstable, and particular to the social sciences. As a result, we encounter the question of causality and logical consequence in a special context. This makes for a number of interesting inversions; in some fields there are rigorous and quite successful deductive theories, but their scope may be narrowly confined, whilst, in others, methodologically less powerful techniques of classification and measurement produce more significant returns than sophisticated procedures.

Though it takes us some way from the style and material of the studies by social anthropologists, it seems reasonable to develop these points by considering contributions to the analysis of social behaviour made by scholars who self-consciously aim at the deductive ideal in their theories.

II

Economic and game theoretic models, like functional models in the anthropological tradition, described systems of rational action. But in terms of their assumptions about factual evidence and its organization, and about prediction and prescriptive recommendation, they introduce a decisive contrast. A later chapter will be concerned with what happens when these perspectives intersect. At this point, however, we simply need to

give some consideration to a tradition of inquiry that takes
seriously the ideal of a positive science, modelled on a version
of the programme of a theoretically mature natural science.

From the anthropologist's perspective, the question of purposive
action is a massive one that cannot be simplified on any grounds
without a serious distortion of reality.[11]

> It would be an absurd requirement to restrict sociological
> interpretation to clear and distinct concepts: these are
> historically a rarity, and there is nothing to make one suppose
> that vague and broad notions, whose logical implications for
> conduct are ill-determined, do not in fact have a powerful and
> specific impact on actual behaviour. We are faced with the
> unfortunate need to interpret just what the concepts in
> question meant to the participants.

Purposive activity may have any number of objectives and all
sorts of unintended consequences. The question is how purposes
are to be identified and described, and how they can be introduced into an explanatory theory. The term 'purposive' has
literary connotations of vigour, of clarity of intention and act—
the suggestion that defined intent can be related to discrete
act, like the deflection of alpha rays by a nucleus in one of
Rutherford's experiments. But the problem is a very different
one. What kind of entity are these determining concepts; how
can we identify them; how do they relate to behaviour? Economic
theory characteristically resolves the problem by means of a
grand simplification.

Milton Friedman has complimented one of his most distinguished
predecessors as follows: 'Marshall took the world as it is;
he sought to construct an 'engine' to analyze it, not a photographic reproduction of it.'[12] Behind this remark are strong
assumptions about the nature of reality and possible ways of
apprehending and controlling it, linked to a precise criterion
for the success of an explanation. We could hardly ask for a
more forceful allusion to the positivist ontology. There is
Marshall, and there is the world, 'as it is', a complex of facts
in a multitude of relationships with each other. These relationships will reveal themselves in any degree of detail if they are
subjected to a systematic method of classification, which will
make possible the description of observed regularities in
terms of lawlike generalizations. This entails a nominalist
account of language, the scientific use of which is to label, distinguish, classify, and compare. In other words, 'every abstract
science is a method of abridging the recording of experiences'.[13]

Standard abuse of the positivist epistemology tends to attribute
to it a belief in a reality consisting of brute facts, which the
scientist tags, as it were, with an appropriate label, so that he
can watch their various interactions and migrations through
space and time. The essence of the analytical method is to avoid
attributing to the facts any unobservable properties, essences
or what the American political scientist Arthur Bentley referred
to as 'spooks', on the grounds that speech adds nothing to what
is observed. Approached without mystification, the observable
facts must display the properties that are intrinsic to them,
and independent of our perception or misperception of them. [14]
But 'the conception of science as descriptive "generalization"
from "brute" facts, as a one way movement of thought from
"facts" to "laws" is naïve and superficial'. [15] Some positivist
thinkers, such as Ernst Mach, have indeed eroded the distinction
between scientific description and scientific explanation, by
arguing that an exhaustive description leaves nothing to be
'explained'. In this view, a rigorous scientific identification of
the facts and their observable connections in itself constitutes
explanation. [16]

But, as Kolakowski points out, another strand in positivist thinking recognizes the artificial element in conceptualization.
Concepts and verbal designations are not simply forced upon
us by empirical realities, but reflect pragmatic, aesthetic and
other considerations. Facts can be described in different ways
and for different purposes. [17] The facts themselves leave us
some latitude for interpretation. Stronger formulations of the
conventionalist point of view were mainly concerned with the
methodology of the natural sciences, but a parallel argument has
gathered force also in the social sciences. Clearly it represented a threat to the positivist epistemology itself, because
it concedes the existence of hypothetical alternatives, theories
which cannot be tested against each other by reference to an
independent substratum of raw experience, since they are alternative and logically acceptable descriptions of that experience.
Even in explicitly positivist formulations of the nature of theory
in the social sciences, this ambivalence in conceptual abstractions has been recognized. Mach's image of an encyclopaedic
Darwinian descriptiveness as the paradigm of explanation is a
long way from Friedman's positive economics. Friedman's
theoretical engine is purposive rather than contemplative, and
this pragmatic determination conditions its reconstruction of
an 'objective' reality. The irreducible and independent objectivity of reality is taken for granted in true positivist style,
but the theory has specific questions to ask of that reality.

It describes certain relationships, but in order to answer the
questions, it can, and perhaps must, ignore aspects of those
relationships. It would not claim to be a comprehensive description or explanation of all facts of economic behaviour.
There is always the possibility that it might provide explanations
that are in some senses incompatible with alternative descriptions of the facts. As a theoretical abstraction it simplifies
reality, and seen in the light of alternative hypotheses, such
simplification may appear as distortion or error. This may
not unduly trouble the economist, however, since the alternative
hypotheses do not engage with his own criterion for a successful theory.

This criterion is a methodological one, and it lies in a certain
relationship between the logical properties of the theoretical
engine and the outcome of observed relationships. For an
economist, the things of the world are commodities, prices,
production factors, the distribution of capital assets and the
like—an integrated series of conceptual categories which
cannot be given discrete translations back into the raw data of
experience. What he observes are complexly interrelated
variations in data having to do with utility transactions of one
kind or another. He begins with a convenient descriptive vocabulary, and ideally concludes with highly condensed statements
about systematic relationships, which can be mathematically
expressed and logically derived in an internally consistent manner. Thus, at the heart of the Keynesian analysis of capitalist
economics lies a complex of interactions which the theory
consolidates into a network of abstractions—investment, national
income, employment, consumption. Each of these categories
requires an operational definition which is an instruction to
make certain observations and provide a summary description
of them in terms of some specific criterion. There are, for
instance, a number of possible ways of defining national income.
Ministers, unions and radical activists notoriously employ different ratios to arrive at figures for unemployment. Keynes's
theory asserts that variations in investment, an aggregate extracted from the records of a mass of individual transactions,
produce changes in the other economic magnitudes, specifically
in national income and employment. Fluctuations in consumption are, in turn, a function of alterations in national income.
Stated in such general terms, of course, we only have a specification for a theory, or a general hypothesis. To create an engine
or model capable of being used to provide deductive computations from an appropriate body of data, we need formulae which
will specify relationships in quantitative terms. How much

variation in one complex component of the model, investment say, will be necessary in order to produce a given alteration elsewhere, in employment, or in consumption? The certification of the engine depends on the correspondence between such reasonably precise theoretical deductions, on the one hand, and predictions about actual observations on the other.

That these specific components and relationships are not forced on to the attention of the economist by an impartial contemplation of 'the facts' is made clear by the history of the consumption function in economic theory. Indeed, it is much closer to the truth to say that it was possible to mobilize the data only because the hypothesis already existed. To quote Keynes's biographer, [18]

> Keynes's treatment had been a priori, abstract, and unadorned by example. In contrast Hansen [a convert to the theory], who had come to value highly the income-consumption relation, first looked at the consumption function from a cyclical standpoint and illustrated his argument with some genuine statistics of family income. Then he applied a long-run secular analysis to the data, computing lines of relationship between recorded income and consumption data.

Keynes had arrived at a way of looking at the aggregate behaviour of a set of distinguishable economic magnitudes, some more manipulatable than others. His definition of these magnitudes entailed certain logical dependencies. Within the general theory, for example, an alteration in national income is a logical consequence of an alteration in investment. The possibility of expressing these functional relations in terms of equations for which data are continuously available in developed economies means that the economist has a predictive theory in the logical structure of his analytical categories. The grand simplification of economic theory, of course, lies in the component of purposive and rational action which is presupposed as the underlying dynamic of the economic system. Keynes recognized a wide range of subjective determinants of consumer behaviour, some of them by no means rational in a narrowly economic sense, but very relevant to other aspects of the individual's social relations. [19] But within a given aggregate of individuals in a developed market economy, these factors are assumed to be stable. The deductive theory is thus made possible by a strong ceteris paribus clause, equivalent to the natural scientist's controlled conditions for an experimental manipulation of selected variables. At the same time the purposive dynamic presupposes a systematic structure of constraints and incentives, which is thereby incorporated into the definition of economic rationality. The evolution of this structure, which insulates the behaviour of commodities from what economists refer to as externalities, has provided the dimension of stability within which systematic relations can be identified between abstract economic functions. Such stabilities may be historically contingent and variable, as Heilbroner points out. 'The dependable regularities of social and economic behaviour on which the great economists from Smith to Marx built their remarkable models of social change now appear as attributes of a bygone age.'[20] But if economists have abandoned the pursuit of large historical prognostications, they continue to provide explanatory theories that justify themselves by deriving predictions from limiting assumptions about motivation within a historically specific complex of institutions.

On the face of it, such a theory or predictive model can claim to have its finger on the threads of a selected, critical process of cause and effect that runs through the seamless web of societal relations. Only on the face of it, however, since we must distinguish between the ability to predict and the ability to specify a causal process. Friedman is clear on this; the relevance of a predictive model is pragmatic, a recipe for manipulation and control. It may or may not provide understanding of causal processes; if it does so it will be in highly abstract and summary terms. It may or may not provide a comprehensive insight into individual or group motivation. Prediction and understanding are not equivalents. Prediction may raise the possibility of acting with foresight, but it need not depend on a full understanding of the complexities that are being manipulated.[21]

Economists candidly acknowledge this limitation. Their successes come from abridging and aggregating, constructing ideal models of narrowly defined systems of relations which frankly ignore associated factors on other dimensions. Such models may make quite inaccurate assumptions about the sociological significance of economic transactions at a micro-level, but the focus does not require an explanation of the behaviour of individuals or of groups, only an explanation of the behaviour of commodities. About individual behaviour the economist is often prepared to be cheerfully unrealistic.[22] It is enough if his simplifying assumptions about purposes and choices are consistent with predictions. He assumes a tendency to make rational choices in the attempt to maximize whatever satisfactions are distributed through market mechanisms. The theory will generally do if people in aggregate continue to behave as if the simplifying, indeed simplistic, psychological assumptions are true. In the economic theory of advanced industrialized societies the principles for organizing the facts are to a considerable extent agreed, and evidence on which richer and more ambiguous inferences about human behaviour might be based make marginal methodological demands. These are defined as external and up to a point extraneous to the system within which the explanatory activities are taking place.

Clearly, then, the demand for economic theory of this kind is based on its instrumental utility. It can provide logical answers to questions about means and ends in relation to the allocation of material resources. But there are other questions to which it is not directed: either it presupposes answers to them, by accepting as given the structure of the commodity relations it explores, or it clarifies the context in which such questions can be asked, by projecting the pattern of commodity relations for alternative structures—where it can do so without abandoning its prior assumptions about rational motivation in economic transactions. But questions about the major political and social choices that have to be made in the allocation of priorities and resource expenditure cannot be answered by any model of the interplay of economic magnitudes or any other designation and classification of the empirical data. Theoretical answers to such questions invoke different criteria, and presuppose a different relationship between the observer and his field of evidence.[23] Any clarification or prescriptive recommendation that may be suggested by an economic analysis will only make sense in the context of a wider, looser and messier process of evaluation and assessment, which will at the same time be a more inclusive and reticulated evaluation of the totality.

In other social science disciplines, where formal deductive theories have been attempted, the influence of economic thinking is obvious. In addition to the exploration of electoral choice in terms of an analogy with consumer rationality, there have been significant applications of game-theoretic models in the analysis of bargaining and the formation of coalitions.[24] The shift of context introduces fresh considerations. The object of the game theorists, for instance, is still formal theory, a set of deductions logically derived from a limited set of assumptions, in the form of 'if...then...' statements, whose validity is assessed by their ability to predict behaviour. But the instrumental appeal of such theory is no longer the same, or at most has an oblique relevance to its main value, which is heuristic or exploratory in a sense that seems to involve a subtle but appreciable shift in underlying assumptions. The game analogy abstracts a structure of rules from a given situation, bargaining in committees, negotiating and threatening in international relations, or engineering party coalitions. The theory, for any given set of opportunities, is a logical declaration of rational behaviour, as prescribed by the universal motive that animates any game—the urge to win.

The rules define all utilities or goals, and these are taken as given and known to the participants. They also define the resources which may be used to acquire them. So in effect they constitute a definition of power relations, and the game is about the use of rules in the pursuit of power. The theory answers two questions about a pattern of competitive relationships: what are the rational moves in a process of interaction (if necessary dealing on a probabilistic basis with uncertainty about an opponent's intentions or resources); and, are the participants deviating from or conforming to this norm of rational behaviour? The answers can be read either for their prescriptive value (if you want to succeed, then you should make one of the following moves...) or as a clue to misunderstanding or confused motivation. Actual behaviour is described by reference to a prescriptive model, which is also predictive to the extent that the actors recognize and accept the logic of the game. The focus, therefore, is sharply on the perceptions, motivation and misperceptions of the agent as he make his choices.

The selection and improvement of game-theoretical models involve some sophisticated mathematical derivations. Alternative formalizations may be compatible with the evidence. The ultimate criterion for selecting one rather than another will be predictive power, but other factors are entailed in the decision, such as assumptions about the structure of the 'game' at stake. So, for example, depending on the way goals and payoffs are defined, the game may take a zero-sum or a non-zero-sum form: roughly, a distinction between winner-take-all and the prospect of a variable distribution of profits and losses. In a case study of Italian party politics between 1953 and 1969, Axelrod found that a theory taking account of non-zero-sum characteristics predicted ten out of seventeen coalitions, whilst none of the zero-sum theories predicted more than five correctly.

Further detail is unnecessary here, since our concern is a general one with the intimate connections between certain assumptions about scientific method, and the intermediate categories that both define and pick out relevant evidence and also form a systematic combination amongst themselves.

Where do such developments leave us, and can they be taken to represent the cutting edge of theoretical development in the social sciences outside economics? From the perspective advanced here, they seem to have a limited heuristic value which is not too difficult to define.

It is sometimes objected that politics is not a game and that the analogy round which such theories are constructed entails a trivializing selection of facts from the political domain. This largely misses the point. At any level, politics concerns relations between differentially advantaged actors. We naturally think of politics in terms of winners and losers, and the question is whether the metaphor can be formalized to some effect. Can it throw a well-directed light on the dynamic process of diverting or securing relative advantages, some of them temporary but some incremental and contributing to emerging distributions of power? The answer is that it may well do so, if both the perceptions and the behaviour of those who are being observed meet certain conditions. They must be institutionalized and given an explicitness that distinguishes them from the vague broad notions referred to by Gellner. In the behaviour of committees, assemblies, conferences, and electoral parties, complex systems of relations are conventionalized, intermediate goals are defined (until you 'win', you do not qualify to make decisions, etc.), rules are more or less agreed, and circumscribed intermediate patterns of motivation generated. To the extent that the theory goes beyond common-sense assumptions, it presents an ideal type, or model of rational activity, which takes account of all the structural and dynamic properties of the system. Prediction, 'postdiction', and comparison of theoretical expectations with actual behaviour may identify facts of some significance. A particular actor may fail to behave 'rationally' under some circumstances but not others. One might want to ask why (ignorance, priority of other values or constraints, his religion, his mistress). Different degrees of deviation from predicted behaviour may point towards combinations of ideology or interest that have not been made explicit at the level of public rhetoric, and such clues take us further in identifying relationships and determining perspectives.

On the other hand, voting and the flux of coalition formation need not necessarily reflect significant shifts in political power. They may, indeed, reflect little more than the gothic decadence of an institution.[25] The possibility indicates the limits on

theoretical and methodological development in this direction.
The reward of an impressive and demanding intellectual
exercise may, to misappropriate a concept from Axelrod's
formal game-theoretical exposition of the dilemma of collective
action, turn out to be the 'sucker's pay-off'. The viability of a
rigorous deductive theory depends on the continuance of
specialized relationships. A schematic treatment of motivation
and rational choice may be justified if behaviour is sharply
constrained by the selective priorities of purposive organization. The assumptions, however simplified, about the psychology
of motivation in such a theory may be realistic, more so than
in some predictive models of economic behaviour. But in the
absence of any substantial utilitarian advantage, it is particularly
necessary to weigh the virtues of elegance, rigour and logical
power against the scope and resonance of the substantive questions the theory answers. Practitioners tend to claim a
heuristic value for such theories. This could mean that they
open up and clarify aspects of a complex situation. It may also
be claimed that they contribute to the development of deductive
theory itself. But it seems quite unlikely that the growth of
methodological sophistication will extend the scope of the
deductive theoretical norm in the social sciences. The wider
the perspective on a field of action, the less likely that it will
manifest the consistencies which a rigorous operational theory
of this type might explore.

III

This does not take us quite as far from some of the other
theoretical perspectives that have been introduced as might
appear. Other types of analysis are groping towards an
abstract identification of the essential structure that lies
behind complexities of observation. Radcliffe-Brown, in particular, seems to be making similar general assumptions about
a scientific method for the organization of evidence and the
testing of hypotheses. There is a major difference. He conceives of the social totality as a dense network of interlocking
systems of actions and interactions, sustained by a corresponding diversity of values and preferences. The achievement of
abstracting one such system of interactions is not accompanied
by the subdued sigh of gratification one detects in the game-
theoretical approaches and others of a related kind. It is
meaningless, for his purposes, to explore kinship in isolation

from other subsystems of value and behaviour, such as economic or ritual. The object should be to integrate a series of analytically distinguishable subsystems of interaction into a comprehensive abstraction of the social structure as a whole, in order to classify, compare and generalize. The research problem involves shuffling data into those categories and sub-categories that will most comprehensively and consistently plot the essential features of a totality of interactions. Clearly, there is a qualitative difference between the raw data of the economist and the field notes of the anthropologist, but the latter are taken to be no less unambiguously 'hard'. Sooner or later this process of classification and abridgment will produce generalizations from which a limited set of general laws, causal in form, may be derived. For example, it will be possible to identify the necessary concomitants of a matrilineal, matrilocal kinship system with a number of additional characteristics. The structure of the whole is to be explained in terms of a logically integrated pattern of such principles. This totality defines a system within which behaviour is meaningful, rational in an ample and complex sense that takes account of collective needs, some of which may be served, but not consciously recognized necessarily, in individual choices.

The problem Radcliffe-Brown sets his colleagues, nothing less than the identification and understanding of all the modes of survival and integration manifested by a certain type of society, cannot be distilled into the pragmatic conventionalization of a predictive theory. Different modes of experience are integral to an analysis, and the beliefs and intentions of individuals have implications that lie outside the pursuit of ostensible goals. As we have seen, the analysis is intensely abstract, but its internal dynamic makes it greedy to incorporate regularities that intersect the basic abstraction of the kinship structure. His theoretical ideal appears to be the classical deductive one, but he concedes that observations of such complexity cannot as yet be described in such a condensed and powerful language. Necessarily, we must engage on a laborious and preliminary activity of identifying, sorting, classifying, as a prelude to connecting and integrating. Initially, the generalizations that emerge from an examination of these regularities will be somewhat fragmentary hypotheses. They can only be tested by further systematic comparison of complex variation among the different attributes in terms of which the structure of a society can be described.

A plausible model for the scientific analysis of such data is to be found in biology, rather than physics. The basis for our understanding of an infinity of natural organisms is their systematic classification and comparison. As a norm for the organization and analysis of evidence, this fundamental device of scientific analysis has been far more important in most social sciences than the classical deductive standard introduced through positive economics, and it is worth taking the risk, which was deliberately avoided in the references to physics, of setting out a layman's view of its significance in biology. The discussion is mainly concerned with positivist assumptions about the nature of evidence and theory, which have already been referred to. It also introduces the more technical discussion of the following chapter, which is concerned with the use of quantitative methods in the analysis of classified data. If the cruder misconceptions about the nature of a systematic classification and comparison of evidence can be avoided, we can then take proper advantage of technique. Quantitative methods elaborate, differentiate and help to justify the classifications and distinctions involved in a theoretical discussion. They are not in any simple sense a set of neutral devices for sieving the particles of actuality. So we need to consider the general properties of statistical procedures and the implications of making use of appropriate procedures on evidence that has been collected and constituted in different ways: biologists and social scientists along with other natural scientists make use of much the same body of statistical theory. But the remainder of this chapter will be concerned at a more primary level with the classification, comparison and analysis of complex evidence, biological and social.

Even a layman's understanding of taxonomy, in fact a distinct field for biologists, can throw fresh light on difficulties that are not always spelt out in comparative studies by social scientists.[26] Methodological loans have been raised rather easily, but without sufficient awareness of the problematic relationship between the hypothetical language of theory and the factual designations and distinctions upon which any system of classification is constructed. For biologist and social scientist alike, what appears on a superficial view to be a logical and technical problem of analytical method turns out to be heavily invested with theoretical overtones. Not even the biologist can claim that his explanations emerge from a systematic description and comparison of the brute or hard facts of organic reality.

General laws by definition refer to the characteristics and behaviour of significantly large numbers of instances of a like or comparable kind. Very broadly, the analytical logic, from a positivist perspective, proceeds as follows. A set of instances or objects is defined, matrilineal societies, city states, or the mythical and repellent 'caminalcules' with which Sokal illustrates his discussion. Within this population there are variations, along a set of characteristics or attributes which are present in different degrees in different instances, or not present at all. Individual instances can be classified into large groups with some range of attributes in common, or into smaller groups with an increasingly high proportion of attributes in common. Of city states, according to Aristotle, there are monarchies, oligarchies, polities, democracies and so on; of biological forms there are many different genera, species and subspecies in formidable nomenclature.[27] The next step is to examine the levels of mutual correspondence or the covariation of different characteristics, and then to consider possible causal and functional relationships between them.

A very simple hypothetical example will serve to illustrate the basic logic of the comparative analysis of subgroups. A sample from a population of fruit flies (Drosophila) shows variations in fertility rate. The problem is to explain the infertile eggs. Do some of the fruit flies consistently produce infertile eggs, or do all of them do so part of the time? If there are relatively infertile subgroups, how can they be accounted for?

A number of the fruit flies are normal (wild type). But the sample also includes some mutants, which have vestigial wings. There are reasons for suspecting this vestigial wing mutant of being abnormal in a number of respects, so it is worth testing to see if it is significantly less fertile than wild type. Obviously, we must compare the two subgroups, wild type and mutant.

The mutants prove to produce relatively more infertile eggs. We can describe this association of attributes by using a simple statistical measure, which will register the strength of the association as a departure from a perfectly random set of combinations between genetic type and fertility. The random distribution can be exactly predicted by calculating probabilities, so this theoretical base line makes it possible to compare the association of variables in different subgroups with some precision, an invaluable asset if we are attempting to assess the relative importance of complex combinations of particular attributes. Where many factors are acting in combination, our problem is less the identification of invariant combinations of attributes than the description of tendencies which can be overridden or diverted by other factors which we may or may not be able to identify. These empirical generalizations allow us to make conditional predictions.

Having identified an interesting (statistically significant) association between genetic type and fertility, what about an explanation? A biologist might propose several. One might be that mutants do not live long enough to produce many fertile eggs. But it appears also that wings are used in the courtship of fruit flies, and small wings may directly influence the chances of successful impregnation. On the other hand, the correlation between wing size and infertility may be 'spurious'. There is, that is to say, a correlation, from which indeed predictions may be made, but, it must be emphasized, a correlation does not establish cause. There may be some third factor producing both vestigial wings and infertility, and there may be no independent interaction between the two. For example, individual genes affect more than one thing at a time: vestigial wings, but also perhaps low resistance to temperature; a predilection for dustbin garbage rather than fallen apples; and infertility. We can only respond to this logical possibility by trying to eliminate some of these hypotheses. So we test hypotheses by 'controlling' for the explanatory factors involved and observing the consequences, in the new patterns of association of the reclassified data. A natural scientist might well experiment by making a drastic intervention. It might be possible to clip the wings of the wild type without impairing any other functions, and thereby to 'control' for courtship behaviour by reducing wild type to the same poor status as the mutants. If, having done so, the variation persists between true wild type and mutant, the hypothesis that wing size is a direct determinant will have lost any support in this evidence. The raw facts have been challenged to provide evidence of a systematic relationship and forced to concede that there is none.

The formal method schematically described here is obviously indifferent to the substantive content of the analysis; any collection of comparable entities can have their variable attributes explored in the same way. Precise statistical expression may not be possible, but on the other hand much more sophisticated multivariate statistics may be in order, and in either case there is a common form to the basic logic.[28] In a perfectly modest guise, it is the staple of the major British electoral survey. In Figure 4, for example, we see the questionnaire evidence organized to indicate the variable determinants of partisan identification. The dependent variable, partisan identification, is, without being invidious as to the direction of the parallel, equivalent to the fertility or the infertility of the Drosophila

(a)   Church of England

	Middle class	Working class
Conservative	82%	b 50%
Other	c 18	50
	100%	100%

b−c = 32%

Nonconformist

	Middle class	Working class
Conservative	46%	b 19%
Other	c 54	81
	100%	100%

b−c = −35%

difference of balance of cross-support in two religious groups: 67%

(b)   Church of England

	Middle class	Working class
Conservative	68%	b 27%
Other	c 32	73
	100%	100%

b−c = −5%

Nonconformist

	Middle class	Working class
Conservative	53%	b 30%
Other	c 47	70
	100%	100%

b−c = −17%

difference of balance of cross-support in two religious groups: 12%

Figure 4   Partisan self-image by class and religion

Note: Middle class is comprised of occupational grades I-III, working class of grades IV-VI. Labour and Liberal partisan self-images are grouped as 'other'. (A) is the group from sample reaching political maturity before 1918 and (B) the group from sample reaching political maturity after 1951.

eggs, and the interconnections between this and three independent attributes are being considered—age, religious denomination and class. For technical reasons that have to do with qualifications about the true representativeness of a stratified random sample, the figures are given in percentages and there is no test of statistical significance.[29] However, we get some indication of the relative importance of religious denomination, in the two widely separated age groups taken from the total sample, by comparing the proportions supporting the Conservative or Opposition parties in each social class, subgroup by subgroup.

The patterns in the first two 2 × 2 tables (Figure 4) contrast sharply. In the latter pair, the association between class and party is not so different in the two religious groups, and it seems reasonable to argue that the significance of this particular attribute for political expression has declined.

But with these two straightforward illustrations we have already slipped past some formidable questions. Which, of an indefinite number of characteristics do we fasten on, and, even prior to that, what is a characteristic? For Aristotle this posed no manifest conceptual problem, though it certainly called for meticulous observation. We can see him classifying in one of the most influential biology texts of all time. [30]

> No mollusc or crustacean can produce any natural voice or sound. Fishes produce no voice, for they have no lungs, nor windpipe and pharynx: but they emit certain inarticulate sounds and squeaks, which is what is called their 'voice', as the lyra or gurnard, and the sciaena (for these fishes make a grunting kind of noise) and the caprus or boar fish in the river Achelous, and the Chalcis and the cuckoo fish; for the chalcis makes a sort of piping sound, and the cuckoo fish makes a sound greatly like the cry of a cuckoo, and is nicknamed from the circumstance. The apparent voice in all these fishes is a sound caused in some cases by a rubbing motion of their gills, which by the way are prickly, or in other cases by internal parts about their bellies; for they all have air or wind inside them by rubbing and moving which they produce the sounds.

But for the contemporary biologist, with scores and perhaps hundreds of possible attributes to choose from, given his microscopy, biochemical techniques and the rest, the problem is not easy. He has too much information. How fast and in what sequence should he throw it away as he simplifies his data? Which attributes are more important than others? How are they distinguished? [31]

> Suppose that in a group of organisms studied substance X, when present, is always produced by a biosynthetic pathway P in which substance Y is a precursor. Should the attribute (X present, X absent) be considered conditional on the attribute (Y present, Y absent) taking the state Y present, despite the fact that X might be derived from other precursors by some other biosynthetic pathway?... the biosynthetic pathway P might be considered as an attribute, and further attributes conditional upon its presence be used to indicate its terminal stage.

This comment from a specialist text makes two most important points. First, every identification of an attribute depends on some prior understanding, based on well-confirmed theory or acceptable hypothesis. Aristotle literally could not have identified a pharynx without some understanding of its function, and an ability to suspect a biosynthetic pathway depends on years of research, by many hands, that has worked its way into a trained biologist's general understanding of his subject. Second, attributes need not be described as discrete 'things'; they may be dynamic relationships. Indeed, to quote from a lucid and important survey of developments in taxonomy, 'reflection will show that all describable characteristics are relations to other objects or concepts; we simply cannot speak meaningfully about the properties of a thing in itself, Plato or Whitehead notwithstanding'.[32] The distinction between wild type and mutant is a distinction between two organic systems, and individual characteristics can only be described in the context of speculations about development and adaptation. And, clearly, the selection of behavioural characteristics of individuals, even such inexorable facts about them as when they were born, entails assumptions about social relationships and social structure.[33] To classify people according to their age, religious affiliation, socio-economic status and political reference group is to place clues to the substantive historical experiences of these individuals in the context of an interpretation that presupposes many more relationships within the social system than are explicitly referred to in the aggregated summaries of particular observations.

The theory impregnation of taxonomy has been a major issue in recent debates among biologists. The advocates of a neutral or 'objective' method of classification, echoing the positivist assumption that all empirical knowledge stems from sense impressions, have pointed out that there is a powerfully circular element in some biological taxonomies. Attributes are selected or weighted according to various assumptions about their significance, derived from evolutionary theory. But evolutionary theory is highly speculative, and there is a risk, therefore, that a classification incorporating its theoretical assumptions, far from being neutral and objective, largely confirms the assumptions by describing and ordering in terms of prior categories. Thus, a taxonomist will have to decide if approximately similar attributes manifested in different cases are in fact homologous, bear the same relation to other attributes in case X as in case Y. His decision will have a strong observational element; for example, is the attribute in the same relative position and

similar in chemical composition? But there are only degrees
of abstraction between such questions and more obviously
theoretical ones, such as, is there some similarity in developmental origin? That the latter (phylogenetic) question should
be excluded from consideration was argued by proponents of
an objective (phenetic) taxonomy based entirely on observed
attributes.

However, whilst treating evolutionary theory with militant impartiality, they were, without recognizing it, discriminating in
favour of any other theories that were inevitably introduced.
The point has been made succinctly by a philosopher.[34]

> Pheneticists make reference to things like wings, antennae,
> anal gills, dorsal nerve cords, enzymes, and nucleotides.
> These are hardly pure observation terms. They presuppose
> all sorts of previous knowledge of a highly theoretical kind.
> For example, a taxonomist working on brachiopods today
> describes his specimens and forgets that at one time con-
> siderable effort was expended to decide whether brachiopod
> valves were front and back, dorsal and ventral, or right
> and left, and that the eventual decision reached was based
> on various theoretical beliefs concerning their ontogenetic
> and phylogenetic development.

No biologist would argue that taxonomy of itself provides explanations or tests theories. It is, on the contrary, an essential
first step towards making problems manageable, by sampling
from an infinity of possible observations and using attributes
to make theoretically meaningful allocations of these into subgroups. It uses quantitative techniques, but these are a means
to an end and not a stable indicator of theoretical sophistication, even in the natural sciences.[35]

In what sense does a taxonomy organize observations? Clearly,
in a loose way it can be said to correlate attributes, but the word
is used in a number of overlapping senses. We might at this
point distinguish four: statistical, taxonomic, logical, and functional. The distinctions do not refer to different types of
classification, but rather to the demands we are making of a
particular taxonomy or the weight of interpretation we are prepared to place on it. The distinctions differentiate between the
more technical and procedural and the more theoretical aspects
of a classification, and serve as a reminder that technical and
theoretical sophistication do not necessarily appear in conjunction. Statistical correlation is, as it were, the creature of a
particular methodology. The taxonomist has made some deci-

sions about the appropriate procedure for sorting the similarities and dissimilarities that concern him. For example, is an
individual to be placed in group A rather than group B because
he is very similar to an individual already in group A, or
because he is similar to an average member of the group?
Taxonomic correlation is rather harder to define without getting
involved in the numerical procedures. It refers to the cluster-
ing of individuals or cases on the basis of sets of characteristics.
So, for example, two cases may both manifest the same numerical proportion of a hundred designated characteristics all of
which occur in some cases in the population. But the content
of the equivalent proportions may not be identical. Depending
on the purposes of the classification, and the significance given
by weighting to different attributes, these attributes may or
may not emerge in the same or adjacent clusters. So, a pragmatic decision about method may also express a theoretical judgment. Logical correlation relates to the problem of decompos-
ing integral processes into analytically distinct characteristics,
and concerns the correlation of characteristics rather than the
grouping of individuals in terms of attributes. Thus, the sub-
stances mentioned earlier as being linked by a particular biosynthetic pathway may be so inevitably and intimately bonded as
to be a virtually irreducible functional unit. Finally, functional
correlation, like linear causal relationships, is necessarily
construed and inferred from ancillary evidence and theoretical
discussion that will appear in the extended argument of an
analysis rather than in the taxonomy itself. Functionally related
attributes are presented as evidence of a systematic or structural process. Thus the size of canine teeth, the size of the
mastoid system, and the size of the sternal system are functionally related in the sabre-toothed tiger (smilodon) whose
'powerful sterno-mastoid muscles were used to wield the head
as a whole in striking prey with the massive canine teeth'.[36]
The fact that no taxonomist has ever encountered smilodon
emphasizes the hypothetical nature of the relationship.

For all its anchorage in fluid and fibre, the biologist's world of
things proves to be an enormously differentiated theoretical
organism, a proliferation of models that are not derivations
from a limited core programme of general laws. A taxonomy
represents the organization of speculations about highly complex
systematic interactions. Though its main practical function may
be to identify the organism on which a biologist is working with
his armoury of experimental and observational techniques, it
consolidates general assumptions about organic life, as well as
identifying unresolved problems in particular combinations of

attributes. It does not sort out facts in a philosophically crude sense.

There are at least two other important elements in this comparison. Obviously the evidence of the biologist encourages the analytical use of highly developed systems of identification, classification, and comparison. Since he has an infinite number of comparable organisms from which to sample, he can still be analysing complex intercorrelations among a large number of attributes when he has extended his classification to make very fine discriminations between subgroups. The social scientist on the other hand, particularly if his unit of analysis is a complex social totality, has a limited universe, within which structural attributes can be combined in a multiplicity of forms. Socio-historical systems are unique in an indefinite series of ways, and manifest verifiable similarities in only a few. For this reason, the systematic comparative classification through which Radcliffe-Brown pursued increasingly comprehensive generalization is inherently limited.

An example which illustrates the very different problems of functional correlation in the two disciplines is provided by Karl Wittfogel's argument in Oriental Despotism.[37] His thesis is that there is a systematic relationship, of a causal, lawlike kind between a whole complex of attributes which, he claims, distinguishes a substantial category of ancient oriental societies, and another complex of characteristics which he defines as oriental despotism. The first set of attributes is drawn from the system of ecology, cultivation and technology, whilst the second describes a system of administrative and political relationships. Leach summarizes the thesis as a circular (functional?) one; 'it was bureaucratic despotism that made the archaic hydraulic societies successful; it was the managerial requirements of hydraulic agriculture which made the archaic societies into bureaucratic despotisms.'[38] The hypothesis calls for a classification of all relevant societies, or at least of a representative sample of them, in terms of the attributes identified by the assumptions. If the relationships obtain, without too much blurring at the edges, there is at least an empirical generalization which a massive and scholarly exploration of historical and archaeological evidence might forge into an explanation of the emergence and stability of these regimes.

Leach challenges the systematic nature of the evidence. Wittfogel's cases are neither randomly selected nor complete. His own criteria should make him include cases which he ignores, such as Burma (pagan), Cambodia, and Dry Zone Ceylon

(Sinhala), and these cases would be as fair a test of his general thesis as any. Leach's consideration of the evidence from Ceylon simply does not bear out Wittfogel's generalization. The massive hydraulic systems are there all right, but Wittfogel was making inferences <u>from</u> them <u>to</u> the kind of centralized and bureaucratic political <u>system</u> which he assumed must be a functional necessity for engineering achievements of such magnitude. In other words, for all his acknowledged penetration and insight, he is here asserting what he set out to prove. There is scant independent evidence of the organizational and administrative attributes which are critical to the thesis. Indeed, archaeological evidence disposes of any facile first impressions. '[The Kalawewa canal system with its reservoirs] <u>looks</u> like a colossal and highly organized piece of bureaucratic planning, the work of one of Wittfogel's idealized Oriental Despots. But if so, the planning must have been done by a kind of Durkheimian group mind.'[39] The system took about 1,400 years to build!

So the systematic analysis of evidence falls down at the level of description and organization, for which there is a model in biological taxonomy. The argument for a functional correlation is invalid, because the population to which the generalization applies is not adequately represented. (Wittfogel also tends to resolve problems of contradictory evidence by creating <u>ad hoc</u> subspecies with exceptional properties.) It is also invalid because key attributes prove to be non-attributes, observations interpreted under invalid assumptions; the evidence has been demonstrably misconstrued.

Leach's critique is part of his war against the positivist hunt for sweeping general laws of society. The point, we are arguing, is not that there should be a sharp distinction between a positive natural science and a qualitatively different type of understanding of social behaviour. Rather, the social scientist must recognize that a different order of evidence forces on him a series of conceptual and methodological limitations.

Another limitation, which affects even the more tightly controlled and narrowly focused functionalist inquiry of the case studies of Radcliffe-Brown and his closer followers, is the question of the equivalence of attributes, such as those he uses as the basis for a critical classification in the analysis of social totalities. Is a particular principle of kinship necessarily a comparable attribute across all cases, or might not its significance for the participants be so different under different types of concomitant variation that the structural similarity is largely formal and disguises all sorts of variations of meaning. Even within the

distinctively primitive subgroups of his comparative analysis,
Radcliffe-Brown is making strong assumptions about the comparability of sentiment, the surrounding beliefs and values,
associated with the institutional structures he abstracts. This
reflects a distinctive orientation towards social facts on his
part, and means that, by implication, he is assuming an essentially
similar system of rational action in societies with a limited set
of key structural characteristics in common. How would the
vague but important intersubjectivities referred to by Gellner
be fed into such a model of social structure?

The point is not to suggest that social phenomena are intrinsically incomparable, simply that they should not be compared
unless it is reasonable to do so, when we are clear about the
level at which a comparison is being made. It is essential to
identify empirical regularities in social behaviour and to
analyse them systematically. But it is also essential to make
sensitive judgments in matching particular analytical methods
to evidence described at different levels of abstraction. The
scientific methods of analytical classification which are standard
in the biological sciences can be used by social scientists for
many purposes. But it seems likely that any functional interdependencies they point to will be historically contingent and
provisional, contributory insights into a systemic process rather
than logical steps towards comprehensive generalization.

Different as they are, the formal models for scientific method
that have been referred to have a similar relevance to the
analysis of complex social systems. By exploring his observations within such conceptual frameworks, the social scientist
can identify, perhaps, 'the principles of operation of partial
systems', as Leach points out in his discussion of logical and
mathematical models. [40] Up to a point, these are matters of
testing, demonstration and verification. Beyond that, at the level
of complex systems and general theory, he is operating with
what is, by comparison, guesswork. The levels are interdependent, but they need to be distinguished.

To take this theme any further, we now need to consider in a
slightly more technical way some of the methodological aids to
comparison and classification which are used both by social
scientists and by biologists.

CHAPTER FOUR

Statistical models and social structures

I

Some specific references to measurement were made in the
previous chapter. They were sufficiently diverse to show that
a consideration of the nature of quantification in the analysis of
social behaviour does not involve a quantum jump into an
independent and methodologically arcane level of thought. We
are concerned with an extension of the elementary analytical
activity of making distinctions, of classifying and comparing
entities which are in some kind of process, and their characteristics. It is of course true that some levels of measurement
are technically simpler than others. The comparisons of voters
and fruit flies called for classification into either/or categories
and the relatively straightforward comparison of percentages
or proportions, with reference to the theoretical base line provided by the mathematical theory of probability. The nature of
the comparisons is essentially no different from any ordinary
day-to-day judgment in which we make qualitative or quantitative
comparisons between groups. But the statistical analysis has
two advantages. It provides a relatively precise statement of
the confidence with which one is putting forward a scrap of
evidence, and it provides a means of exploring the implications
of that evidence by placing it in formally similar conjunctions
with other observations. An economist will generally need to go
further than this (nominal) level of classification and comparison, because his conceptual categories refer to the relationships between continua, linear processes, such as fluctuations
in investment, production and employment. He could say very
little about any of these if he were forced to make nominal
classifications of each dimension into High and Low. He needs
at least measures of ascending value (ordinal) and preferably
measures that can define the evidence in terms of equivalent or
comparable units of measurement (interval). In general, each
of these levels of measurement improves on the previous one;
it provides greater precision and is associated with more
powerful and flexible statistical techniques. Though, as we shall

see, this is not to say that subjecting a body of evidence to measurement at a higher level will necessarily provide answers to pertinent questions.

But we should emphasize that what we have in statistics is an integrated body of mathematical theory, which is in itself entirely indifferent to the substantive content of the material it may process. It imposes certain specific formal requirements, but whether or not any particular body of evidence is taken to meet these will depend in large measure on the observer's assumptions about his evidence. As a result, any decision to pursue an analysis of relationships by taking advantage of the resources of logic and discrimination that are stored in statistical theory will, or should, provide the observer with a further occasion to consider the nature of his conceptualization of the evidence. This was an issue discussed in the last chapter, and we can develop that discussion by considering the relationship between statistical models and evidence constructed at different levels of generality.

Since we are concerned very broadly with the relationship between one type of abstract model and another, theories about real relationships on the one hand and the internally consistent logic of a body of mathematics on the other, it does not seem too irresponsible to be casual about detail. So this discussion will tend to be evocative rather than technical, with apologies to sophisticates for any violence committed on mathematical structures in the process. [1]

The logical analysis of relationships among a limited number of attributes presupposes extensive preliminary work in sorting out and organizing the confusions of a field of evidence. It is necessary to be clear that this is a uniformly theoretical activity, but some theoretical constructs are better confirmed and more integral to our understanding of reality than others. As a matter of practical necessity, apart from anything else, there are wide reaches of evidence which any scientist must take for granted and use in his investigations as accepted facts in the reality he is concerned with. Individually he may not treat them as problematic, but in combination they are bound to be, unless some pattern and order can be detected in their combinations and permutations in different organisms or populations. So there is a sense in which statistical analysis and simplification is a way of allowing the facts to speak for themselves. Once the relevant attributes have been defined, empirical truths can be established about their covariation by counting them and presenting the calculations in a suitably condensed form, graphs, clusters, maps, tables. The counting rules for a statistical taxonomy are not difficult to grasp at an intuitive level, and the complexities are largely in the sheer mass of observations that have to be reduced to their instrinsic regularities. There are increasingly powerful mechanical solutions to this in the use of computer software.

What the statistical models propose is the transformation of a field of observations into an appropriate mathematical or geo-metrical analogue. Thus, a case may be represented by a point on an ordinary graph, one axis of which represents magnitudes of one attribute whilst the second represents magnitudes of another. Any number of cases can be compared in terms of their relative positions in this attribute space. They can be grouped into similar and dissimilar clusters. Many taxonomic procedures do this by using as a summary measure the Euclidean distance between points (see Fig. 5).

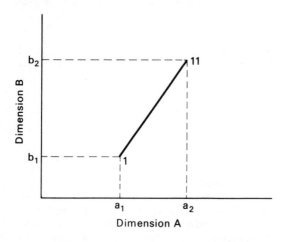

Figure 5   Euclidean distance between two individuals on two dimensions

In this case, the length of the line 1-11 gives a measure of simi-larity of the two observations with respect to dimensions A and B. It is possible to visualize the addition of a third dimension. There would be another axis, as it were from the eye of the reader, joining the origin of A and B at another right angle. Each point now will have a location in three-dimensional space, as if it were floating somewhere in the corner of a room. Accommodating further dimensions is no problem for the mathematician, who is accustomed to moving in an n-dimensional hyperspace which is impossible to visualize. However, such complex relationships can be measured and their general features condensed into summary relational measures. It is easy to see the value of such a descriptive analysis for the biologist who needs to keep distinct a multitude of functional complexes, among organisms which may even be quite similar superficially. He is concerned with a very large number of observations, most of which will be interpreted in similar terms by his colleagues, so there will be a high degree of professional consensus on the meaning of the different dimensions.

Other statistical models make a different interpretation of the space in which observations are located. Regression analysis is concerned with the strength of the relationship between attributes, and asks how likely it is that attribute A will appear with attribute B or, more precisely, for a 'prediction' of B from A at a given level of probability. (Or of A from B; such statistical predictions are structural and 'ahistorical', and their dynamic interpretation takes place in another context.) If the points are scattered at random across the space, it will be impossible to infer any association between the variables. However, if they are condensed into an ellipse round the 'line of best fit' it will be clear that increases along one variable tend to be accompanied by increases along the other. For a given swarm of points, a regression analysis will define a line (a plane if we are relating more than two dimensions) which might be described as a moving average of the distribution; more precisely, it transfixes the swarm of points in such a way that the sum of the squared distances of each point from the regression line is at a minimum. (See Fig. 6.) This summary abstract of the relationship between two attributes can also be given a geometrical expression as the angle between two lines, which represent the magnitude and direction of the two variables relative to each other. (The correlation coefficient which measures the strength of the relationship is mathematically equivalent to the cosine of this angle.)

Of course, it will generally be assumed that many other variables are affecting a bivariate relationship, and the analysis provides an indirect indication of the impact of these interactions in the 'residual term', an associated mathematical expression of the extent to which the points are scattered or condensed around the regression line. [2]

For the moment leaving aside any comment on the interpretation of a multidimensional space in this context, the effect of other measurable variables can be further explored by completing a

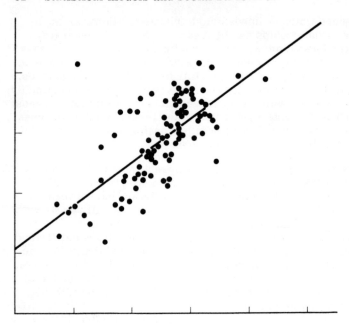

Figure 6   Scatter-diagram of observations on two dimensions

Note: This distribution represents a relatively high positive
correlation of 0·68.

series of pair by pair comparisons. The results will appear on
one of those bewildering matrices of intercorrelations which
psychologists and social psychologists in particular are liable
to prepare. Each entry will be a coefficient for a pair of
variables, lying somewhere between −1·0 (perfect negative
correlation) and +1·0 (perfect positive correlation). The interpretation of the intermediate values is not entirely straightforward, but where they are comparable they do at least point the
way towards empirical generalizations about clusters of
attributes which appear to interrelated through some functional
or causal interdependence.

A perusal of the texts referred to will show that, whilst these
allusions to the more visualizable features of statistical theory
need a great deal of elaboration and amplification, the sophisti-
cations are grounded in a very few basic ideas, in particular the
idea of a representative value and the theoretical interpetation
of distributions around such a value. For example, a representa-

tive sample is assumed to have the same shape as the 'universe' from which it was drawn. That is to say, it manifests the same attributes, and these are distributed in the same combinations and proportions as in the universe from which it came. In a genuinely representative sample, a measure of dispersion, which tells us, say, how wide the gap is between rich and poor in a national sample of individuals, tells us within a specified margin of error what the picture is for the country at large. The theoretical relationships between sample size, and sample mean and dispersion for any given variable are the fundamental elements in a form of analysis that can condense and explicate interrelations in an otherwise indigestible confusion of evidence.

II

Some examples should clarify possibilities and limitations. Comparative studies at the cross-national level can call on enormous quantities of data collected by governments and international agencies. Such studies invariably register a paradoxical complaint. Much of these data (and, worst of all, an unknown proportion) are inadequate (fabricated, unreliable, full of gaps, not reflecting theoretically important characteristics, not assembled on uniform principles and therefore of dubious comparability). But even in the absence of these limitations, they are almost indigestible and represent every degree and shade of interpretation and variability. The facts are enormously difficult to condense and many of them are of dubious quality, scratched negatives from photographic plates exposed more or less at random. However, the problems of modernization and development do not wait on our understanding of their dynamics. The raw data must be 'cleaned' as far as possible (to borrow the clinical and ambivalent jargon of survey techniques), and constituted into categories which will reveal the underlying regularities of structure and process.

So a representative study of some 112 countries, both underdeveloped and advanced, offers the 'best available' comparative data in the form of forty indicators. [3] A random selection of these shows that they are thrown up by many different aspects of the total social process: per capita gross national product at factor cost (in 1964 U.S. $), newspaper circulation per 1,000 population, nurses per 10,000 population, daily cereals and starches as proportion of total calories consumed per capita, per cent female enrolled in third-level education, recurrent cost of education per unit at third level, life expectancy at birth, population density measured in terms of square kilometres. Where whole nations are involved, the apparent concreteness of such 'facts' is undeniably deceptive. For the most part these are summary measures of central tendency, and give no indication of the range of variation or the social and geographical distribution of the observations from which they are extracted. As evidence, therefore, they are limited in a double sense. They are abstracted from the structure of relationships in any of the senses we have referred to. Second, as quantitative measures they are poor material for statistical exploration; a well-rounded representative value in statistics is a compound of a summary measure of central tendency and a summary measure of dispersion, since without the latter we have no clue to the diversities that have been condensed into the mean.

It might be argued that the first limitation is not really so serious. It is not the differences between countries but the broad processes they have in common that are of interest here, general socio-economic determinants and constraints that operate across cultural variations. Also, it may be possible to compensate for the second limitation by the sheer weight of data. Despite the limitations of the data, there may be enough of it to set groups of countries beside each other in meaningful comparisons. Chapter 11 of this survey by the Industrial Relations Section at Princeton introduces a taxonomic analysis. [4]

However, it is significant that we find here a step that would be unusual in a biological taxonomy. The raw variables are combined into groups so that a series of composite indices can be extracted from the original data, giving each country a score for each group of characteristics. Thus, a cultural development index stands proxy for (their phrase) the 'process of modernization'. Suitably treated measures of variation along six attributes (newspaper circulation, literacy, annual cinema attendance, etc.) combine in a single statistic which places each nation in its relative location along a continuum, which has a complex but unitary definition—the word refers to a distinctive emergent process. Comparisons are made between countries in terms of the distance between their respective indices, of cultural development, economic development, level of strategic skills and knowledge, educational effort.

One justification for treating the evidence in this way would be that it avoids placing too much weight on too few relatively unreliable observations of a very gross nature. But the selection and compositing of attributes would also have to be justified on theoretical grounds, and it is perfectly obvious that the play of speculation around the specific observations is very loose compared, say, with the dense concentration of theoretical assumptions around each selected attribute in a biological comparison. Behind the organization of the evidence there is a general theory, or at least a collection of theoretical assumptions, about development and modernization. Compared with the admittedly speculative and untestable evolutionary theories in biology, these general assumptions are vague and contentious in the extreme, as the most cursory consideration of the bulky literature in this field will swiftly reveal. The correlations do manifestly reflect gross processes of change. But they have been organized on the assumption that there are certain general tendencies and patterns implicit in them, that a general theory of change is a conceivable outcome of a systematic comparative description of a number of cases, and that the essential social facts are caught in the quantities that are manipulated. The structure of the systematic description is built around these assumptions. The general theory is invested in a small group of highly abstract theoretical categories, educational effort, cultural development and so on, which are taken to be the critical dimensions whose interactions describe the course of history for these countries. The problem for such an analysis is to find opportune operational indicators, 'facts' to be subsumed beneath categories.

But this seems to be a questionable procedure. The objection is not to the statistical methods, which are used with great professional skill, but to the status of the evidence on which they are working. The observations are lopped from specific social structures. As we have seen, the identification of different aspects of a complex of social relations is a problem that demands considerable conceptual subtlety. A given relationship or social performance can be seen in different aspects, and its implications can only be made clear in context. Any sense of this recognition is lost when observations, derived from social interactions, are assigned to separate inventory headings such as 'economic' or 'social', and then treated as the interacting elements of a large systemic process.

To make this objection is not to say that gross figures organized under such headings are not meaningful, or that inferences cannot be productively made from their intercorrelations. The suspicion is of an analysis that provides no persuasive grounds for seeing in its statistical and taxonomic relationships the exceedingly complex functional interrelations which the implicit general theory needs to validate. Highly distilled and, as it were, chemically unstable data have been further refined by a series of conceptual distinctions that seem intrinsically specious because they imply that the sets of observations are invested with mutually exclusive properties. The taxonomic analysis only makes sense as a first move in an attempt to place the categories of an economic analysis in relation to gross and aggregated measures of various 'externalities', factors introducing variation other than those abstracted into the definitions of the economic model. Somewhere implicit in these factual conjunctions, presumably, are the telling generalizations that will describe the progress of underdeveloped countries towards a Western, industrialized model. The facts have been identified through a whole series of 'common-sense' assumptions, whose normative overtones would be hard to disguise, and then turned over to a process of condensation on an analytical assumption that is positivist in an unreconstructed sense: that the facts are discrete, have an independent objectivity and are comparable.

The Princeton volume uses only 'hard' data—a very misleading phrase, indicating non-subjective, demographic, 'economic', etc—and the authors make economists' assumptions about psychological states, traditions, ideologies, values and the like. There is no suggestion that these are unimportant, simply that an economic analysis should take economic facts and make sense of them in its own terms. One should add, also, that this 'workbook' is presented with modest claims and that the authors place all their cards on the table, both in connection with uncertainties about the reliability of the evidence itself and as regards the methods they use. They see themselves as developing a form of comparative analysis which is intrinsically capable of improvement and development, and they would presumably accept the suggestion that an analysis that absorbed yet more data of another kind, provided it met the formal requirements of a quantitative method, would be more productive empirically and conceptually.

Two other authors, in an earlier study, have produced a methodologically similar analysis that does attempt an inquiry of wider scope. [5] They are not prepared to accept that the essential structural features of a process of change can be traced by examining 'hard' variables in isolation. They recognize that these 'hard' facts mean different things in different contexts, and that the relationships between subjective orientations, the productive process and political and social institutions are variable and entirely problematic. In their theoretical discussion, they in fact cite anthropological studies which they use in interpreting their data. So they incorporate measures of 'soft' or qualitative variables, such as degree of modernization of outlook, degree of social tension, and the extent of leadership commitment to economic development. These are interrelated with the other economic variables in a factor analysis. The result, for all the care and technical skill that went into it, seems discouraging and, again, its failure is related to its epistemological and theoretical assumptions about the structure of societal relations and the dynamics of change.

There is nothing intrinsically dubious about pushing the description of subjective states to the point of measuring them. Whatever their limitations, we have learnt a great deal from sample surveys that have attempted to do so. [6] And the use of quantitative measures in psychological testing is highly developed. Indeed, in this area the picture of a primitive social science adapting the second-hand models of the natural scientist needs to be corrected. Some important developments in statistical method, particularly in principal component analysis and analysis of variance, both of which will be described in this chapter, must be credited to psychologists and have been adapted by mathematically minded biologists. [7] Obviously there are very substantial difficulties which would take us into arguments that are far from being resolved, in the field of personality theory for example. In order to fit subjective states to statistical models, for instance, we will generally have to think of them in linear terms, such as continua of Liberalism-Conservatism, ascending 'scales' of neuroticism or ethnocentrism. This may or may not be a reasonable convention to accept. There are also problems of dimensionality. Scores on the scales will be compared, standardized, added and correlated. It may or may not be a reasonable convention to think in terms of equivalent units of psychological space and to classify people in terms of the degrees of psychological distance that lie between them.

However, such subjective measures as Adelman and Morris use are decidedly rough compared with the aggregate scores of psychological tests, and their debt to the psychologists is a general methodological one. They use a statistical model which is frequently used with exclusively, or largely, psychological data, to find order in the confusion of their total weight of data, hard and soft alike. The general description of the model is factor analysis, of which the method of principal components is a representative variant.

As a systematic instrument for a theoretical analysis, this particular set of statistical models has some quite astonishing pro-

perties. In a most intriguing manner it offers the possibility of
locating in the manageable confusion of a large number of
interacting variables the features of a limited number of
components. These can then be described by the appropriate
intermediate theoretical categories. The facts, to caricature
elementary positivist expectations, will be organized and waiting
for a suitable designation. If the evidence is appropriately
presented in a formal sense, a factor analysis guarantees to
organize its confusions into a limited number of categories,
which have at least a clear mathematical significance.

In educational psychology, the home base of this comparative
method in the behavioural sciences, the concept of intelligence
is of central importance, but it is notoriously difficult to define
with precision or to test simply. A popular operational definition is the one which says that intelligence is whatever
intelligence tests measure, with the implication, which is not
entirely fair, that the concept in practice finds itself reduced to
the prior categories of the educationalists who devise the tests.
It is not entirely fair, because they in fact assume that they are
investigating a multifaceted as well as variable capacity in
individuals and they have devised many different tests to try to
capture different elements in the psychological make-up of the
individual which affect his ability to handle problems and
situations. It is assumed that these different components will
interact in systematic ways, and the problem is to describe these
interrelationships. So the factor analytic technique can be used
to discover connections amongst the psychological elements
that are measured by the primary tests of capacity. The factor
analysis starts with a matrix of intercorrelations such as was
referred to earlier, pair-by-pair correlations between individual
tests of one kind and another.

By a further sleight of hand, as was hinted earlier, these correlations (indeed, any correlations, including 'partial' and
'multiples') can be represented as geometrical relations, and
in these terms it should be possible to describe the model without getting lost in the formidable but necessary computations.
A given correlation can be translated into the cosine. Thus, a
perfect positive correlation (1·0) corresponds to a situation in
which there is no angle at all between the vectors, one is
superimposed on the other. A total absence of any correlation
(0·0), whether positive or negative (for present purposes we
need make no special reference to negative values) corresponds
with an angle of 90°. At this point the dimensions are described
as orthogonal, at right angles to each other. The conversion is

made through a table of cosines; the value of the correlation is the cosine of the angle.

The geometrical analogue for a relationship between two tests, then, would be two intersecting lines. If they intersect at an acute angle, the correlation will be relatively high—there will be a tendency for individuals scoring high on one test also to score high on the other. But as the angle approaches 90° we will know that there is less and less pattern to the distribution of individuals between the two dimensions. (Beyond that point, as the angle becomes increasingly obtuse, we are registering negative or inverse correlations. Individuals high on one test tend to be low on the other. The direction of the tests is obviously arbitrary, but it does have to be consistent.)

If we add more variables to this picture we will need a space with more dimensions. Each vector will have to be so placed that the complete range of particular comparisons is translated into the appropriate angles of incidence. With a great many dimensions we might find ourselves regarding a kind of battered and uncanvased umbrella, with ribs at every conceivable angle to each other, but, alas, without a handle.

A factor analysis proceeds to invent a handle. In the case of the intelligence tests, the logic would be as follows. You observe a high degree of correlation amongst some of the tests; though they are each measuring something different they all seem to be on to some common underlying element, which is reflected in each in different degrees. One can imagine an ideal test, which would exactly measure an individual's position on this elusive common attribute. If it existed, the tests employed would be redundant approximations, confused by error and contaminated by other factors. But they are all pointing towards, and indicating, the composition of this complex common element. Such a test is inconceivable in practice, but what the factor analyst does is to estimate the score each individual would get if it did exist. He does this by considering in mathematical combination each individual's score in each individual test and the established correlations between all the tests. The result is an exact specification of the location of a new vector in relation to all the others. Gripping it, metaphysically, he is claiming that this is indeed the umbrella to which these ribs belong. Each attribute can be described in relation to it, and so can each individual. We have one condensed summary of a large number of complex interrelations.

There will be more than one factor, and there may well be more than three, each one uncorrelated (orthogonal) to all the others, so that we are left to make what we can of the image of a multi-handled umbrella in multidimensional space. It will have served its purpose if it makes sense of the critical question in factor analysis. The factor has a mathematical reality; it is the inevitable outcome of a number of purely abstract considerations. But what is it that the evidence has identified for us in reality? The test-scores are intercorrelated, but can we really conclude that they are bound together by a distinctive dynamic of functional interactions simply because we can condense these elements into a representative value? What name do we give this new fact? The analysis itself can provide no guarantee that this abridgment of the evidence has any significance whatever in a theoretical sense. All one can say is that if the categories that come to be attached to these condensed patterns of evidence are theoretically significant, then the analysis will have provided a systematic and meaningful connection between the theoretical language and the complexities of a field of evidence. There are uncertainties here which cannot be resolved internally. They will have to be referred to informed judgments within a field of general assumptions. These may well be modified by what emerges from such an analysis—it would be pointless going to the trouble if one did not expect them to be—but the results cannot determine assumptions.

This is the powerful analytical technique, in any event, which Adelman and Morris use to organize an enormous quantity of data from seventy-four underdeveloped countries. Where Harbison and his colleagues had been relatively tentative and exploratory, the analysis in this case raises higher expectations, that internal comparisons of the data will point the way towards theoretically interesting generalizations, statements about general relationships, which would be supported by a great many narrowly focused observations of functional interdependencies at an operational level.

But, once again, it is not clear what we learn from the analysis. The extraction of the factors stimulates no startling hypothesis, points to no fresh conceptual formulation. The conclusions reflect the assumptions that ordered the raw data, assumptions embedded in the use of broad theoretical terms such as 'economic' and 'social' to designate observational elements that are thought of as being in some objective sense distinct. [8]

> The degree of intimate interrelationship found in this analysis between the economic and non-economic concomitants of a country's historical evolution is rather surprising. It lends support to the view long held by development economists

that, in the last analysis, the purely economic performance of a community is strongly conditioned by the social and political setting in which economic activity takes place and that the less developed a nation is, the less powerful is economic policy alone in inducing economic development. It would appear that the splitting off of homo economicus into a separate analytic entity, a common procedure since Adam Smith in theorizing about growth in advanced economies, is much less suited to countries that have not yet made the transition to self-sustained economic growth.

But there is nothing surprising about the interrelationships between economic and non-economic concomitants, not at least to students of less developed nations or societies. The factor analysis reveals that seventy per cent of the intercountry variations in the levels of economic development is associated with differences in non-economic characteristics, and the authors conclude that it therefore appears 'just as reasonable to look at underdevelopment as a social and political phenomenon as it is to analyse it in terms of intercountry differences in economic structure'. As an insight this is on the banal side. And it seems reasonable to object that their statistical correlation is an inevitable function of the mechanistic conceptual distinctions between types of attribute, economic, social, political, which they had adopted. The data are at best a record of usually obvious logical correlations, and provide little fodder for a genuinely functional hypothesis. There is not much weight to the inferences this elaborate abridgment provides. We are that that[9]

the results of the factor analysis neither demonstrate that economic growth is caused by sociopolitical transformation nor indicate that variations in development levels determine patterns of social and political change. Rather they suggest the existence of a systematic pattern of interaction among mutually interdependent economic, social, and political forces, all of which combine to generate a unified complex of change in the style of life of a community.

'Systematic pattern' refers to the statistically significant inter-correlations and factor loading among arrays of attributes, the general direction of which one would have anticipated, leaving aside the main interest in the relative strength of association among different empirical attributes. What we have no clue to is the systematic relationship between spheres or systems of interaction at a structural level. Gross generalizations from aggregated evidence of this kind are not the tentative building blocks of a theoretical analysis. They are the terminus of a

methodological procedure which has confused the idea of a
structured totality of functionally dependent social processes
with a general but untheoretical sensitivity to the interconnectedness of things.

In slightly different ways, these two studies seem in their
limitations to suggest a methodological rule of thumb, which
in turn reflects the general view of a scientific method in the
social sciences that is being advanced in these pages. The
quantification of evidence presupposes a theoretical understanding of it, not in the first instance in terms of broad abstractions
and generalities, but in a sense much closer to what is intrinsic
to formally similar studies in biology. That is to say, we need
a theoretical understanding of what is being identified as an
attribute or variable at a primary level, and its immediate
relationships. The studies that have just been discussed seem
to lack this, partly as a result of the substantial abstractions
involved in their primary evidence, partly because of the ways
in which this evidence is then described. Economic magnitudes,
which have indeed been split off from other factors, because
they have operated as commodity relations within the institutional
structures which have emerged since the time of Adam Smith,
are measured against other magnitudes which are not isolated
and defined by institutional structures in at all the same sense.
On the other hand, factor analytic studies of psychological data
in intelligence testing, contentious enough in all conscience,
manipulate the results of carefully prepared tests given relatively homogeneous samples.[10] Factor analytic studies of
legislative behaviour, like the game-theoretical approaches to
behaviour in such settings, presuppose interactions and choices
that are understood in much the same terms by the participants,
and the extraction of summary factors from the massive output
of votes may well reveal basic alignments and ideological
preferences which are not explicit or easy to observe in the
raw run of voting.[11] And much the same point can be made of a
more exploratory and heuristic use of such techniques. If the
field of data has a manifest homogeneity, if we can reasonably
claim to understand at least the salient definitions and constraints within which the participants organize an aspect of
their behaviour, we may be able to pursue such an understanding
further to good effect by making judicious transformations,
even elaborate ones, into statistical models. The result can test
assumptions in a number of limited senses, by uncovering surprising juxtapositions, raising new questions, qualifying emphasis.[12] We are back with a point made in the last chapter. There
appears to be something of an inverse relationship between the

sophistication of multivariate quantitative methods and the scope of the problems to which they can be directly related. They may tell us more than we would otherwise detect about the principles of operation of partial systems, but arguments pitched at a more comprehensive and general level necessarily make use of intermediate concepts of some complexity which raise intractable problems of operational definition, comparability and dimensionality.

III

It has been suggested that it is a mistake to impute particular epistemological or general assumptions to an analysis simply on the grounds that it makes use of particular formal methods. Indeed, it is by examining the fit between a general theoretical model and its statistical analogue in each particular case that we can see more clearly the fundamental assumptions lying behind the former. However, it does seem to be the case that particular statistical models tend to invite or accommodate distinctive general assumptions about the nature of evidence and the analyst's relationship to it. Not that such assumptions can be categorically identified. The criticisms of factorial methods in comparative studies of change imply that this statistical model runs the risk of being seen as the paradigm of an inert and unreflecting version of one positivist tradition; it organizes facts that are confusing in combination but unproblematic in themselves, in order, it is hoped, to uncover their causal and functional dependencies. In drawing a contrast between these methods and analysis of variance, Hope balances two other philosophical traditions. 'Factor analysis is akin to medieval scientific method in that it allows Nature to dictate the explanation, whereas analysis of variance has the modern, Kantian, spirit which "puts Nature to the Inquisition", imposes unnatural conditions upon her in order to wrest from her the answer to preconceived questions.'[13] In any event, whatever philosophical correspondences one might wish to draw, we have in factor analysis and analysis of variance two models which presuppose differences in the form in which data have been assembled and theoretical questions pitched at quite different levels. We can be precise about the mathematical differences between the two models and then turn to their implications for the analysis of any given body of data; it is[14]

not that one is related to experiments and the other to observations, because in fact either may be related to either of
these, but that in the analysis of variance the criteria for
dividing the total sum of squares are given externally, while
in principal component analysis the criterion is strictly
internal, namely that each successive parcel shall have a
largest possible sum of squares and be orthogonal to the
preceding parcels.

The description of the missing umbrella handle was an attempt
to indicate the strictly internal criterion for extracting successive factors; a projection from the matrix of correlations determines the only place where it can be located.[15] Whilst in
analysis of variance, a sample is broken into two or more sub-
samples, and these are compared with respect to whatever
attribute is of interest to the observer. He may, for example, be
interested in 'modernization of outlook' as a variable that could
have contrasting values in different parts of a society. He
extracts the two groups from his sample and compares the
representative value of this variable in each group. By doing
so, he will have created on his own criterion two groups, each
with a mean value for the attribute, and each (assuming, as was
pointed out, that he has collected the relevant data from individuals) with a measured dispersion around that mean. The measure of dispersion indicates the extent to which, in either subgroup, the attribute is erratically distributed or is something that
most individuals have in common to more or less the same
degree. He is asking a specific question: Is there a meaningful
difference between the two groups with respect to their 'modernization of outlook' (however that may have been assessed)?

Every statistical analysis tests a hypothesis—analysis of
variance tests the null hypothesis that there is no difference
between the representative values in the two groups. However,
this is not the form in which hypotheses in some general theory
of change are likely to be formulated. We would be more likely
to find ourselves arguing whether it was because one group had
a modern outlook and the other did not that their relations developed the way they did. In the context of such questions an analysis of variance may be an invaluable ancillary in establishing
the credentials on which the argument is based. Assuming
agreement on the significance and measurement of the attribute,
the analysis will identify something that the argument is prepared to accept as fact. There appears to be a difference
between two groups with respect to an observable characteristic: but is there really a difference? How likely is it to be an

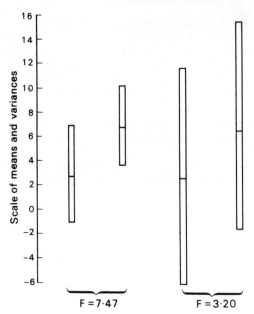

Figure 7   Diagram of ratios for analysis of variance

Note: 'F' is a ratio of two variances (a) the variance of the
means and (b) the error variance, estimated from the variance
within the samples. In each of these two pairs the variance of
the means is the same, but the error variance is larger in the
second pair.

unrepresentative observation, the result of contingent factors
or poor measurement?

Hope's diagram (Fig. 7) represents two pairs of comparisons.
In each case the horizontal line bisecting the block stands for
the mean value for the observation in the subgroup. The length
of the block stands for the relative size of the distribution
about that mean in each subgroup. In each pair the difference
between the means of the two subgroups is the same. But there
is much more homogeneity in the first group; people are much
less likely to be widely different with respect to the observed
characteristic than in the second pair. The mean in the second
pair is something of a statistical fiction. There is so much
overlap that the comparison between groups is not one on which
a strong inference could be based. In the first case there is
much more of a distinction and there are grounds for advancing

it as consequential in an argument. If the observations themselves are representative, the analysis offers a judgment on the comparison in the form of a probability statement; there are so many chances in a hundred that the difference between sets of representative values (means/dispersion) would be as appreciable as it is observed to be on a purely random distribution of characteristics.

It is not always the case that the implicit comparisons in factual assertions are given the validation an analysis of variance can provide. The possibilities, particularly for an analysis that is focused on a common set of structural parameters and social meanings, are only beginning to be realized.[16] They focus attention inescapably on the interpenetration of strictly statistical and substantively theoretical assumptions in any application of quantitative techniques.

CHAPTER FIVE

Causes and structure

I

Statistical applications necessarily reflect theoretical decisions about the nature of the evidence, and the causal or other relations of interdependence within it. Bearing as they do on matters of choice, they cannot be insulated from the observer's interpretation of the rationality of those choices, from the normative framework within which the social scientist must identify the relevant detail of his analysis, whether it is quantifiable or not.

Certainly there are ways of treating mathematically widely different sorts of observations, in order to establish facts and in order to identify different configurations of attributes. But there also seems to be a caesura between these empirical explorations and the problem of explaining the maintenance, interplay and transformation of whole systems of social relations. It is true that classification and analysis in Radcliffe-Brown's hands is implicitly statistical—his discovery of concomitant variations of structural attributes in whole classes of society leads him on to comparative generalization. At a rather different level, Leach has insisted on the value of giving mathematical expression to the kinship problems which the structural insights of Radcliffe-Brown had already pushed to an abstract and comprehensive level. His point is that by doing so we can specify precisely the interdependence of particular structural attributes. 'In talking about "function" in a generalized way it is not sufficient to specify relationships between particular empirical facts; we must give a genuine mathematical sense to our concept of function and start thinking in terms of ratios and the variations of ratios.'[1] But, again, the advantage is heuristic, to 'get away from excessive entanglement in empirical facts and value loaded concepts'. Mathematization is not, as it were, the matrix out of which a functional explanation of the total process of structural stability and structural change can in principle emerge. It may be a useful ancillary device which

integrates evidence to the theoretical argument. But such an
argument is necessarily generalized and imprecise with respect
to the entire field of interdependencies it identifies, a fact that
is fully reflected in the medley of applications the term 'functional' has acquired[2] and in the variety of senses in which social
scientists refer to 'structure'.

However, even the cursory comments on a couple of quantitative
studies of the gross processes of economic, social and political
change should make it clear that the use of quantitative methods
raises problems that cannot simply be referred to the pragmatic
ingenuity of the researcher when confronted with burdensome
collections of data. They raise pervasive and fundamental
philosophical issues. Whether a social scientist is attempting to
extract from his evidence general statements about common
processes affecting many societies or many individuals, or to
establish the operating principles of a particular social system,
or to locate historical factors that transform relations within it,
he cannot avoid taking a position on the central epistemological
problem of causation. What he is prepared to accept as an
explanation is contingent on that decision.

It is a painfully difficult decision to take, and social scientists
have been understandably reluctant to leap in where philosophers
move with caution, and often at great length. [3] Brisk clarifica-
tions have been put forward, such as Spiro's observation that
'causal explanations attempt to account for some sociocultural
variable by reference to some antecedent conditions—its
"cause". Functional explanations account for the variable by
reference to some consequent condition—its "function".'[4] But
this leaves us pretty much on our starting positions. A variable,
we have recognized, is a theoretical construct, and so are what
he calls consequent conditions, whilst the distinction here
between the dynamics of cause and function seems to be purely
formal and unilluminating. Surely statements about functional
interdependencies are causal statements of a certain kind, and
the mystery that has often surrounded the distinction is partly
a reflection of the social scientist's uncertainty about how to
identify precisely interconnections that are both reciprocal and
multiple, interactions involving indefinite series of factors. It
has also of course been compounded by the teleological and
organicist assumptions referred to in Chapter 1. Under these
assumptions, the philosophical and methodological premise of
the interconnectedness of structural components of society was
a sleeping pretext for overlooking asymmetrical relationships
between variables. Many processes are irreversible and can
only be represented in a unidirectional model. Physicists do

not describe the transformation of pions into muons and
neutrinos as an interaction, because the energy for the event
is an attribute intrinsic to pions. There is no shortage of equivalent examples from developmental biology. Likewise, endo-
genously generated processes of social change seem to force us
to think in causal terms. Though, even here, vague philosophical
reservations about the standing of the concept of cause have
tempted historians into the evasion of referring to 'factors' that
have variable degrees of importance in conditioning subsequent
developments.

Quantitative studies, influenced by empiricist assumptions about
scientific method, have developed their own neurosis. They have
tended to deal with covariation, along the lines outlined in the
previous chapter, and with prediction, whether in the context of
the theories of a positive economics or more modestly by extrapolating from empirical generalizations. But as far as the main
question goes 'The statistical literature, it seems, is almost
schizophrenic in its approach.... While I have not made a
systematic content analysis of the language used in various
statistics texts and writings, there seems to be considerable
confusion of terminology and almost a conspiracy of silence in
dealing with the problem of causality.'[5]

The schizophrenia Blalock refers to is quite general to the
statistical literature and by no means only to what has come to
be called social statistics. The reason is the traditional and
familiar one in discussions of causality, that constant conjunctions of events, variables, characteristics, can be established by
observation, but this does not <u>prove</u> necessary and causal connection. Statistical methods can be very precise about degrees of
covariation, and there may be much to be gained from translating
observations into an appropriate mathematical generalization.
But there is only a speculative bridge between this language and
the language of causal explanation. In the natural sciences, this
limitation on causal inference was a telling one for Mach and the
neopositivists who followed him. Accordingly, they argued that
causation should be replaced by interdependence, and that mathematics should be used to establish functional statements which
would identify a 'static net of reciprocal dependencies like that
among the parts of a steel frame'.[6] This clearly excluded the
type of irreversible relationships referred to earlier. The
implications of making a naïve transfer of this epistemological
position to the statistical analysis of social behaviour are plain.
It does, however, fit a literal and unadventurous reading of
statistical data. Causal inferences are regarded as unwarrant-
able, because undemonstrable, additions to objective reality.

Uncertainties about the philosophical validity of causal connections have been introduced on other grounds as well, and reflect
other aspects of the positivist's search for reality. As one
philosopher points out, in the course of an attempt to put the
concept of causality out of business in any field whatsoever, [7]

> science, instead of establishing connections between facts
> as such, rather analyzes them. This analysis consists of
> decomposing (in thought) the unique course of actual events
> into elements which are simpler, recurrent and capable of
> measurement. The 'uniform' relations of which philosophers
> are so fond are to be found, not between the events them-
> selves but rather between the elements into which they have
> been dissected.

How much sense does it make to relate analytically convenient
categories to each other in causal terms? The 'imposing of
"names" and the "connection" of them' is a social and intellectual activity, and the boundaries of such conventional entities
are not some sort of cellular grid that corresponds to unquestionable boundaries in objective reality.

The issue of causality seems to be unresolved for the philosophers of natural science, and the importance of causal explanations for the practising scientist probably varies considerably
from field to field. These discussions throw some light on our
own problems but they do not take us very far. An encounter
with the problem from two strongly contrasted perspectives, that
of the generalizing, quantitative study, on the one hand, and that
of the particularizing historian or social anthropologist on the
other, seems to indicate a distinctively messy solution for the
social scientist. Unless he is prepared to provide explanations
in causal terms, he is destined to produce castrated explanations. However, he has to operate with a notion of causality that
is not unitary or philosophically rigorous. Causal explanations
are uniformly speculative, and this is merely underlined by the
way the generalizing and quantitative studies emphasize what
I have called the caesura between the language of mathematical
relations into which observations have been transposed and the
theoretical language that is necessary to interpret their relationships. But causal explanations are speculative with respect
to qualitatively different categories of fact and at different
levels. Generally, we need causal assumptions when we explain
in terms of 'impersonal' determinants (population change,
technological development, etc.), when we explain in terms of
motivation and decision, when we explain in terms of the intermediate level of Durkheimian 'social fact' (ideational structures

that define awareness of a social situation), and perhaps in
another sense again when we explain in terms of the possibilities
introduced by normative political theory. This chapter will
attempt to indicate the necessity for such an untidy interpretation of the notion of cause in social explanations.

II

The previous chapter understated the possibilities of comparative quantitative analysis of social and political phenomena. It
was suggested that an ability to make elaborate internal comparisons of bodies of evidence could very usefully reduce complexities, select crucial factors, identify relationships, challenge
discrete factual assumptions and provide reliable evidence for
the categories of a theoretical argument. But the value of a
method is a function of the conceptual orientation working
through it. It is, for example, an illusion, or even an evasion, to
suppose that a 'scientific' method for making refined comparisons and discriminations will of itself generate a coherent
interpretation of 'an unanalyzable muddle consisting of an
infinity of "factors", all of them standing on the same footing'. [8]

However, it is not necessary to relapse into this assumption of
an impenetrable global functionalism; and data virtually identical
with that used by Adelman and Morris can be analysed com-
paratively and statistically in the light of leading questions or
hypotheses that presuppose significant and identifiable causal
chains operating through the broad processes of change. Putnam's attempt to explain military interventions in Latin American politics uses statistical analysis to pursue explicitly causal
hypotheses. [9] He shows the scope and limitation of the concept
of causality at one level of analysis, where the abstraction and
analysis of comparative evidence perhaps represents a less
gross destructuring and reconstitution of reality.

There exist, in the studies of Finer, Gutteridge, Huntington and
others who have considered the relations between military and
civil institutions in different types of society, various hypotheses
that might explain structural tensions characteristically leading to an invasion of the civil functions of the state by the military apparatus. The mere fact of a military intervention can of
course have a variety of implications. There are substantial
differences between, say, the reformist military regime of Peru
in the 1970s and the regime in Paraguay in the 1960s. But

Putnam does distinguish between different degrees of military involvement in terms of a rough continuum, so what he has to explain is a differentiated variable. At the same time, it seems reasonable to argue that these events are frequent enough and have significant enough features in common to be comparable. These features can be described with reference to colonial histories, the nature of the struggles for independence from the original colonial powers, the nature of secular and religious authority and relations between the two. In terms of a number of dimensions of social organization, Latin American countries obviously have more in common with each other than with the states of Africa or South East Asia or the Middle East.

The more important hypotheses tested by Putnam have to do with economic and social underdevelopment, namely that the propensity for military intervention is likely to decrease with increased mobilization, and that, economic development, especially industrialization, diminishes the propensity for military intervention. There is no need to repeat comments made in the previous chapter about operationalizing (finding proxies for) general concepts of this kind. The concepts identify for him highly complex general trends, of which there is a wide variety of observable manifestations. He selects a number of such indicators, for example, percentage of literate adults and percentage of labour force employed in industry. He standardizes the raw data, and extracts indices of Social Mobilization and Economic Development for each country. From here he can proceed to correlate the distribution of scores on each of these indices with the series of historical events (conventionalized in a Military Intervention Index) which reflect the forms of structural change he wishes to account for. The results are interesting and not a pretentious statement of a truism. The hypotheses are confirmed. However, it is possible to respond within the terms of the statistical model to an obvious objection, namely that 'Economic Development' and 'Social Mobilization' are analytical constructs which indicate different, theoretically interesting, aspects of an empirically compounded reality. So the data for the two sets of indices are bound to correlate. But it is the fact that they do so imperfectly and variably that provides the social scientist with opportunities for making plausible inferences. The empirical confusions find themselves translated into the mathematical model in the form of a correlation between the two indices (ED and SM), which is very high at 0·89.[10] It is possible to use some mathematics to distinguish the variability within each of the two sets of observations, in other words to remove the effect of the variability along one analyti-

cal dimension whilst calculating the association between variations on the other index and the dependent variable (MI). When
this is done we are forced to reflect back on the common-sense
assumptions the original hypotheses embody, because we now
find that 'if we remove the effect of social mobilization, economic development itself turns out to be positively, not negatively,
correlated with military intervention'.

This analysis simply develops for data above the nominal level
of classified observations the logic set out in the fruit-fly
example of Chapter 3. As it happens, and despite the limitations
of such data and the indefinite possibilities of local variations,
the complicated statistical result seems to throw light on a number of specific histories. Putnam cites Colombia, El Salvador,
Venezuela and Costa Rica. The same statistical procedures are
applied to other hypotheses, for example one concerning the
historical importance of foreign military missions in Latin
America. The useful general outcome is, first, that a number of
frequently invoked explanations are ruled out of court because
they are contradicted by the evidence, and, second, that we are
obliged to make more sensitive and discriminating distinctions
between broad categories which are frequently used to describe
and account for change. 'The direct effect of economic development seems to be to encourage military intervention, although
there is also a strong indirect effect linking economic development and military abstention, by way of social mobilization.'[11]
Whatever objections might be raised to the theoretical categories
themselves (and Development, particularly Political Development
as Putnam identifies it, invokes normative criteria which are
very much in dispute), their content has been specified and the
implications systematically explored, with the effect of producing a conceptual shift. Though the categories are analytical
and to that extent limit observations, and though the observations
themselves are to a degree logically and functionally correlated
amongst themselves, the analysis provides better pointers than
may be provided by individual historical accounts to the evolution of general determining processes which penetrate specific
social structures.

But the essentially heuristic value of comparative statistical
analysis is even more explicit in the balance of the paper,
because here Putnam fits the statistical data to a causal path
analysis which picks out particular patterns as candidates for
an explanatory complex of cause and effect. This entails making
candidly unrealistic assumptions about the relevance of variables not abstracted into these patterns. In fact it is necessary
to ignore entirely the impact of variables that are not being

considered, if one is to fit the data to the formal requirements
of the model. He uses the analysis to overcome another general
limitation of the aggregative comparative study, that they are
synchronic and that there must be uncertainties about the
apparent coherence of the evidence that are analogous to those
referred to in connection with the synchronic systems of the
anthropologist. He distinguishes two historical phases during
which military interventions took place, takes literacy data as
a respectable proxy for the construct of social mobilization,
excludes on a priori grounds seven of the logically possible
causal links within this set of factors, and establishes the
relative strength of the associations among the remainder (see
Fig. 8).

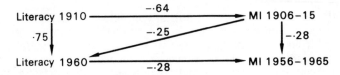

Figure 8   Path coefficients for relationships among literacy rates,
            1910 and 1960, and military intervention, 1906-15 and
            1956-65

A brief inspection will indicate the various a priori reasons such
as temporal sequence and general implausibility for excluding
particular causal paths.

Evidently, we are no nearer demonstrating a causal process
than we were before, but we have been provided with an internally balanced appraisal of evidence for the particular hypothesis, which may converge with other threads of evidence in a
more comprehensive analysis, or may simply indicate other
questions or gaps in the evidence. It is thus possible systematically to explore a speculation about elements in a complex process in ways that lead one to modulate the emphases of a more
general explanation. Such an analysis is necessarily oblique
and in a sense artificial. 'Complex multivariate models require
a good many assumptions in order to estimate the parameters
of the model. These assumptions are often not testable, and they
do not, of course, "emerge" from the analysis of the data, and
should not be reported as empirically grounded conclusions.'[12]
In this case the limitations are well recognized. The statistical
rigour is most decisively valuable in disposing of the off-hand
speculations of various observers. But it also makes tentative
and interesting contributions to a more constructive analysis.

Firstly, it indicates a certain bias or causal flow among factors that can be described in terms of generalizing abstractions, at least as these embody historical transformations in the Latin American subcontinent. Second, it is used, not as a methodological ante-room leading on to the more ample accommodation of abstract and highly inclusive general laws, but, on the contrary, in order to open up entirely new questions about particular societies, above all where they seem to demonstrate structural relationships that do not correspond with a general trend. The identification of very general configurations considerably enlarges our understanding, but only to the extent that we continue to think of what is common and what is distinctive in terms of particular social structures. Statistical generalization provides a frame of reference for further inquiry, which may take the form of quantitative analysis of different data, of historical analysis, or of an analysis of particular structures of roles, economic factors or what not. Tufte has argued persuasively that this is the main value in statistical analysis at any level in the social sciences, and that it has been seriously neglected. [13] This view does not exactly correspond with arguments that are commonly advanced for a scientific method in comparative studies. We find Przeworski and Teune, for example, summarizing their position on comparative research and social science theory by saying (in part) that[14]

> explanation in comparative research is possible if and only if particular social systems observed in time and space are not viewed as finite conjunctions of constituent elements, but rather as residua of theoretical variables. General lawlike sentences can be utilized for explanatory purposes. Only if the classes of social events are viewed as generalizable beyond the limits of any particular historical social system can general lawlike sentences be used for explanation. Therefore the role of comparative research in the process of theory building and theory-testing consists of replacing proper names of social systems by the relevant variables.

In other words, we are arguing that the systematic discovery of empirical regularities is an essential activity of the social sciences, which may be particularly productive when it is pursued in the light of explicit causal hypotheses.

But the value of the generalization is not simply in itself, a manifest lawlike statement. This is reflected in the potential importance of prediction from such empirical generalizations. Of course prediction underwrites generalization in the conventional sense. Electoral surveys (as distinct from opinion polls)

are capable of making very impressive predictions, and this
certainly supports their claims to have identified the relevant
general 'determinants' of voting behaviour. [15] But it is equally
important that the prediction emerges from what is in effect a
system of classification, and one that can only take account of
those dynamic properties that have been specified and observed,
so that it is also a vehicle for making qualifications and distinctions. An analysis of the failure to predict a specific historical instance may be the most significant outcome of establishing
a relatively successful lawlike generalization. Why is it, for
example, that Bolivia, Costa Rica and Argentina seriously dis-
turb the general pattern that relates Social Mobilization and
Military Intervention in the 1956-65 period? The question
emerges from the broader comparative analysis, but the
explanation must lie in the particular historical conjunctures
and decisions. In fact, inspection of these particular deviant
cases suggested to Putnam that the development of class anta-
gonisms might be an important factor missing from his analysis.
The suggestion finds confirmation in what is known about the
1973 military coup in Chile, where the military have not, historically, been deeply involved in politics.

The method is not necessarily good for evidence at any level of
generality. Reasons have already been given for uncertainty
about the validity of comparative generalizations based on data
aggregated from a wide variety of situations. The suggestion
that even ostensibly 'hard' data may have quite different implications in different situations, touched on in the last chapter in
connection with Harbison's study, should be considered more
particularly in the context of a discussion of causal analysis.
Forbes and Tufte have pointed out that 'especially those aiming
to give a causal interpretation of their findings should consider
the possibility that different causal processes operate in different subgroups of their data'. They go on to suggest that 'this
may be formally incorporated into the model by using statistical
procedures that take interaction effects into account'. However,
at first sight, the limitation also suggests that the statistical
analysis of data on causal assumptions can proceed with greater
confidence in relatively more narrowly defined situations. If
we abandon the grail of generality in social science explanation,
at least as it has been thought to emerge from analytical procedures of this type, we can involve the methods in testing and
consolidating insights into complex particulars. The real bene-
fits might lie in making statistical comparisons within societies
rather than between them. With this suggestion the statistical
models we have touched upon could come very clearly within

the reach of the anthropologist, and combinations of them, from analysis of variance to the assessment in a correlational analysis of abstracted causal connections, could be used to develop the precise and particular statements Leach calls for in his criticisms of a generalized functionalism.

But quantitative methods, as Leach himself points out elsewhere, cannot necessarily be assimilated to the anthropologist's perspective by a decision about the scale and type of the social entity that is being analysed. [16] Discussing what he insists is an important contribution to Ceylon studies, he finds himself describing a crux in interdisciplinary perspectives for which there is no obvious resolution. He and a survey team from Ceylon University had independently considered strictly comparable data, but the facts that they placed in relation to each other suggested anything but a converging interpretation of causal or functional relations. The reasons for this stem from a basic methodological difference, which in turn reflects different working assumptions about the explanation of social behaviour, rather than some ideological difference between their perspectives. The comparison, of course, is invidiously in favour of his own discipline, but not without reservations. From his own, particularizing, perspective he can make damaging criticism of some of the statistical 'facts' assembled in the survey, facts which are intrinsically polemical, since they describe widening economic disparities between different categories of person in rural Ceylon. For example, the survey finds that, out of 506 households, 335 owned no paddy land at all. The anthropologist has to 'convert the figures back into facts'. This means indicating the relationships that lie behind the numerical categories. Thus:[17]

> (1) Sinhalese village girls tend to get married very young, but... every married woman, however young, has a separate cooking pot. Thus every married couple constitutes a separate statistical household, whether living in a separate house or not. (2) Property may be transmitted to an individual's descendants either by inheritance at death or at any time by gift inter vivos. In practice, except in the case of dowry to the daughters of the relatively wealthy, most property is handed on only when the original owner has become elderly. Thus if a man of means is living on a single compound with three married sons, the sociological analysis might record this fact with the statistic that 'three out of four households are landless'.

So a proportion of the landless were landless because they consisted of[18]

young recently married adults who were heirs to still living
parents. I have arrived at this conclusion by making the
typically anthropological assumption that a social field does
not consist of units of population but of persons in relation
to one another.

Leach goes on to make comparable points about the survey's
use of sharecropping as a critical structural characteristic. If
we take account of the generational relationships, synchronous
observations of the pattern of land holding as between proprietors
and (sharecropping) heirs take on a specific sociological significance. This dimension, a structure of persistent interpretations of the nature of personal property, are not statistical facts
within the context of an equally synchronous but more abstract
survey. It is not immediately obvious how such observations
could be presented statistically. At the same time, they hardly
encourage us to take up the statistical analysis as a basis for
causal inferences. The accumulation of empirical facts, as
these present themselves to an inquirer trained to identify
relationships among roles or jural persons, seems to work
against the grain of generalizations derived from random
samples, in which by definition (a requirement of the statistical
model) the sampled units are unrelated to one another. If we
are to talk about determinants and causes in the evolution of
behaviour within these relationships, the statistical facts will
have to be interpreted in terms of an apprehension of structure
and social organization, and determining conditions will be
identified in a complex of constraints. Causal speculations are
based on another type of description of empirical regularities.

Set beside each other, Putnam's use of statistical methods to
make broad causal inferences, and Leach's critique of a
representative contribution to empirical sociology suggest some
tentative conclusions about the extraction of causal inferences
from numerical categories at different levels of generality.
What Putnam's theory identifies are broad and general variations, at the level of population growth, technology and industrialization, basic consumption, etc., together with a broadly identified type of structural change in the distribution of power and
authority. Specific structural variants are deliberately ignored
for the sake of precision. Each category of fact is immensely
complex and carries with it variable implications for different
situations, but it is at least the basis for serious argument that,
in combination, they provide an intellectually coherent identification of a field of forces that conditions the performance and
the opportunities of a large number of societies. It would be
absurd to imagine that his oblique identification of these patterns

is a first step towards establishing a body of laws. But such an analysis does help to establish certain emphases in the evolution of these processes. The empirical confusions are that much less opaque when we have evidence to support assumptions about some determinate historical trends. The dissection of reality into numerical categories at this level of abstraction is a constructive intellectual activity, capable of testing assumptions within its own frame of reference, and at its chosen level of generality a rough and ready, but not positively distorted, reflection of actual social experience.

Leach's argument, however, suggests that a causal analysis of behaviour at the micro-level of particular societies will be much nearer to the game-theoretical models of rational behaviour referred to earlier. It will be more amorphous and open-ended and will have, overall, a more limited capacity for prediction, but the analysis depends on an insight into the rules and meanings (whatever their ambiguities) which people implicitly recognize in their relationships with others. The dissection of reality must start with them, and any statistical analysis will have to be articulated to this analytical core as an ancillary element in constructing the power map, the distribution of resources and rights, in a given structure of roles and relationships. The question of causality is set in the context of a discussion of the meanings, justifications, reasons for behaviour. As MacIntyre has argued, this basis for a causal analysis of action is not as remote as some have claimed from the Humean concept of causality[19] but the consequences for empirical method do take us outside Humean parallels with the observation and analysis of natural phenomena.

III

From the social anthropologist's angle of vision, dominated not only by the unique intersubjectivities in the society he observes, but also by the interpretation of different dimensions of social organization, kin, economy, religion, and so on, the concept of causation can appear as a dangerous luxury. It is perhaps no accident that Winch's well known admonitions to social scientists to exempt social life from any causal dynamic sets up the social anthropologist as their prototype.[20] In the Malinowski Memorial Lecture of 1971, Ardener generalizes the

Humean problem, though his scepticism about causal explanation is pragmatic and does not endorse Winch's philosophic position. [21]

> We are in the position of one person who imitates another. While person X performs some repetitive or patterned activity, person Y, the imitators (in computer terms the simulator) acquires some degree of skill in predictivity. When X̄ changes to another mode of activity Y flounders. The predictivity fails at the only moment at which it is truly important. It seems quite likely that human beings in society do tend towards periods of repetitive inertia for varying lengths, along various measurable parameters. The pattern of these stretches may then be recoverable by observation. The biological and environmental infrastructure will impose regularities such that a resolute attention to these in particular is an honourable study. Even with their help, however, the mere 'observer' of social events, even with further assistance of some probabilistic dialogue with the participants, is truly ... in a position comparable to a Maxwell's Demon, a being on the same scale as the molecules in a thermal system. The Demon's problem is, essentially, that he cannot command the information to map the system of which he is a part. He is a goal-keeper in the fog trying to intercept footballs kicked from all directions.

That is to say that the social scientist deals with histories and not with determined systems or confined configurations of change. He must expect to be betrayed by behavioural regularities and should learn to pursue speculative insights that will never provide the explanatory closure of a deterministic, or dependably effective predictive theory. Other social scientists, economists in particular, have a heavier investment in the type of causal theory that extrapolates from empirical trends. A theory of economic change which can take the form of soluble equations represents at least the possibility of intervening purposefully in the development and distribution of resources.[22] However, where political, administrative, ecological, even religious systems, can intervene on imperfectly institutionalized market systems, even economists are ready to make quite restricted demands of a theory of development. Some of them would be well satisfied with provisional diagnostic tools, which might at least predict broad and stable equilibrium paths for specific periods of time with a reasonable degree of frequency. 'Briefly put, we should expect a conceptual framework that would facilitate the creation of theories or models that contain manipulative variables whose dosages can be raised sufficiently to obtain accurate directional predictions for a limited period of

time. This leaves many unsettled issues. '23 The unsettled
issues have to do with the nature and impact of systems of
relations that have not been abstracted and composed into the
causal model, and with the free play of choice open to different
groups at different points in time. The point is not that we
cannot look for the causes of the interruption of an analytical
equilibrium within a particular pattern of variables—we might
do so in terms of the logic of a structural contradiction—but that
we cannot extrapolate, except in a loose probabilistic sense,
from present conditions to new states that have yet to be interpreted by human agents. (Extrapolating backwards to make
sense of historical change is equally problematic. We cannot
demonstrate structural determinants.) Such interruptions of
an equilibrium may indeed be 'overdetermined', like any other
event or development, in the sense that many factors, some of
them dispensable, provide the conditions for them. But, by
definition, we cannot say much about the elements of chance and
choice till the histories have been acted out.

Leibenstein is requiring more of a theory than that it should
serve as Friedman's implement for pragmatic economic engineering, which means that he, like Putnam in his rough assessment of empirical regularities, is prepared to turn the limitations of a predictive, causal explanation to further account. It
should be possible to integrate the heuristic theory and an
account of the actors' behaviour. Apart from logical consistency,
he wants his theory to have 'sound assumptions' about
behaviour, and to be consistent with what he takes to be relevant
past experience. He wants a theory to describe real relationships, and recognizes that, whatever the degree to which commodity relationships can be abstracted from a social totality,
they are still functions of that totality. Whatever questions are
begged in his short-list of requirements for a causal type of
theory, he does, in consequence, make clear that he sees the
possibilities as being very open. The pursuit of causal explanations, validated by some measure of predictive success, does
not necessarily entail determinist assumptions or aspirations.
A theory of development may provide the opportunity for some
degree of successful intervention by locating a salient set of
variables during a period in which the society is, in the analytical sense, in a state of equilibrium. But that is all. It clarifies
the range of choices open to actors in a particular situation, and
perhaps the social and economic costs of following one course
rather than another. It will sooner or later be the victim of
other forces, the more nebulous parameters of the wider frame
of reference, relations of power, bureaucratic structures,

beliefs, values of various kinds developed by new élites and so on. But its partial and relative success, in a given historical setting, may enable us to bring into focus both the functional dependence of these other spheres of activity and their significance as determinants. A theory that attempts to integrate these different elements in a more comprehensive understanding of historical change will also deal in causality. But it will not repeat the analytical fragmentation of reality which was the basis for a causal theory derived from a severely abstracted pattern of empirical regularities. Causal theories of that type are perhaps most useful when they serve as flying buttresses to more amorphous theoretical structures.

A philosophical concept, rationality, together with a sociological one, structure, take us beyond the constraints of this notion of causality. But before trying to relate these two categories of explanation through various examples in the next two chapters, we need to reconsider the contrast that has appeared and been questioned at several points in the discussion, between historical explanation and social science theory.

IV

We have an interesting point of departure for this reconsideration in just such a theory of economic development as Leibenstein envisages, an exploratory deductive model of limited utility that fits a particular series of empirical regularities. However, though the theory involved is predictive, it is applied to the past; it has no pragmatic justification, but brings established historical assumptions into the open and tests them, and in addition explores the limits of alternative paths of (irreversible) economic development which were not in fact taken. These studies are generically referred to as the 'new economic history'.[24] Fogel, for example, has taken rent theory, which asserts a systematic relationship between transport and the rental value of land, to an analysis of the development of the American railroad, a technological innovation with large consequences for relations of production in the United States.[25] The theory demanded hitherto unconsidered data on production and consumption as evidence, and the quantification of certain variables which had not previously been given a statistical expression, in order to construct an economic model of the commodity trade within which specific alternative predictions could be made.

One of the results of the analysis is an alternative 'postdiction', what he calls 'counterfactual statements', which establish the general shape of viable commercial agriculture had the railroads not existed. Clearly, this involves an explicit rejection of determinist assumptions about development, and to the extent that they are systematically supported by the relationship between the 'postdictions' of theory and the available data, they plot alternative causal paths. But, no less interesting, though such might-have-beens remain, in Eliot's words, [26]

> a perpetual possibility
> Only in a world of speculation,

they raise questions about the agents of the choices actually made, their motives, their power relative to other groups, the institutional structures that supported them or facilitated one kind of choice rather than another. A rigorous causal theory is here a means towards the historian's ultimate goal, the assessment and evaluation of the past, as a field of opportunities lost and taken. The specific causal theory reaches beyond itself to a consideration of structure and the rationality of social action in more senses than one. It contributes to an understanding of what happened historically, but in the process presents implicit questions about other systems of relations, the parameters of the causal model.

Gluckman has identified one pair of horns on the dilemma of contrasting modes of explanation, whilst claiming its kinship with a celebrated methodological crux in physics.[27] 'Our dilemma is that the more the detail in which we describe change, the less we grasp the structure of social relations; the more we grasp that structure the more change and movement elude us. This is the principle of sociological indeterminacy equivalent to Heisenberg's principle of indeterminacy in physics.'[28] The dilemma is there, if the analogy is somewhat strained. But it is intersected by another which is much harder to cope with systematically, very broadly the fact that the language of generalization in the social sciences, particularly concepts identifying structures, is frequently, and simultaneously, the language in which normative judgments about societies are being conveyed.

The contrast with which we left pre- and post-revolutionary Rwanda, between a functional explanation of persistence and a narrative explanation of change, was clearly simplistic. It was not, however, all that remote from the common stereotypical distinction between history and the social sciences. This is sometimes invoked on a live-and-let-live basis by historians,

as in a recent guidebook to historical explanation. 'The familiar
platitude probably overstates the case but it nonetheless contains a vital kernel of truth: the historian must always accommodate the unique and the contingent, the social scientist is essentially oriented towards the universal, towards the recurrent
pattern.'[29] Elsewhere the stereotype appears as something of
a straw man in the process of setting out an account of a differentiated historical explanation.[30] The legitimate butt of these
quizzical interdisciplinary tours, 'vague jargon-obscured,
typologies, or so-called general theory stating indeterminate
relations between immense abstractions, untested by present
realities and awaiting instead "the syntheses of its over-
receding maturity", '[31] is not the sole product of an academic
industry. The polemical use of the stereotype is misleading if
it suggests that crude taxonomies, a speculative functionalism
and a lame form of causal analysis represent the limit of what
these disciplines have to offer, or that the only meaningful
accounts of change are to be found in the narrative histories of
unique events.

The idea of narrative is far from simple, and a recent series
of discussions among historians echoes, with differences of
language and emphasis, the questions around which our own discussion has revolved, description, abstraction, explanation and
normative judgment. For a start the writing of history and the
writing of narrative are not conterminous.[32] Historical narra-
tion is a species of historical description, and some outstanding
historians, such as Huizinga and Burckhardt, have been very
little concerned with narrative.[33] Furthermore, a narrative
account and a causal account should not be confused, for causal
efficacy in history is not simply a matter of antecedents[34] and
the value of a good narrative, as Dray points out, lies in its
ability to stimulate sensitivity to 'a host of subtly different
relations' which an exclusively causal explanation will miss.[35]
These relations constitute the context of the narrative and
sustain two essential explanatory functions. They make the
narrative credible in terms of the perspectives, knowledge and
beliefs of the participants, without necessarily indicating that
this was the only possible or potential course of events. They
also throw light on analytically distinct aspects of the events,
their implications for a variety of logically or functionally
integrated spheres of activity, their internal contradictions and
unintended consequences.

Finally, it has been pointed out that the action which finds its
way into historical narrative is not a self-evidently distinct
category of fact that steps forward to the observer from out of

a diffuse background of 'conditions'. The distinctions between underlying conditions, actions and consequences are analytic distinctions. Neither conditions nor consequences can be described except with reference to potential narrative statements, statements about actions. For the historian, as for the anthropologist, underlying conditions, actions and consequences must form in some sense a totality. What is to become part of the narrative, and whether the history is to be envisaged from the perspective of one or other of these three analytical components reflects a judgment by the historian which itself must be referred to the state of our understanding of the material, to research priorities and to underlying assumptions about the nature of the events and their significance.[36]

The discipline of history provides a tradition, or a set of traditions within which social continuities and transformations are explored. But its distinctiveness is not at all easy to summarize. The kernel at the heart of the platitude really contains very little, unless it contains a clue to the forms of recurrence and universality that are distinctively a preoccupation of the social scientist. If this is to be found simply in the scientism of the search for general laws, the discussion is already over or not worth pursuing, and the ironies of practising historians like Stretton are conclusive. It is clear that in a range of ways the social scientist lives off a compulsion to classify, and to compare and generalize from his classifications. This is the basis for assembling evidence for certain kinds of causal connection, for predictions at a certain level, for the identification of structures of belief, hierarchical relations of authority, and segmentary relations of power. But over virtually this entire range historians match social scientists with parallel apprehensions of the evidence. Fogel's 'predictive' modelling is more sophisticated and rigorous than most causal analysis by social scientists. Statistical methods have come to be an element incorporated into historical methodology. Any distinction between narratives of action, its context and its consequences, would be quite meaningless without an elaborated understanding of recurrent interdependencies of every kind. The platitude, at this level, does little more than distinguish a useful ancillary activity that complements historical analysis.

The polarization of orientations does seem sharper if we consider the explicitly evaluative element in historical writing. Unlike some of their remoter predecessors, contemporary historians do not draw straightforward exemplary morals from history. But they necessarily pass judgment on what they identify as significant action, and to the extent that they suppress

their own or their readers' awareness of their canons of judgment, they necessarily blunt analytical penetration of their
material.[37] They are concerned both with understanding and
assessing specific actions within a specific frame of reference,
with the rationality and irrationality of particular actors in
relation to the constraints and opportunities presented in their
particular situation.

Marwick credits the social scientist with the more regular use
of models and theoretical constructs. But Stretton sees in this
a positive limitation. In the actual practice of social scientists,
he says, the abstractions of such intellectual devices as conceptual frameworks and general theoretical categories select and
institutionalize an inflexible and insensitive set of diacritical
attributes as the relevant facts for analysis. The models are
the trappings of a more or less residual positivist ideology,
theories that do not declare themselves, disguised as programmes for objective observation and analysis.[38] However, the
structural models and general constructs have other intellectual
origins, though these may often have been obscured in the
thought of some modern social scientists. The construction of
abstract models was the first and has been the most consistent
form in which normative theorists presented their arguments.
The function of these models in the dialectical relationship
between the observer and empirical social behaviour takes
several different forms. The grand abstraction of Plato's
Republic is a perfectly tautological model of social relations
that excludes any possibility for political action. It establishes
criteria for social organization against which empirical societies
can be measured, a statement of the principles that should
inform social organization, rather than an idealized description
of its form. In The Laws, principles are accommodated to
realities to an extent, and the normative prescriptions appear
more pragmatic: even, one might argue, compromised. Marx, to
rush to the other end of the conventional Political Theory course,
works two models, if we distinguish the relative simplicities of
the Communist Manifesto from the complex fusion of norm and
material history elsewhere in his work. Various static ideal
types of political community provide the fulcrum of Aristotle's
empirical comparisons and for his theory of structural change.
A point not always stressed in conventional genuflections to
Aristotle in contemporary comparative studies is that these
'ideal' types include both good and bad. Within his frame of
reference Aristotle cannot distinguish between qualitative and
structural dynamics; within the constraints of general structural
tendencies, there are better and worse choices to be made, and

these determine outcomes. The structural coherence of Hobbes's Leviathan is the product of a normative injunction—'to endeavour peace'—and a distinctive psychological theory. And so on. The various organic analogies we referred to earlier, with their latent normative connotations, are a subtype in this idiom.

We can make one simple point about what all these normative models have in common. Each of them combines a series of definitions in such a way as to specify the preconditions and characteristics of rational action, individual and collective. The energy behind the definition of rationality comes from some core value, Plato's vision of a harmonic fulfilment of individual and totality, which he elaborates in the concept of Justice, Aristotle's solider sense of various forms of the good life, Hobbes's anxieties about civil disorder and his vision of civilized peace. But the definitions that are assembled as the normative elements of the model are essentially structural categories, prescribing certain divisions of function and status, hierarchies of authority, structures for composing the relations of power, programmes for articulating norms and beliefs in apposite balance, the concentration of sanctions, the allocation of resources. They are predictive in a specialized sense. They all argue that, if we desire to realize a given value or values, then it follows that we shall have to invent certain kinds of persisting relationship, which integrate the incentives, constraints and habits that sustain ideal patterns and regularities of behaviour. Plato and Hobbes, of course, provide 'static' or nondevelopmental normative models, whilst Aristotle thinks in terms of the logical tendency for a given type of structure to shift in a limited number of directions. But transformative models, Marxist or other, obviously present analogous arguments. Giving the models themselves a somewhat different place in relation to the explanation of empirical change, we have a pessimistic variant in Weber's ideal type of bureaucracy, which assumes certain structural developments as an inevitable consequence of a particular historical process.[39]

All such theories have an empirical substratum or make some empirical reference, but their appeal is universal in that they are attempts to persuade their readers into a point of view, to accept certain assumptions and to recognize the presence or absence of certain principles of organization and interaction in any situation. They cannot be directly tested, since they are in themselves highly complex definitions that seek to impose a hypothetical coherence of the most comprehensive and therefore abstract kind on reality. Their impact on empirical analysis is inevitably indirect and fragmentary. They are often referred to as standards for comparison, and where this means more than habitual academic allusions to Hobbes's war of all against all and the like, it entails a process of tentative, and often piece-meal, extrapolation from the intermediate categories of such theories, and their modification and incorporation into other combinations. In a sense, every innovative study raises a death duty on this literature, appropriating what it needs for its own purposes and circumstances. Depending on the scope of what was attempted and the extremity of the confusions and tensions that normative theories have attempted to resolve, some bequests are more rapidly exhausted than others, and some categories drift through more reconstructions than others.[40] The point here is simply that empirical analysis can, as a legiti-mate matter of emphasis, be directed at the categories, their validation, their interdependence. The exploration of categories in this sense, and the explanation of particular processes are not independent activities. One function of models and theoretical constructs is to keep this conceptual dimension in focus.

To anticipate an illustration from the next chapter, the model in Riggs's prismatic theory[41] is an ideal type in a double sense. It is a highly abstract representation of social and political change, and it incorporates a normative ideal for the relations between 'the political' and 'bureaucracy'. It provides cues for the accumulation of evidence, and at the same time criteria for applying the normative assumptions on which it is based. The model itself represents a hypothetical structural balance, and certain logically possible deviations from it. These deviations explain empirical situations in which some individuals are forced to compromise contradictory goals, or in which collective objectives are frustrated by specific structural irrationalities. So, in his work on Thailand, Riggs sees a major structural transformation beginning with a bureaucratic reorganization in 1892, which increased the differentiation of the bureaucracy and the centralization of the regime.[42] There was in consequence an apparatus for moderating and controlling modernization, but this forestalled and ultimately impeded the emergence of any autonomous centres of power, such as interest groups and politi-cal parties. The structure was inherently malintegrated, and inevitably generated tensions and frustrations, with increases in population and urbanization, the consequent problems of food production, and a growing basis for a revolutionary intelligentsia among graduate students. Self-defeating frustrated pressures reflect structural contradictions which he explains in terms of a failure to approximate his ideal hypothetical balance between political and administrative relations in Thai society.

Similarly, in other studies, theoretical constructs such as 'stability', 'compulsion' and 'participation' are constituted into theories of political development in ways that accommodate their author's anxieties about survival, or viability, or democratic norms.[43] Seen in this light, the theoretical abstractions belong to a repertoire out of which different analytical programmes are repeatedly being drawn, both as a means to an end, and as a matter of concern in themselves. The relevance of this preoccupation to the understanding of specific historical processes is of the first importance, though it is not an integral part of historical method. The abstractions of the programme offer the possibility of comparison and evaluation, not in the first instance on the basis of the taxonomic and comparative methods we have discussed, though these may for supplementary purposes be useful or essential, but through the use of concepts that help us to identify structural principles operating in highly diverse empirical situations. These structural principles have to do with relations of power and authority, material advantage and disadvantage, the contexts that structures establish for purposive action, and the productive or unproductive, 'rational' or 'irrational', consequences of such action. They do not represent any ultimate syntheses from factual data, so much as intersecting criteria for the selection of evidence to explain empirical relationships in ways that compel evaluation and assessment.

CHAPTER SIX

Rationality and structure

I

Rationality is a distended philosophical concept, and there is no point here in attempting to integrate all the senses in which it may legitimately be used by social scientists. [1] But, given the variety of situations in which we tend to use the term, we need to reassure ourselves that we have not got into the way of referring to different categories under the same heading. There are manifest differences, for example, between referring, as a Marxist does, to the rationality or irrationality of entire economic and social systems, or, as an organization theorist does, to the rationality of correct administrative decisions, or, as anthropologists and philosophers repeatedly do, [2] to the rationality or otherwise of the Nuer 'belief' that a human twin 'is a bird'. One statement refers to a value judgment about society and the nature of social change. Another refers to the relationship between means and ends in a defined situation. The third has to do with the nature of the credence given to an ostensibly factual statement. And yet, there is a connection between the three uses of the word. The issue of rationality is complex for the social scientists, and it is as essential to maintain continuities of meaning as it is to make use of qualifications and differences. We must, if we are to do this, think simultaneously in terms of rationality and of structure. This in turn is the basis for insights into the social causation operating in particular events.

Without foreclosing on the many complexities, we can at least begin by setting out what is intended by the suggestion that the grand abstractions of rationality and structure are complementary dimensions in the analysis of social relations and social change. From this, certain methodological consequences follow. The previous chapter touched on the dead-end that a numerical approach to sociological evidence can, at certain levels, lead the observer to. The relational aspects got laundered from the evidence. So, the question now is, how can explanation be organized round the analysis of relationships? The two main illustrations, M.G. Smith's analysis of the West African Kingdom of Zazzau and Riggs's attempt at a general theory of development administration, represent in a new guise the contrast between the particularizing approach (this time fusing historical and anthropological perspectives) and the generalizing. They are compared and contrasted in the light of the introductory discussion.

We can begin by asserting that there must be a series of independent questions about what makes sense in general which we can bring to bear on any situation or statement. These are criteria of logicality and false reasoning.[3] However, these criteria cannot be drawn in compact order from some universal Euclidean text, because there is no point at all in applying them to individuals to whom they were simply not available in a highly developed form. They can only be applied in a spirit of understanding, necessarily an historical understanding, of the intellectual resources in principle available at a particular time and place. 'A man who uses the best canons available to him may behave rationally in believing what is false, and a man who pays no heed to the rules of evidence may behave irrationally in believing what is true.'[4] Even at this most basic level, whilst rational behaviour is the responsibility, or achievement of the individual, it is contingent on a given pattern of social meanings. In order to understand it, the observer must be able to place behaviour in relation to its context or conditions. He may judge it in the light of general criteria, but these are qualified by his understanding of the intersubjectivities of the actors within the limits of the knowledge available.

The attack on crude evolutionary theories of social development led inevitably to an acute preoccupation with this intersection between the general criteria of rationality and the societal terms under which they were to be applied. There was always the possibility that the discrete facts of behaviour and belief that had demonstrated the irrationality of primitive man to an earlier generation could, in context, be part of a coherent pattern of behaviour. This standing hypothesis, as we have seen, was the prime mover of functionalist method. It has been extraordinarily productive, leading, for example, to a far richer sense on the part of social scientists of the use of language in maintaining and transmitting different types of social meaning.[5] The bird-twins of the Nuer is just one of many bizarre expressions of belief that can actually contribute to our understanding of Nuer social relations if we can recognize it as a symbolic statement, which means something in the context of the structure of relations and classifications explored by Evans-Pritchard. In terms of what it does in this system of meanings, we may not see this as an irrational belief.[6] Turner's analysis of Ndembu symbol and belief is a classic illustration. On the other hand, rationality ceases to be any criterion at all if it is assumed, as it sometimes has been in functionalist studies, that every belief and every action can, as it were, be justified by being placed in context at some appropriate level of intrinsic meaning. In every society, beliefs that are false and actions that are unrelated to their intended objectives flourish in defiance of reason. Indeed, they may be so pervasive that we can only describe them as part of the generally shared structure of beliefs. This situation in itself requires explanation, so that here too, in a more complex way, the issue of rationality is entailed in the issue of structure. How do these beliefs come to be maintained or these actions continue to be sanctioned; what are the consequences of such beliefs for the relations of different groups and social categories; is there any connection between the answers to the first and second of these questions? To explain the existence of recurrent objectively irrational interpretations of reality in a society in terms of some residual quantum of irrationality in human nature is simply to explain them away. Psychological theories attempt to do rather more than this, but they also presuppose a society with structured relations of authority, control and learning.

To identify the significance of specific actions, with reference both to the general criteria of rationality and to the historical conditions in which they are partially realized, need not necessarily involve the broader evaluative criteria which are also invoked in the name of rationality. However, discussions of rationality by organization theorists show how these normative judgments are entailed in the analysis of means and ends. The rationality of behaviour within a formal organization is by definition a function of its structure; an organization is a purposive unit, even if it has many and even contradictory purposes, and its structure is a means to the achievement of ends, directly or indirectly securing desirable consequences and avoiding undesirable ones. However, as Simon makes clear, it is as cramping to think of discrete means and ends in this context as it is to detach specific beliefs from their general setting.[7]

First, the ends of organizational activity are not a consolidated terminal category which makes sense of all the activities of the organization. More often than not it is the case that one objective is important because it is itself a means towards

another or others. It is much more realistic to think in terms
of hierarchies of means and ends, which in practice interlace
and react on each other in complicated and not always predictable ways. What are means and what are ends is, therefore,
a matter of definition for a given sequence of decisions in a
structured situation. If it is at all possible conceptually to
isolate systems of relations, then the organizational and other
determinants of consequences can be compared and assessed,
and even adjusted in order to modify outcomes. This is what
organization theory attempts to do. But the abstraction of an
'isolated' system is an analytical one, and the system can be
placed in indefinitely larger series of societal relations. As
with the game theorists, who have been an important source of
inspiration for Simon himself,[8] a decision is made to accept
as given certain parameters, rules of the game and objectives.
The causal sequence of ends and means is pursued within those
terms of reference. But if the terms of reference are expanded,
the issue of rationality is unavoidably reopened. Second, there
is no guarantee that multiple and interweaving hierarchies of
means and ends can be reconciled. The result of this is that,
even within an organization that has clearly defined goals, there
will be competition and inconsistency. Such 'irrationalities'
may, in point of fact, be very important in helping the organization to discover what some of its objectives are and what its
internal limitations are, so they may not simply be a cost on
efficiency. But the point here is that we can hardly talk about
activity in terms of rational motivation without reference to
the persistent structure of relations and behaviour within which
choices between alternatives are made, and without at some
point relating that structure to others. The pursuit of objectives at the individual or sectional level in an organization may
be entirely rational, but the relationships combining these
activities may be so organized that only unsatisfactory consequences can emerge, despite co-operative good-will and high
intelligence on the part of the decision-makers. Rationality and
irrationality is an attribute of organization and systems of
organizations no less than of individuals. There may be many
ways of pursuing an (intermediate) objective, and these may
either threaten or enhance other values irrelevant to or incidental to the objective. It is a very real consideration whether the
process of decision-making is so organized as to reduce the
chances of the more damaging alternative courses being followed.[9]

Simon makes a further important observation, which emphasizes
the structured context, as far as we are able to identify it,

against which we assess the rationality of action. The choice
of particular behaviour alternatives itself helps to determine
the range of alternatives that will be available subsequently.
From the point of view of the organization theorist this is a
necessary condition of rationality, because it narrows down to a
manageable field the alternatives on which a decision-maker
has to bet (probably against a time schedule and heavy information costs). [10]

> This time binding character of strategies deserves the
> greatest emphasis, for it makes possible at least a modicum
> of rationality in behaviour, where, without it, this would be
> inconceivable... an organization that is manufacturing shoes
> does not need to reconsider every day (though it may need to
> reconsider at intervals) whether it should be in the auto-
> mobile business instead.

But the implications in a large context may be much more dis-
turbing, because the time-binding strategies may have limited
choices to alternatives with ruinous consequences for clients
or dependants, or for objectives that are being pursued in the
larger extent of structures of which this is a part. It may be
possible and necessary to isolate closed systems of decisions
and consequences, but there is no logical basis for this in a
qualitative difference between behaviour classified as means
and valued states classified as ends.

In brief, to adduce reasons in order to provide causal explanations of behaviour is not to assume that the reasons are necessarily true or good. The first task of the social scientist or
historian is to make them intelligible, and this means identifying
them as the products of a specific history, both in a general
cultural sense and in the sense that they are drawn from a range
of possibilities that are historically limited by previous
policies, strategies or choices. This leads directly into an
analysis of the structure of social relationships, and a concern
with the overall consequences of the pursuit of a plurality of
goals by groups in various relations with each other. Social
organization differentiates and counterposes purposive activity
into elements of variable scope. A differentiated use of the
concept of rationality enables us to identify and evaluate the
process at different levels of abstraction or particularity.
Thus, within the confines of administrative behaviour, Simon
suggests that we can clarify the complexities of action by [11]

> using the term 'rational' in conjunction with appropriate
> adverbs. Then a decision may be called 'objectively' rational
> if in fact it is the correct behaviour for maximizing given

values in a given situation. It is 'subjectively' rational if it maximizes attainment relative to the actual knowledge of the subject. It is 'consciously' rational to the degree that the adjustment of means to ends is a conscious process. It is 'deliberately' rational to the degree that the adjustment of means to ends has been deliberately brought about (by the individual or by the organization). A decision is 'organizationally' rational if it is oriented to the organization's goals; it is 'personally' rational if it is oriented to the individual's goals.

At a much more comprehensive level Weber makes his distinction between formal and substantive rationality, between which there is a dialectical and problematic relationship.[12]

> the very rationalization of social life... has consequences which contravene some of the most distinctive values of western civilization, such as those which emphasize the importance of individual creativity and autonomy of action. The rationalization of modern life, especially as manifest in organizational form in bureaucracy, brings into being the 'cage' within which men are increasingly confined.

At this level the distinction identifies what he sees as a structural contradiction, namely the impossibility in a certain type of society of organizing to secure two distinct sets of values, which are, for historically determined reasons, in a contradictory means-ends relationship to each other. Weber identifies in the intrinsic antinomy between formal and substantive rationality, at a very abstract level, certain operating principles of social organization in western society, and at the same time he shapes a judgment in terms of the possibilities that are forestalled.

II

This general discussion suggests a brief for empirical analysis. The generalizations that emerge from empirical studies may be about particular societies, parts of societies, or types of society. But they will show action as the plausible, even predictable, though not necessarily the inevitable, outcome of complex but identifiable regularities of behaviour. This is as true for accounts of change as for accounts of stability.

One important answer to questions about how in fact this may be done is offered in different interpretations of the concept

of role. The loose common usage is familiar enough. In my
role as a university teacher I should report your gross indifference to things of the mind, but as a friend I cannot; should
I resign, or default on professional expectations, or get drunk?
As a sociological concept, it describes the regular expectations
about behaviour that confer specific qualities on a relationship.
Every individual lives out distinguishable aspects of his life
within different patterns of relationships, family, community
and so on: he participates in different sets of roles. So the
concept can be used to show how an individual may be involved
in intersecting but mutually incompatible systems of expectations, and to explain his behaviour when he cannot rationally
resolve the contradictions that are presented to him. It may,
on the other hand, identify ambiguous expectations, which allow
a great deal of latitude for interpretation and manipulation.
Above all it can be given an operational interpretation in
empirical analysis that enables us to identify whole patterns or
systems of relationships. At the level of the individual, we are
trying to discover the various social performances he has reason to believe people expect of him in his dealings with them.
It is obviously important to know to what extent these are inter-
nalized, so completely absorbed that they have become integral
to the individual's sense of who he is and what life is about, or
to what extent dependable behaviour on his part is maintained
by external sanctions and incentives, so that it would only be
predictable whilst these sanctions continue to operate.[13] But
at the level of collectivities of individuals, we are seeking to
generalize about relationships and networks of relationships,
about consistent asymmetries of power or status or influence,
the scope of sanctions, incentives and legitimating beliefs in
this sector or that sector of an entire system.

It is hardly surprising that the most rigorous operational use
of the concept is in studies of the type of formal organization
with which Simon was concerned. They are, in a sense, artifici-
ally isolated social systems, with more or less explicit and
certainly limited purposes. They are organized to meet these
purposes in a suitably complicated division of functions, so that
each individual is, in principle, given clear instructions about
where he stands in the hierarchies of information and control.
Ideally, a formal organization insulates itself from those aspects
of its members' lives that are irrelevant to the goals of the
organization. Of course, no organization can do this completely, and no organization is more than relatively efficient and
co-ordinated, so the official description of the organization will
miss the undercurrents. There will be informal, even subversive,

expectations and norms built up, severe tensions for officals
in certain positions, tensions deliberately built into the system
but formally unspecified, failures of information of a systematic
kind, perturbations resulting from the personality characteristics
of employees. All these confusions—irrational from the point
of view of the organization—must become part of a description
of the actual, as opposed to the official, patterns of interaction.
An ambitious work by scholars from the Michigan Survey
Research Center provides case studies of a number of organizations along these lines.[14]

The bulk of raw data for the studies consists of responses to
long open-ended interviews with samples of employees. These
reveal a great deal about how each individual thinks about the
job, those he works with, his superiors and subordinates. There
are answers to many straightforward but important questions,
such as whether what an individual thinks he does, or should
do on the job corresponds with his colleagues' or his superior's
expectation of what he should be doing. But the questionnaires
revealed more than the respondents perhaps realized, because
the authors also drew on a body of theory from experimental
psychology in order to classify respondents in terms of their
personality characteristics. There are well-developed scales
and other verbal response tests to measure the relative position of individuals along a number of clinical dimensions, such
as psychological anxiety, neuroticism, guilt-proneness, tolerance and will-power. These hypothetical dimensions are conceptualized in linear terms, so that the scores of individuals
can be intercorrelated and factor-analysed. The statistical
summaries that emerge can then be related to an individual's
success, his job position, superannuation prospects, and so on.
By these means the authors generate in systematic fashion a
body of evidence that invites inferences in response to a number
of questions. How do the purposes of the organization impinge
on the private purposes of the individual? At what points does
the organization create logically (or emotionally) impossible
situations by forcing individuals to fuse incompatible expectations? Do 'irrelevant' personal or social characteristics in-
filtrate and modify the functional requirements of the organization?

Such questions, and the list could obviously be extended, can
make use of the evidence to explore the counterpoint of rationalities which Simon formally describes. At the same time, they
are searching out the existential reality of a functionally complex system of relations which has to be projected on to the
two-dimensional scheme of the official design. It is a structure

with dynamic properties and if its features have been accurately caught in the analysis, it might be possible to identify the range of directions in which its internal contradictions and tensions are most likely to take it. It would also be possible to place the whole empirical analysis, if not sub specie aeternitatis, at least in a much wider frame of reference. Organization theory is primarily pragmatic, assessing structure in relation to performance within a conceptually closed universe. The Michigan study shares this perspective. But the evidence it so skilfully assembles could be brought up before the Weberian perspective, which sees a causal sequence at another level of abstraction, and revalues the elements in it in terms of a structural contradiction that is historically and geographically vast. The established facts are facts still, but as evidence they are transformed. For the organization theorists the role structure presents problems of social engineering. For Weber, even its limited success as a purposive organization of activity is evidence of a structural failure of western society. From his position, the refinements of analysis are irrelevant to the main point that it is objectively possible to abstract and anatomize behaviour conditioned by such intensely specialized functions; whilst the pragmatic orientation of these social scientists is itself a symptom of an historically determined rationalization.

Within the closed system of the formal organization, causal hypotheses can be argued with some conviction. Many of the purposes involved are explicit and functionally specific. Others can be discovered, because survey interview techniques are powerful when interviewer and respondent share some common frame of reference, and when both respondents and the organization itself have an interest in collaborating in the generation of relevant evidence. Strong patterns of intercorrelation among those attributes of individual and organization that have been abstracted for observation from a densely articulated system can give relatively clear indications of what combinations of conditions tend to produce different types of consequence. Clearly the quantification of data of this quality makes it possible to pursue elaborate internal comparisons, to test causal hypotheses in order to rule out or reformulate some of them, and to build up a working model of the organization out of the mutual perceptions and behaviour of its members.

The society that traditionally concerns the social anthropologist is also a densely articulated one, but in a radically different sense. Consequently, his operational use of the notion of role in exploring relationships will be different. The obvious dif-

ference is that we are not now concerned with a highly specialized subsystem of relations abstracted from the total field of
relations in which individuals are involved. Roles, patterns of
expectations guiding different aspects of the individual's behaviour as he moves between one social status and another, fuse
and overlap. It may be difficult to make analytical distinctions
between different roles; they may be exceedingly difficult to
disentangle empirically, since the analytical distinctions are not
recognized by the individuals concerned. Thus, in the context
of our own society, we find no difficulty in distinguishing 'the
law' as a subsystem of relations, institutionally distinct, working
according to a highly differentiated rationale of its own, and
constraining with ritualistic formality the behaviour of judges,
advocates, police, litigants and criminals. This occidental
institution has had a chequered colonial history, and Bohannan
fulminates against 'the grossly ethnocentric practice of raising
folk systems like "the law", designed for social action in one's
own society, to the status of an analytical system, and then
trying to organize the raw social data from other societies into
its categories'.[15] Both empirically and analytically, the law is a
much less isolable system for the social anthropologist.

However, there is no simple regression between the empirical
fusion of role structures and their analytical separateness. The
Barotse have a total known corpus of law, and Gluckman claims
that they have in fact 'developed the law by employing all the
methods isolated by Cardozo', the United States Supreme Court
Justice, 'for Anglo-American adjudication'. However, Barotse
judges do not simply apply the law or even look systematically
for precedent in a juridical sense, as we would understand it.
Rather they explore the relevance of generally accepted and
understood norms of reasonableness and good behaviour. What
is in effect a criminal or administrative trial may be pulled out
of a civil action, with the judges deliberately using the occasion
to reinforce customary standards of a quite general kind.
Furthermore, the judges do distinguish between their own
judicial and other roles, legislative and administrative, but their
actual behaviour, in maintaining customary relations amongst
their kin, and occasionally sanctifying changes with a customary
gloss, simultaneously embodies all the functions.[16] On the
other hand, there are some situations in which it is difficult for
the participants to demarcate different sets of purposive
relations, and there is reason to believe that one function of
ritual performances is to clarify and reaffirm subsystems of
roles within the multipurpose relations of such societies.
Ritual can serve the purpose of clarifying the structure of

relations both for participants and for observers. Seen in this
light, the observation of ritual provides one point of entry into
the structure for the social anthropologists.[17] Under these
circumstances, there is not much scope for the analytical
rigour that can be applied to the analysis of more differentiated
systems.[18] Though, again, roles can be differentiated to quite
different degrees in societies of various sizes. In general,
smaller societies have fewer and less differentiated roles, but
some small societies manage to combine little technical and
economic specialization with considerable proliferation of
political roles.[19]

Having indicated that the essence of an empirical role analysis,
whatever the society or organization, is to construct a model of
the dominant relationships based on the interpretations and
mutual perceptions of those involved, if that is at all possible,
diversities such as these serve as a warning that we cannot
afford to assume a simple correspondence between how a
society classifies its relationships and its actual structure.
'Different forms of classification are found with identical types
of social organization, and similar forms with different types
of society.'[20] Indeed, we may fail entirely to discover the
significance of certain critical political relationships if our
empirical distinctions between role systems are not informed
by other theoretical insights. For example, Leach's analysis
of political change in Highland Burma depends on his theory
about the two incompatible, but simultaneously available, interpretations of political relationships which individuals in this
culture can invoke (gumsa and gumlao). There is a logical contradiction between these two systems of political roles. Roughly,
gumsa is an authoritarian and monarchical type of ideal structure, whilst gumlao reflects an ideal of egalitarian republican-
ism. Historically, each of them has dominated different communities at different times. Leach explains the creeping trans-
itions between these alternative logically incompatible, structural norms in part through his conceptualization of myth.[21]
Instead of reading myth as a code or metaphor for relations in
an established social organization, it seems to him to be much
more like a repertoire of symbolic expressions and beliefs
which can be drawn on expediently by individuals and groups
as the pattern of political advantage develops. This development follows the structural logic of a cyclical or pendular
drift, analogous to Turner's, which is generated by recognizable
structural tensions.[22]

My general proposition is then that while it is analytically
correct to regard the gumsa and gumlao systems as separate

patterns of social structure, the two types are, in their practical application, always interrelated. Both systems are in a sense structurally defective. A gumsa political state tends to develop features which lead to rebellion, resulting, for a time, in a gumlao order. But a gumlao community... usually lacks the means to hold its component lineages together in a status of equality. It will then either disintegrate altogether through fission, or else status differences between lineage groups will bring the system back into the gumsa pattern.

What Leach has done is to identify the principles underlying political change in an exceedingly fluid politics by describing the rational pursuit of political advantage within a context that offers specific shifting alternatives to individuals who have incentives for exploiting them and are able to do so. Roles do not express given and necessary functions which certain individuals must perform in order to maintain a structure of relationships, so much as a legitimate or self-legitimating expression of the current political map. A synchronic identification of this political map would tell us very little. The dynamic is only recognizable over time, as one configuration leads into another through a limited series of variations.

Economically, demographically and politically, Highland Burma happens to have a history of endemic turmoil and change. But the point about the potential fluidity and ambiguity of social relations, the possibilities for creative innovation or manipulation, is of general importance. In empirical description, a role has the characteristics of a measure of central tendency. It anticipates future behaviour in the light of past observations, but within a margin of confidence that need not be a constant. There is a depressing aridity to the many role analyses that are insufficiently sensitive to this.[23]

Whatever the fundamental differences between the formal organization in a Western society and the range of 'primitive' societies that have concerned anthropologists, there are important similarities in the evidence available to the investigator. The relationships that have to be identified are generally face-to-face, and the participants can be directly observed and questioned. In the one case, the structure of relations is contrived to meet at least some of the purposes and goals of the organization, which means that it is possible quite easily to specify some of the causal mechanisms involved. In the other case, teleological arguments are more dubious, but for other reasons the task of describing structural characteristics in dynamic terms is a manageable one. As Gellner points out, 'the technological limitations of "primitive" society were a considerable help in narrowing the range within which one could seek the causal mechanisms which maintained the social structure. What are the sanctions, the multiple swords of Damocles, hanging over any society? Above all, starvation, anarchy, external aggression.'[24] The operational use of the concept of role, in order to identify or contribute to an identification of structures and the purposes they shape or embody, has obvious applications at this level. However, in modern societies as a whole, political, economic and administrative relationships are very much less direct, perceived in very different terms. Sociologists tend to resort to more diffuse relational categories, such as the 'reference group', and structures are more usefully described at a more abstract level, in terms of caste, for example, or class or the notion of plural society used by Furnivall and others

But there is a wide intermediate range of situations where the interface of important elements in a process of structural change can be explored in terms of structures of roles. Characteristically, they are situations that lack the functional integration of the relatively isolated society or insulated organization. They tend to be impacted societies, where a colonial intruder or an urban political élite, for example, work their own purposes into existing relationships. The result is a new and complex system, organized round unique and almost arbitrary internal contradiction. Its features can be identified with historical particularity. Fallers, for example, has described the position of certain Ugandan chiefs in terms of the logical contradiction between their roles as symbolic and political heads of traditional societies bonded by kinship and clientship ties, and their roles as proto-Weberian bureaucratic administrators under the aegis of colonial authority. The values expressed by each complex of expectations are incompatible (partiality to kin versus administrative impartiality etc.), and often the consequences are psychological stress and resignation of office, or the forms of compromise that district officers tended to define as corruption.[25] What we see here is manifestly a general feature of the colonial and post-colonial situation. It can be identified in combination with many other variable attributes, economic conditions, interethnic relations and so on. The identification of particular situations in terms of types of role structures is the analytical basis for a general comparative analysis, such as is proposed by Riggs.

III

But before turning to Riggs's attempt at a logically integrated comparative general theory, we should look in some detail at an attempt to explain structural changes in a particular society through an analysis of specific relationships. This example should pull together threads from the preceding discussion. M. G. Smith is writing history, and he makes use of narrative. But he is writing it as an anthropologist preoccupied with structures, in which he identifies the constraints and possibilities that fashioned the purposive behaviour of men. Through his identification of roles, he locates the perspectives and opportunities of political actors, and he appraises the entire configuration by means of a parallel analysis at a more abstract level. An explanation of change in terms of a differentiated use of the notion of rationality is implicit and we are left with a compelling sense of an intelligible causality giving a shape to events.[26]

The history Smith documents concerns a much more highly differentiated society than any considered in the studies by anthropologists referred to so far. It encompasses the invasion of the pagan Habe kingdoms of central Nigeria following the 1805 jihad of the military-religious leader Othman Dan Fodio, the establishment of the kingdom of Zazzau as a feudatory of Sokoto, dominated by a Fulani élite of three royal dynasties (Mallawa, Bornawa, Katsinawa), and the adaptation of existing Habe political and administrative structures, followed by a substantial modification of them as the British presence came to be felt. The narrative is far from placid. It includes two transformations of major importance. In the first, an ethnic and religious majority came to be dominated by a religious-military élite. (Following the invasion Habe were allowed to hold office, but they were gradually excluded as the Fulani dynasties proliferated.) In the second, the élite not only survived the arrival of the British, but consolidated its position through a number of structural modifications.

The two invasions, Islamic and colonial, precipitated change, but the problem Smith sets himself is to account for the course and tempo of that change. A narrative account would fail to do this unless it emerged from an understanding of a series of social relationships. The interests of individuals and groups were bonded and differentiated in distinctive ways. Supplementary processes supported or modified these relationships and had their own logic. There were clientship relations between Fulani and Habe, and there were detailed and somewhat rigid sub-hierarchies which ranked individuals within the dozen or so orders of society. Relations could be manipulated over time by the use of marriage alliance strategies among Fulani partilineages. So the events of a narrative become coherent as passages in an historical landscape, in which incentives and constraints that are of general and, within historical limits recurrent significance, direct competitive energies and the demands for security and material advantage.

Smith freezes the shifting contours of his history in three synchronic functional analyses. Individually, these are not unlike Maquet's account of the social and political system in Rwanda. Thus the first, the analysis of Abuja, the capital to which Habe leaders retreated and where they retained control, and the structure of which is presumed to derive from the prototype of pre-Fulani Zazzau, discloses an intricately balanced system of patronage and office. Ranked round the king were a series of promotional offices, with different degrees of access to him, different degrees of control over other appointments, external functions, economic resources and influence over the succession. The relative autonomy of these positions is finely adjusted. For instance, the senior civil administrator (galadima) was a eunuch and therefore had no hereditary ambitions; officials of the royal household had opportunities to control appointments through their access to the throne, but they were economically dependent and the chief official (sarkin fada) was much lower in rank than the military commander (madawaki); the mallams were economically dependent, but important in the electoral council for the succession; certain hereditary chiefs had considerable autonomy in their fiefs, but were remote from the courts, vulnerable to royal intervention and had to fulfil military and administrative functions. More generally, a stratified system of closed orders determined absolutely the range of opportunities open to any individual within the structure of relationships of which these ranks (sarautu) were the apex. The closed orders were royals, freemen, eunuchs, and slaves by inheritance or capture.

This structure of offices was more or less retained in Fulani Zazzau as a convenient means of exercising control after the conquest, but with highly significant modifications. These are caught by the second synchronous analysis. Unquestionably the most important change was the introduction of three dynasties as groups which filled the throne in rotation, out of their own endogenous process of competition. Whereas the function of the king in the context of pre-Fulani Zazzau (on the evidence from Abuja) was to maintain a stationary equilibrium, balancing

the internal competition among the different offices, the kingship in Fulani Zazzau becomes a coveted political prize. Its
acquisition brings in a season of advantage for the dynasty,
but within the dynasty advantages are selectively distributed,
much as they are within American politics by the successful
presidential subdynasties. Competition within the dynasties
is intense, and the king uses his short-term autocracy through
the structure of offices to set up potential candidates for the
throne in good starting positions. The functional consequences
of this innovation, the competition between dynasties, reverber-
ated throughout the society. Competing patrilineages increased
their support and resources, but also their obligations, by incorporating Habe into clientship relations. For Habe these
affiliations meant opportunities for employment at certain
levels, and certainly greater security. At every level involvement in the working of the system was heavy.

The functional integration of the system as a whole hangs upon
this extended, intense but stable structure of relationships,
which slotted whole series of compatible and competitive individual and group interests into recurrent patterns which
particular categories or groups either saw no gain in challenging or quite lacked the political resources to challenge. The
structure was stable because it was to the advantage of those
who concentrated political and economic resources to keep
it so. The subordinate Habe had no alternative basis for
organization and every incentive to compete for relative advantages within a clearly defined system. Intense as was the
rivalry between dynasties, there was always the accessible
authority of Sokoto to chill the gamblers' instincts of individual
dynasties and provide insurance against civil war.

This is slender detail from a massively documented work, but
it serves to introduce a conceptual distinction which is fundamental to Smith's analysis. He is concerned with public affairs
and political action as the focus for the analysis of significant
change. The two synchronic analyses describe governmental
institutions in the sarautu, but clearly, despite a number of formal continuities, they are quite different in each case in the ways
in which they interact with wider forms of activity. A narrative
of institutional change by itself would be pointless and tedious.
We need to be able to describe the infiltration of the system of
offices by forces that cannot be defined solely in institutional
terms.

To do this we must fragment political action analytically. The
components that result cannot be identified with different

institutions, since they will be present in varying degrees in particular institutions. They correspond to no discrete fact or set of facts, since they are meshed principles of social action, and the analytical distinctions they introduce allow us to hold in focus different aspects of substantive action. This basic analytical distinction is between power and authority, power being 'the capacity for effective action despite material or social obstacles', and authority 'the right and obligation to take appropriate actions in certain situations subject to conditions and procedures set out in precedents or rules'.[27] The distinction is related to the one made by Riggs between political and bureaucratic sectors, though he tends to see the differences in terms of particular institutional structures. It is most important to Smith's analysis that he is distinguishing between types of relationship, interpenetrating sets of roles, in terms of an abstract summary of their basic operating principles. He arrives at his conceptualization of the structure as a whole by integrating to the formal structure the arena of behaviour his distinction allows him to describe. Thus, the exercise of power (the pursuit of support and compliance) does take place within a context of procedures, precedents and rules, or those involved would not be able to understand each other at all. But, what the concept distinguishes is the open-ended, variable and contingent basis for power. Political relations express and translate into action relations of power, involve the invention, accumulation, consumption and wasting of resources that can be used to increase autonomy and effective action. Many variables, from luck to the possession of technological innovations, come into play. Political relations, therefore, are labile and intrinsically generative of structural change. Administrative relations (though, again, not necessarily particular administrative structures, which may be arenas for largely political activity) 'express and mediate the forms and the operation of public authority'. So, administrative relations constitute one structural component embedded in the total system, political relations another. To make sense fully, both will have to be described in terms of ramifying networks of interaction of every kind, but Smith's argument is that ultimately we must compare political systems in terms of the ways in which these structural principles interlock or play off each other, 'the forms and scope of public authority within them and... [the] distributions, bases and modes of public power, together with the conditions of their combination'. A further point is that such comparisons serve the purposes of identification of types of political system, rather than their classification for the comparative purpose we have been concerned with earlier. The goal is less comprehensive generalization about types of society, than inclusive generalization, which uses comparisons to identify more precisely what is distinctive and particular.

In Abuja we find political and administrative action taking place within the closed arena of the sarautu, for the most part. Political resources are mobilized within the structure of offices, so that it embodies both the structural principle of hierarchy, and a political component of segmentary competition between offices, in particular at the higher levels, between household officials and senior public officials, where feudalistic and contractual relationships between individuals are involved. The more strictly administrative offices are involved in relationships of a different kind. Mallams, chamber eunuchs and slave officials are tied to the structure by norms described in terms borrowed from Weber's ideal type for a bureaucratic structure. They have clearly defined spheres of competence, identified by impersonal rules, and stand in clear relations of superiority and inferiority to each other. The changes in Fulani Zazzau lifted political competition to a great extent out of this hierarchical structure of offices. They created great concentration and solidarity of interests in the upper reaches of the administrative hierarchy. But they intensified and greatly extended the scope of political competition and involvement between the patrilineages, and reached out to involve Habe clients and their dependants as subordinate parties to a common political interest. Some of the implications can be summarized. The drift in the role of the king, from a mediator among palace influentials to the much more autonomous head of an administrative structure, increased the autocratic nature of the system. Administrative activity came to be at one and the same time functionally differentiated from political relationships and employed as an integrated instrument for certain political ends.

The third synchronic analysis is of the structure under British administration. External relations of the system, analogous to the external relations of the Nuer in that they present problems for which the existing structure is well adapted, now involve the attempt by the northern Hausa emirates under the Sultan of Sokoto to retain a dominant position in a united Nigeria, or at least to hold off the southern Yoruba and Ibo. But internally in northern Nigeria the political balance responds to the ignorance or indifference of the British, who wanted a 'depoliticized' administrative structure, and accordingly assimilated permanent technical offices to the sarautu and permitted the dominant lineage to establish an alliance (Bornawa-Katsinawa) that consolidated its political dominance of the administrative machinery.

The nature of this domination was reflected, for instance, in the political nature of the judiciary, a situation consistent with indirect rule but not with the constitutional and institutional imperatives of the Westminster model. In a larger sense, the British presence affected the structure of political relations very little. Ex-slaves, for example, were still pinned to their relative position in Hausa political society by a whole series of constraints. There were, for instance, the complex and crushing traditional status implications of not having the resources to acquire or keep a wife. The dynasties had become an official class, which protected itself by traditional means, through marriage, clientship and kinship.

The synchronic abstracts from three widely spaced periods identify social changes and certain structural continuities. To explain this loosely in terms of 'system maintenance' is an evasive tautology. But, equally, a precise causal theory would seem to be out of the question. Narrative, on the other hand, needs to be placed in a dynamic context of relations, and Smith offers an explanation for the shape of the continuities which relates narrative evidence, discrete non-repetitive events, to an abstract specification of structural principles. His argument is that this apparent departure from the hard historical data in fact increases the precision and comparative scope of the analysis, because it relates specific events to a logically inter-related set of particular structural principles on which this system is based, and which can themselves be ranked in an asymmetrical hierarchy. It is this ranking of principles that provides the key to the direction and degree of change in the political system over this span of time. From his historical analysis he abstracts seven formal principles, which he sees as an irreducible minimum definition of this type of government.

1 Status differentiation
2 Offices differentiated as perpetual statuses
3 Differentiation of office by status conditions of eligibility
4 Kingship as the most senior of such offices
5 The rank organization of offices
6 The role differentiation of offices
7 The organization of offices in exclusive promotional series

Some consideration of the list will be necessary to see in what sense they are logically and asymmetrically related. Starting with the fundamental principle of a system based on status differentiation, they represent increasing degrees of specification and differentiation. In political terms, the evolution of the system, as over time it develops and institutionalizes this series of principles, reflects the increasing consolidation of the structure as interests and opportunities crystallize, demarcations are traded, and the rules of the game are refined. Conversely, the later principles are the easiest to reverse or modify, and it is this recognition that makes sense of stray historical incidents. For example, allocation of territorial fiefs to <u>mallams</u> was not a major perturbation for the structure or the interests of the participants, whilst an attempt by one king to abolish vassalage led to his deposition.

We can also describe these structural principles in terms of the context for rational action they provided the participants. There is a rough inverse ratio between the logical position of a principle and the scope and the necessary intensity of any action intended to reconstruct the substantive relationships that embody it. A number of unsuccessful initiatives were taken by the British, for example, who characteristically defined the colonial situation in strictly administrative terms and attempted to introduce administrative reforms that were simply not 'conformable', were logically incompatible with the nature of the structure, and presupposed political changes which had not taken place. Such attempts were substantively irrational; they represented changes that could not follow in any eductive and logical way. They challenged fundamental and obstinately defended structural principles which eluded the grasp of the constricted functional categories of the colonial administrator. As Smith points out, 'the form of a political system changes as a consequence of the political actions within it, and such action can never be unilateral. In consequence, political systems change by a process of structural drift.'[28]

Such a structural analysis of a particular historical process amounts to a severe judgment on certain kinds of comparative theorizing. By identifying the dynamic of change and adaptation in the logically constrained, but in the last analysis unpredictable, actions of individuals and groups, it demonstrates the limitations of causal explanations of processes of such complexity. Equally, it places functional analysis as a programme, a way in to the evidence, rather than the basis for a comprehensive theoretical explanation. As Barth has pointed out, we have the one case where[29]

> a social form, or a whole society, is seen as a morphological creature with certain requirements that need to be ascertained, in the functionalist tradition, the better to understand how it is put together. In the other case, a social form is

seen as the epiphenomenon of a number of processes, and the analysis concentrates on showing how the form is generated. Only the latter view develops concepts that directly promote the understanding of change.

Some writers in the former tradition of explanation, which was presented in the first chapter as inevitably stunned by a substantial shift in the course of events, have attempted to redeem the situation by invoking loose developmental assumptions, which would presumably have to be represented in terms of a series of quantum jumps from one situation to another. Thus Levy has asserted that 'once the penetration [of modern patterns] has begun, the previous indigenous patterns always change; and they always change in the direction of some of the patterns of the relatively modernized society'.[30] However, as another student of northern Nigeria points out, this particular piece of crude shorthand is intricately contradicted by the history of northern Nigeria. Change is not an integral process, and when it takes place in one aspect of social activity, that will itself create opportunities as well as constraints for particular actors in other directions. In the Nigerian case, a society notable for its intensively integrated structure of political domination, indigenous patterns were solidly reinforced during 'modernization' as a result of the manipulation of advantages created for the political élite by the conditions of external dependence and the introduction of administrative and technological modernization.[31]

The thrust of Smith's argument, none the less, is still comparative and generalizing. It is focused by two main preoccupations. He requires an adequate descriptive analysis of a type of government, but this means that he must go well beyond the observation of a few obvious social forms, to look in detail at many types of relationship, including the religious and economic. He is also concerned with the clarity of a few essential abstract categories, because it is through them that he, first, identifies the implications of situations for the individuals in them, and, second, arrives at his judgments about these situations in their full historical context. If illuminating description can only emerge from a meticulous and comprehensive structural analysis, comparisons will be limited to small numbers of similar types, and they will not be directed towards generalizations about broad paths of development or change beneath the undergrowth of contingent variations. The concern is more with an explanation of the behaviour of groups and individuals that can be seen simultaneously as making sense to them, in terms of the knowledge, beliefs, and values that are theirs, and also as part of a totality whose performance and potential may be assessed with reference to a number of appropriate evaluative criteria. Possibly these cannot be realized simultaneously, stability and order, subjective identification with the collectivity or subgroups, the distribution of material advantage and individual autonomy, to name the most obvious. Within the context of one society's history, we are offered a structural analysis of change which is at the same time an assessment of the performance of the society in terms of the production, distribution and use of resources, the control of groups and individuals, and the quality of the community for different categories of person.

IV

Smith explains change in a particular historical structure by identifying, in the behaviour of kinship segments and office-holders, the organization of political and administrative roles, and the opportunities, incentives and constraints they defined for a specific élite. A comparative theory, generalizing from the structure of relations, would need to classify a substantial number of societies in terms of critical differences in their systems of roles. The taxonomy would be the basis for an analysis of the different processes associated with characteristic forms, and possibly for a comprehensive causal theory explaining general patterns of change at a level of some abstraction. Riggs's work is an attempt to encourage the development of such general comparative explanations. As a more extended discussion of his work points out, his evocative and inventive qualities suffer from being boiled down, [32] and the skeletal outline that follows is invidiously selective. The comparison with Smith's study is concerned with the implications of the most obvious difference between their respective recipes for explanation. Formally, each one follows a different sequence. To put it crudely, Smith allows his model of the structure of Zazzau to emerge from what he finds people actually did and do in the orders of interaction he identifies. His major theoretical insights work their way out of this material, as it were. Riggs, on the other hand, begins by thinking about different types of role structure, considering their internal logic and their representative functional correlates. Having organized these reflections, he proposes we canvas the evidence, for confirmation and modification. (He is already, of course, very familiar with the evidence, but we are referring here to the formal sequence in his explanation.) To what extent can a logical structure such as this, a classification of abstract types of role structure together with certain assumptions about organized activity that relate the types in a developmental sequence, be used to generalize about a messy and diverse reality?

The answer depends on how far observations can be interpreted in terms of the system of ideal types which constitute his a prioristic theoretical framework. Such ideal types are not abstract and summary descriptions of actual situations, nor, of course, are they ideal in the sense of being ideally desirable. They are arrived at in consultation with reality, as it were, in the light of whatever leading questions interest the theorist. In Riggs's case, the most general question might be, under what circumstances is it possible for a society rationally to pursue collective purposes? It is an organization theorist's question, but with a difference. It cannot be answered simply in organizational terms, since he is concerned in the main with societies in which the necessary administrative roles are far from solidly established, and where their performance is affected by other factors which are at best irrelevant to an efficient realization of administrative objectives. So his perspective is what he describes as an ecological one, a concern to identify for whole categories of societies the representative complex of significant role structures, within which administrative functions are embedded. This is an ecological context which conditions within the social system the performance of administrative roles: he is rather indifferent to the ecological context in Sahlins's sense of an international economics and politics impinging from outside on the development of these societies. Another theorist, such as André Gunder Frank, might see that as determining, and conclude that Riggs is playing with a comparative theory about epiphenomena.[33] However, Riggs constructs his model out of the internal counterpoint of rationalities. The logic of this counterpoint is built into the structure and can be identified in the organization of roles, not because it has been found in some prototype, but because one can imagine the consequences of establishing contradictory or non-contradictory patterns of expectations and rules for behaviour, with respect to competition for power and influence and the formation and implementation of legitimate and authoritative decisions.

The typology echoes other familiar ideal types used to explain social change, such as traditional-transitional-modern, or Durkheim's organic and mechanical. The difficulties of actually applying such ideal abstractions in the course of empirical analysis have often been pointed out. Raymond Apthorpe, for example, has claimed in connection with Durkheim's analytical distinction, that[34]

> Neither the organic nor the mechanical image may satisfactorily characterize a society or a social structure, because both may be applicable to different aspects or sectors even at the same time. The value of the image may be less at fault than the error in trying to apply it to a non-existent totality. Hierarchical social relations may indeed 'be organic' in several important respects, just as competitive relations 'are mechanical' also to some extent. But an actual social system is not reducible to only one kind of social relation or another, however much prominence it may be given in an ideology.

This restates in terms of structured relationships a point made by statisticians like Blalock and Tufte, that the social scientist can expect different causal mechanisms to be operating in different subsets of his data. But the ideal type raises, in addition, the problem of the comparability of the component roles and sets or systems of roles. The discussion so far has suggested that role is a somewhat indeterminate category. In any given situation it serves to organize a range of observations, depending on factors specific to that situation. There is at least a problem over the degree of empirical precisions that is possible when classifying role systems for comparative purposes. Below a rather general level of description there will be degrees of messiness to a taxonomy depending on general diacritical terms such as 'achieved roles' and 'prescriptive roles'. Achievement is supposed to determine qualification for political roles in advanced western societies. But it is hard to believe, for instance, that the proportion of Etonians in Mr Macmillan's cabinet could wholly be accounted for on grounds of achievement. So it can only be in approximate terms that Riggs's continuum of ideal types, fused-prismatic-diffracted, can be used in empirical analysis. They are a logical series of references for the identification of structures and structural change. However, it is not clear if his core concept of the prismatic society is in fact an ideal type in this sense. The ambiguities here are of some importance to his theory.

Riggs's fundamental intuition about the rational integration of role structures is expressed in what Dunsire ferociously characterizes as a 'grossly ill-fitting analogy' with elementary optics. White light can be described as fused: there is no distinguishing its components. But it can be diffracted, and its rainbow frequencies clearly distinguished, by the intervention of a prism, the internal properties of which, in the interests of Riggs's theory, we should overlook. So, applying the analogy, we have at one extreme the criterion type of a fused society, familiar to the anthropologists, in which roles are intensively blended and structures (religious, military, political, administrative, etc.) are quite undifferentiated. At the other extreme, the diffracted model represents a maximal differentiation and proliferation of roles, with their specialized skills and highly institutionalized support structures for selecting and training people to meet these role requirements. The corollaries of these models are elaborated at great length. Thus, in the fused situation, the élite commands most bases of influence—wealth, even if this is translated into prestige by redistribution, skill, learning, military resources. In the diffracted situation, there is pluralistic competition between various élites representing more diffuse interests; the potential bases of influence are dispersed—horizontally, if not vertically—and political authority itself becomes a specialized function, instead of the concomitant of a comprehensive kind of social eminence. All this entails, for the diffracted society, elaborate channels of social mobility, specialized ambition structures with limited possibilities of transfer at different levels.

This brief summary must serve to convey the gist of a highly inventive exposition of the general characteristics of the two polar ideal types. The essence of their relatedness is that structural transformation across the continuum they define, the proliferation and differentiation of subsystems of roles, entails changes in the nature and quality of relationships within a society, the range of options open to the active and the dissatisfied, and the consequences of their pursuit for the entire social system as it moves through time.

The evocative energy of the approach is generated by creating a logical combination of the two extremes. If he has set up adequate limiting criteria to represent twin constructs very like Durkheim's mechanical and organic, then the logical consideration of an intermediate position should reveal a number of structurally significant contradictions. The prismatic ideal type is a mixture, a type of social organization containing characteristics both of the fused and of the diffracted. The amalgam is not random, because it emerges from historically fused societies, and structural drift is affected by the objectives and resources of existing interests. We are concerned here with societies which are self-consciously transitional, at least in the eyes of their élites. However, the prismatic society may, because of its unique structural contradictions, have reached a dead end, and be quite incapable of co-ordinating the complex systems of incentives and rewards that would be necessary to take it further towards the developmental goal of a rationally ordered diffraction of functions.

So, for instance, the previous example of northern Nigeria provides us with a representative prismatic case. Institutional development is fostered in the colonial situation, according to the highly diffracted norms of British local government. But these structural principles are grafted onto a social totality which is persistently interpreted in terms of ethnic and religious stratification. The criteria for the administrative career, hard work, honesty, impartiality, formal administrative rationality, are competing with a completely different interpretation of the social reality, in terms of group and kinship solidarity, the hegemony of an Islamic political ideology, semi-feudal relations of clientship and mutual obligation. The competition between the two is not on equal terms, at least in the intermediate run. The traditional élite adapts to inducements and pressures towards structural change with a highly rational conservatism that accepts most of the new behavioural requirements of a role structure based on achievement. But it avoids opening recruitment to any outside its own élite stratum. So individual success can take a larger number of forms than before, whilst continuing to depend partly on skill, luck, energy and so on, but the participants come from an exclusive administrative class. To a greater degree than in twentieth-century Britain, no doubt, we encounter an anomalous combination of traditional and modern, as academics have tended to define those terms.

The field of speculation illuminated by the reflections on prismatic logic is more rewarding and intrinsically more interesting than what emerges from the aggregative comparative studies referred to in Chapter 4. The speculative argument about the interaction between systems of relations brings into relevance a wide range of variables, but in terms of comprehensive relationships, rather than as a seamless web of inter-correlated abstractions. By identifying the constraints and options built into relationships of different kinds, it exposes the paradoxes of intention and consequence that defeat the eupeptic optimism of those politicians, planners and others who 'are inclined to see all policy issues in the context of an overall transformation of society which they hope to see accomplished. In this picture, all fields of public policy will play a part— education will spread, welfare services will expand, consumption will rise, but so will investment, productivity will go up, and

so on; growth in each sector of life will stimulate and be
balanced by growth in all the others.'[35] Societies that can be
identified through the prismatic ideal type have economic and
administrative structures that are functionally inefficient:
budgets are uncertain, prices highly variable and determined
by political criteria; groups are treated selectively, there are
selective opportunities in politics and administration, and
authoritative decisions tend to have paradoxical unintended
consequences (or no consequences at all) when they are made
by a 'sala' type of bureaucracy.[36]

But Riggs makes unWeberian demands of his central ideal type,
and the confusion he creates as a result illustrates the limitations of the analytical ideal type when it is turned upon essentially historical problems. It is useful to remind development
theorists that to be 'transitional' may not mean that one is
being pushed along a developmental sequence to anywhere in
particular. Prismatic structures might well epitomize a substantively irrational and insoluble bind. It might in principle be
possible to describe the essence of such a bind, and one might
then have the basis for a valid ideal type. But societies with
prismatic characteristics are not necessarily involved in a
functional vicious circle. Riggs vividly describes possible
cycles of such reciprocal causation. Economic growth, a
prerequisite of any meaningful economic redistribution under
contemporary circumstances, is contingent on certain systematic
relationships holding between capital and factors of production.
The development of models of economic growth may still be
in a stage of 'reconnaissance exercises',[37] but in a general
sense there is not much doubt about the relevance of capital
formation to growth. However, capital formation is a function
of only some types of social structure. It is incompatible with
massive and unproductive short-term consumption by a minority. There will be no incentive for the emergence of an entrepreneurial class unless it can work in a context that has some
degree of security and predictability from the point of view of
investment and its returns. In a situation in which those who
produce economic resources are prevented by the existing
principles of social organization from achieving eminence and
political influence on the basis of their activities, the economy
will be vulnerable to the impositions of the political élite,
and to the side effects of its internal power struggles. Of course,
some political élites may become economic entrepreneurs, but
in many situations survival for the entrepreneur may mean
consuming wealth in purchasing protection or in buying his way
into politics, rather than in investment rationally adjusted to the

priorities of development. Riggs describes as 'penury' one of
the symptoms of such 'negative development', meaning the
inability of a prismatic economy to match its level of productivity to the exponential increase in the costs of proliferating
institutions. There is no salvation in the process of diffraction,
since its functional correlates elsewhere in the prismatic
system are likely to include diminishing productivity in some
sectors, increasing inequities and economic disparities between
groups or regions, and the sapping or suppression of mobilizing
institutions capable of producing a new and substantively more
rational political formula. At least as measured by the frequency with which it has been disregarded, it is an important
general insight of the ecological perspective that merely
administrative reforms will provide no short-cuts to development, and might do the reverse. Administrative structures are
in a variety of possible ways dependent on others in prismatic
societies, and the model generates a coherent account of these
mechanisms.

And yet, prismaticness is not necessarily self-defeating. To
talk about the logical consequences of structural forms as a
general matter is only a loose manner of speaking, for there
is no ineluctable logic, only what is perceived in given situations, with more or less conviction or bigotry, as being logical
and rational. There is always some latitude for free-play, the
success of alternative interpretations in the particular historical conjuncture, of new élites discovering both new resources
of political support and new priorities. So this ideal type is,
after all, a brilliant, enlightening generalization from the evidence, but inherently imprecise, the best that can be done with a
state of empirical confusion.

This inherent looseness in such general theorizing about
structural change focuses on our two recurrent methodological
difficulties. One is the question of the theoretical entities that
are being used as the basic units of the comparative analysis.
The second is the question of comprehensiveness; crudely, is
this about all developing or transitional societies, or just some
of them?

We find that the concept of role is an indeterminate one at an
operational level, as soon as we come to the point of making
broad structural comparisons. Role is what it does in a given
situation. Just what gets included in it, in terms of expectations,
norms, values, and just how clear, compelling and unambiguous
these appear to the reasoning individuals who learn them is a
question for the specific historical conjuncture. In a well-
explored context, the counterpoint of rationalities may emerge

with great force from an operational analysis of role structures, despite the limitations of cultural distance and scrappy
evidence. But to attribute determining force to a general
pattern of roles is another matter. The problem is compounded
by the use of other categories to which Riggs gives a predictive and universal form, as when he proposes hypothetical
relationships between the degree of prismaticness (or the extent
of role diffraction), and the 'scope' or'weight' of bureaucracy.
If one is to talk about degrees of such theoretical dimensions, in
order to locate particular societies along a continuum, then
definition and measurement cannot usefully be distinguished.

But given the indeterminate, relational nature of the basic
observational element of roles, what convention might one
propose that would not be too crude for the refinements of the
argument for giving numerical values to differences? This is
not a methodological problem that can be postponed, pending a
technical solution, but a theoretical question of primary importance.

The second difficulty is underlined by Smith's analysis of
Zazzau. What he identifies as the logic of certain structural
changes emerges from an intensive assessment of the evidence
in the functionalist tradition of the social anthropologist. The
elements in the logical mix are particular to the society and
its history. Riggs's argument gives a spurious solidity to
generalizations about the logical constraints operating within
types of structure, though these are hard enough to identify
even within the framework of an extended monograph on a
particular history. One review of his book quotes six dominant
values of Thai bureaucracy, as identified by Siffin. Unlike
Smith's they are not placed in logical series, but they are constraining principles at the same level of abstraction.[38]

1 Open access, but status expressed by rank
2 Hierarchy more important than functional responsibility
3 Predominance of personal and paternal relations over impersonal relations between superior and subordinate
4 Little emphasis on productivity or the initiation of new
   activities
5 Great importance of family connections and school friendships
6 Transcendence of the material realm as the ultimate goal

Suggesting that Riggs's model has the bias of his South East
Asian specialization, Kasfir points out that Thai culture is
highly integrated, and that this list would have a greater relevance to it than any single list would have to the various
syncretic cultures of Africa. In short, a rigorous analysis in
terms of the logical constraints of a set of structural principles

must stay close to the particular, since the addition of one factor, such as the egalitarianism of African solidary descent groups, will alter the nature of the mix and its internal logic.

These methodological criticisms need not lead us into an entirely negative conclusion about such a comparative approach. We are not provided with an empirical theory, consisting of operational criteria for classifying structural types. Neither are we given an analytical logic for specifying causal mechanisms and the principles behind structural change that would identify what is common and fundamentally important in the histories of a large number of societies. But we are stimulated into an awareness of a wide range of relevant considerations which are in a general sense connected, and which can contribute to an understanding of systematic configurations. This stimulus certainly derives from the normative core of the theory, an argument which incidentally reminds us of the contemporary relevance of classical political theory. Riggs in fact spends a little time on Plato's seminal contribution to the literature on socialization, in the context of the training of administrators.[39] The Republic is a model of a simple but diffracted society, with a few clearly differentiated and functionally integrated roles. They are simple roles, without ambiguities or tensions, since individuals are to grow into them in a simultaneous process of education and self-fulfilment. The total structure is a perfectly integrated complex of values and activities, with a specialized guardian class administering and sustaining a worldly replica of the divine order of Justice. There is no power in this structure because it is not needed, and therefore no politics.

That was the Socratic prejudice. But Riggs places the administrator in a context that can only achieve an optimal dynamic equilibrium by integrating energies not licensed by Plato. Political relations are seen as the mechanical governor of administrative structures, picking out the historical path a society takes. These complementary aspects are to be identified in the different criteria for rational action expressed in distinct but related structures of roles. The attempt to run out the 'logical' consequences of the analytical distinction for a large number of contemporary societies invokes a standard of substantive rationality for social organization as a whole.

Certainly the model for this is highly abstract. So are the structures erected for such purposes by the political philosophers from Plato to Marx—but it does provide a set of bearings for the empirical analysis of complex patterns of purposive action.

CHAPTER SEVEN
Levels of theory

I

The ultimate concern of the political and administrative activity which Smith and Riggs describe in their different ways is the control of economic resources. At this point we need to reconsider the analysis of the economic dimensions of social organization and the interpenetration of economic and other facets of social behaviour. It is a convenient opportunity to review the different senses in which the idea of theory has been used hitherto, since each of the studies with which the discussion will conclude draws on more than one form of theory, and an analysis of economic structure is central to all of them. These studies blur schematic distinctions, but they do suggest that the strength of a persuasive explanation depends on a conjunction of theoretical activities, appropriate to the particular formulation of a problem and making the most of the available evidence, an analytical counterpoint, in which the limitations of one pattern of conceptualization are to some degree balanced by the strengths of another.

We have referred to abstract or pure theory, which describes a causal or functional process within a logically complete system of relations. The implicit ideal is to be found in the predictive laws of the natural sciences. Its guardians and high priests in the social sciences have been economists, but acolytes and postulants have appeared in other disciplines. In problematic contrast, since economists have made significant contributions here too, is what we could call empirical theory. This includes more than simply the generalization of empirical observations or even the extrapolation of predictions from actual trends, since such 'middle range theory', as it is sometimes called, is concerned with processes that are conceptualized in abstract terms. Particular insights into electoral behaviour, or the specific hypotheses tested by Putnam would fall into this category. Riggs introduces a third form, a general normative theory, in this case embodied in a typological construct. This was presented as a logical analysis of types of structure, fed by assumptions about the pursuit of a plurality of goals in complex and open organizational systems. It was prescriptive in the sense that it was organized around assumptions about effective and rational administration. It incorporated a number of assumptions about causal tendencies, but offered logical criteria for the evaluation of any given situation rather than a model of precisely defined interactions following a determinate course. The typology is a vehicle for a general perspective, a framework for bringing general considerations to bear on particular historical situations. Finally, the social anthropologist is characteristically concerned with the custom-built model of a partial system which throws light on a particular society. Smith's administrative hierarchies, or Turner's patterns of kinship, residence and marriage, for instance, each have characteristics that may be compared and generalized, but the achievement in these studies is to identify the implications of systematic processes in a specific setting and in unique interdependence with other internal and external forces.

The major studies we will be referring to, work by Geertz on Indonesia, Alavi on Pakistan and Balandier on groups in the Congo, all owe a great deal to the anthropological tradition. But they all draw on the other theoretical approaches as well, invest their particulars with general significance and explore comparisons at different levels in order to develop insight into situations of great complexity.

II

The condensed, predictive formulation of fundamental relationships, associated with the deductive model of the natural sciences, is evidently at some distance from the empirical complexities confronted in the anthropological and historical studies, or from general structural theories of the kind proposed by Riggs. Some allusion has been made to the development of such 'pure' theory by economists. It is not something that emerges from 'the facts'. On the contrary, what is looked for here is a complex of definitions, or a language system, which is logically complete and internally consistent. [1] Keynes proposed a series of abstract and mutually defining categories, as one way of enabling us to understand and to control transactions in an industrialized economy. There is an arbitrary, conventional element in such theorizing, which Friedman exaggerates in stressing the pragmatic criterion of predictive success. But, as subsequent discussion of Friedman's essay has made clear, there are separate issues involved here.[2] Nagel points out that the elements out of which a predictive engine may be constructed can be realistic in more senses than one. If Friedman is referring only to the most obvious of these senses, unrealistic in the sense of false or probably false on the available evidence, then the mysterious potency he attributes to theory employing such assumptions cannot exist. On the other hand a theory is an abstraction and not a total description. The question is whether the particular complex of concepts can be related effectively to realities at its chosen level of abstraction. Nagel cites the familiar example from physics of the Law of the lever, which refers absolutely only to the completely unrealizable conditions of a perfectly rigid rod turning without any friction about a dimensionless point. The elements of the system can be given quantitative values which are logical functions of their mutual variations, and these can be used to describe and predict invariant behaviour with a high degree of precision. Economic theory also employs ideal entities in logical combination, perfect competition, indefinitely divisible commodities and the like. The strength of a theory which links such constructs depends on its fertility in producing logical derivations, and on the empirical manifestations which these anticipate.

Lack of realism becomes a limitation in the context of the application of pure theory to specific situations. Powerful theories in the natural sciences succeed in identifying systemic behaviour which does not vary at random and which is in a certain sense independent of forces outside the system. That is to say that other factors, friction or flexibility in the case of the lever, introduce variations from predicted values in specific observations, but their magnitudes can be identified and accounted for and they are relatively marginal to the process identified in the theory. Theoretical stability of this kind provides a powerful instrument for probing reality, and this is one of the contributions which Nagel claims for pure or abstract theory in economics. The theory can be used to pin down the sources and the relative importance of distortions and irregularities. Observed variations can be distinguished in an appropriate taxonomy, which may in turn suggest more detailed inferences about functional or causal mechanisms operating within different subsets of the data. The abstract theory, therefore, becomes an instrument for probing a reality that is far more complex and diverse than it can, as it were, admit to itself. However, the economist is not dealing with distinguishable phenomenal systems which associate with but do not interact with extra-systemic forces. So the logical simplification, from the point of view of an applied economist, has a more important intermediate or heuristic function. Thus A.K. Sen picks up a discussion in which he had 'assumed away all complications' in order to illustrate clearly the problem of choice of capital intensity in relation to the Indian economy, by releasing, as he puts it, seven restrictive or unrealistic assumptions.[3] These range from assuming the absence of factors of production other than labour and fixed capital to assuming the absence of external economies. From this point on, the analysis takes account of such factors, which complicate the problem of choosing paths for the particular economy. There is a transition from logical certainty to conditional empirical generalization in which the ceteris paribus qualifications to a set of predictions are specified as clearly as is possible under the circumstances.[4] Sen justifies the shift to an applied analysis, [5]

> the perfectionist attitude of orthodox economics is not the only possible approach. Indeed, the object of the exercise is not perfection but minimization of imperfection, and by trying to make some reasonable assumptions we may go some distance in aiding the decision-makers (economists, or politicians or planning experts) who have to make some assumption or other to get anywhere at all.

His rationale for an empirical theory, however, conceived in a moment of logical clarity but proceeding to assimilate the complicating factors forced on it by reality, skirts round epistemological issues raised by historians of economic thought. He seems to be implying here that abstract theory is an exclusively logical construction and this suggests a distinction between abstract logical theory and specific historical circumstances that is misleadingly sharp. It is as if some timeless verities are being frustrated by the pathology and irrationality of a confused society. In his view, the economist confronted with the task of formulating a development strategy continues to think as an economist: a model that idealizes a limited set of logically interdependent and measurable functions is pitted against the empirical processes it is intended to identify. But the analysis is provisional and its context is recognized as an uncertain one in which a large number of local factors may be operating.[6] This requires the identification of these local factors, through a structural analysis that is not primarily economic, certainly not exclusively so. Such an analysis will be integral to the interpretation of abstractly defined economic functions, since on it depends the possibility of describing behaviour as meaningful, rational or otherwise.

But the difficulty of preserving theory for some practical purpose is not simply intrinsic to the peculiarities of under-developed economies, as Lowe has shown in his account of the evolution of economic theory in its historical setting in the industrialized world. He begins by noting an historical fact about the actual correspondence between predictive theory and predictive capacity, 'our ability to explain and to predict has not improved in proportion to the exactitude of the methods applied'.[7] And he relates this anomalous association between methodological investment and predictive dividend to a form of periodicity in the history of economic thought. The 'unrealistic' assumptions of abstract economic theory have not been uniformly unrealistic over time. Thus, abstract 'economic man' is a genuine abstraction from the substantive social experience of the classical period, from the mid-eighteenth to the mid-nineteenth centuries. There existed over that period a whole complex of historically contingent circumstances, which would include mass poverty, the social isolation of the individual in a competitively organized civil order, and a cultural climate in which economic success had become a prime source of power and prestige. Demographic and technical factors ensured that the factors of production could react swiftly to changes in demand. In a large sense there was a consensus on what economic rationality consisted in, deriving from a convergence of complex natural, social and cultural forces. Description and prescription fused in classical theory to an extent that has not been recovered in subsequent adjustments of the model and its basic assumptions. None the less, in the face of tenacious survivals, adjustments have been made to cope with emerging economic phenomena, such as the progressive reduction in the elasticity of supply in the neo-classical period, the development of monopolies and modern forms of governmental control of the economy.

What the history of these adjustments reveals is that an effective logical theory presupposes a motivational pattern, and that this is an historically contingent quantity. Developments in economic theory which have detached themselves from a concern with the structure and evolution of a distinctive society, in the pursuit of a pure, positive theory that would generalize any form of economic motivation, have tended inevitably to sophisticate method but accumulate failures where the methods have been applied to specific problems.[8] As the proliferation of special theories shows, it has become increasingly difficult to assume

common motivational patterns or shared priorities and preferences, and in its practical application economics raises the
paradoxical requirement that the economic system be manipulated in order to produce appropriate motivational patterns.
This is not for the trivial purpose of making untidy facts fit an
elegant logic. The point is that the logic has always been
instrumental and prescriptive.

Adam Smith, Lowe points out, based his theoretical construct on
a normative commitment to specific collective goals, a common
object of rational activity, namely economic growth, to maintain
the population and supply the state with an adequate revenue.
The social preconditions for this common pursuit he described
as 'natural liberty', and he gives a good deal of attention to
possible, but menacing and undesirable, institutional alternatives
such as mercantilism or an unbalanced emphasis on agriculture.
He was, it appears, quite clear that motivational patterns are
politically determined. The logic of theoretical constructs in
macro-economics is bonded to political preferences, which the
economist may or may not share with, or be able to impose on
a particular society. The Keynesian macro goal of full employment, which was serviced by a revolutionary transformation of
economic theory, was acknowledged by Keynes as part of a
social philosophy. The empirical theory of Sen's planners and
politicians is similarly instrumental and may well, as Alavi's
work will indicate, conflict with the political goals of other
groups in the society. Planners may call for analytical tools
that will take them beyond traditional forms of analysis, in order
to plot in detail interdependencies between different sectors of
the economy and lay out choices on a realistic time scale,[9] but
the choices made will reflect preferences and objectives, whilst
the analysis that succeeded in distinguishing them will have
excluded some possibilities from consideration entirely.

Lowe's proposed resolution for economic theory, confronted by
the empirical disorder of patterns of motivation at the micro
level and the impossibility of making assumptions that are
parsimonious, logically comprehensive and at the same time a
realistic abstraction from historical realities, is a controversial
one. But his historical review throws light on the limited
applicability of abstract theory. Even where the claim that
realistic assumptions are being made can be sustained, as Lowe
claims they can for neo-classical theory, the basis for the logic
of the theory is instrumental, prescribing for one complex of
social motivations and preferences rather than another. Where
cracks appear in the consensus on the 'economic action directive', controversy inevitably starts to revolve round ideology

rather than logic and technique. For many, the Western science
of economics is part of the ideological superstructure legitimating the contemporary version of a laissez-faire market
economy. It provides no theory to deal with the ideologically
central issue of distribution. The resilience of its basic
assumptions, protected by special theories and techniques for
making marginal adjustments, reveals an intrinsic bias.[10]

Abstract theory is not in itself tied to particular basic assumptions, but where there is extensive social change, or forms of
social organization that lack certain institutional patterns or are
fragmented by plural economies, the parameters of abstract and
comprehensive theory cannot be readily established. Economic
rationality can be identified in only a partial sense at the
individual, psychological level. Theories of change that attribute
a fundamental causal dynamic to entrepreneurial rationality as
a motivating characteristic raise more questions about social
organization and historical circumstance than they answer.[11]
Rational economic man, as the ideal fiction in neo-classical
theory, is a displaced person in some societies, not because
people have failed to develop an urge for personal economic
advantage, but, for technological and other reasons, because the
social organization of their economic transactions is quite
unlike what neo-classical theory presupposed. Thus Pospisil
writes of the very primitive Kapauku Papuans that 'lacking an
authority or a binding custom that could determine and fix the
value of certain commodities, the Kapauku market relies
heavily upon free and automatic adjustment of prices to the
supply and demand'.[12] Uncontrolled by customary sanctions
in economic transactions, Kapauku were rational, calculating
individuals, but only in the loosest sense did that involve them
in a market economy. The spirit in which the Siane of New
Guinea engaged in certain economic transactions was so
clearly determined by a rational pursuit of profit that Salisbury
appears to have gone further than was justified in interpreting
their economy in the language of the market model. In an
illuminating analysis of the consequences of the introduction
of steel axes to the economy of the Siane, he equates 'capital'
with real goods, the durable instruments of production, which
seems to introduce a confusion between what economists would
describe as capital and what they would describe as factors of
production.[13]

On the other hand, careful consideration of peasant behaviour,
often on the face of it wilfully indifferent to manifestly
'rational' techniques and habits of cultivation, suggests that it
may in fact be consistent with shrewd assessments of the pros-

pects of material gain and survival, taking into account local factors of risk and uncertainty.[14] But it does not fit theoretical assumptions about economic rationality. Worse still, as Riggs's analysis suggests, one might have to 'release' a number of restrictive assumptions about the economists and planners themselves. In developing societies, the official embodiments of economic rationality may well be a thoroughly unrepresentative professional élite, formulating goals from a sectional perspective or, quite possibly, isolated from central decision-making and administration, and serving a largely ornamental function, of seducing the major powers into a liaison sweetened with economic aid.

The complexity of the problem is compounded where economic transactions take place across interlocking, partial systems, operating on different premises and realizing different social objectives. 'Primitive' and advanced economies seldom exist in total isolation from each other. Where they interact they develop into larger systems of relations, exposing entirely new opportunities for enterprising entrepreneurs, for instance. European economic activity has frequently changed local circumstances, with the result that existing social systems have been rapidly modified and the customary management of economic transactions discarded in order to accommodate the manipulation of new opportunities.[15] There emerges a new and distinctive structure, whose economic aspects can be described, but not subsumed under an ideal type susceptible to rigorous operational interpretation. All this is not to say that the economist abandons precise theoretical definition and measurement in favour of impressionism. It does mean a different level of theoretical activity.[16]

III

The normative commitment to an economic action directive is implicit in economic theory. Formal theories in other fields similarly presuppose certain criteria of rationality. But disagreements and uncertainty over such assumptions invoke a looser, more explicitly evaluative and philosophical type of theory. This is necessarily comparative, offering criteria which distinguish types of structure. These may be crystallized, as in Riggs's prismatic theory, in a language of ideal types, and an analytical framework of ideal types may provide at least a way of clarifying the problem confronting an economic analysis. It might sort out distinctions between qualitatively different patterns of economic interaction and their structural correlates.

One attempt to identify the principles organizing economic life in different types of structure emerged from a Columbia inter-disciplinary project in the 1950s, particularly in the work of Karl Polanyi. The philosophical perspective is fundamentally at odds with the scientific objectivity attributed to the methodology of positive economics, and his work is a peculiar combination of schematic thinking infused with insight into the conditions of social change. He has a Marxist vision of the fully developed market economy, as the skeleton of a maimed society, irra-tionally organized round contradictory purposes. This combines with a belief in the historical reality of Aristotle's philia, the general good-will which is supposed to link together the mem-bers of the ideal city state, as a natural component of customary relations in primitive society.[17]

He makes reference to Maine and to his disciple Tönnies for the well-worn ideal types that define a continuum of structural change, between relations based on status and relations based on contract, or between Gemeinschaft and Gesellschaft. The continuum drawn between these analytical end-stops is obviously closely akin to the one adapted to Riggs's purposes in the pris-matic theory discussed in the previous chapter. For Polanyi, the essence of the conceptual distinction is that it provides 'ideal' descriptions of two systems of economic behaviour that are quite distinct in the normative quality of their representative social relations. In the former, relations of production, land and labour are integrated into an economy through kinship, with all that that implies, or through personalized relationships of a feudal kind, or, in the case of the hydraulic empire states, through a centralized state. The market economy emerges from these patterns. Land and labour cease to be organized in terms of a structure of solidary relations and become commodities that can be freely purchased. This summarizes a massive and complex historical process, but his large generalization is, Polanyi claims, more accurate to the historical facts than the historically untenable theory of stages which had become part of Marxist doctrine, since that dogma is conditioned by assump-tions about the status of labour and overlooks the historical significance of land.[18]

In terms of this macroscopic perspective, what we normally describe as the rationality of economic man is a consequence of the institutionalization of only one possible economic mode. An

evolved market system, the availability of credit as the basis
for contracts involving long-term planning, implies a system of
relationships governed by impersonal criteria. This economic
system can be understood in terms of its own dynamic properties. It has ramifying functional consequences for other
kinds of relations in the system as a whole, but increasingly the
role of these other structures in determining the nature and the
flow of economic transactions is reduced till they can be
regarded as externalities, more caused than causing. Given
this development, it was in the interests of an apparently
attainable rigour that the post-classical economists between
Marx and Keynes, such as Jevons, Menger and Walras in the
1870s, searched for a pure theory, positive and comprehensive,
and shifted attention away from the moral and cultural aspects
of economic exchange.[19]

At the other end of the continuum the economy is embedded in
other structures, and the criteria for rationality must be different. Aristotle's philia links the members of the society
affectively. It also defines the unequal standing of the
differentiated roles through which the community survives and
has continuity. In the Platonic tradition, 'justice' consists of the
functionally effective, and therefore normatively good, model for
the structure of relations of authority and obligation. Economic
transactions are embedded in this totality, so the 'just price'
expresses philia; it does not emerge out of an impersonal com-
putation of the exchange value of goods, but expresses a shared
understanding of the needs and obligations of different statuses
within the community. Within this sociological perspective
'normativity ... is inseparable from actuality'.[20] The huck-
sterism Aristotle identified in the developing patterns of trade
in his time was not only a premonition of economic development,
but had ethical consequences for changing social patterns in
general.

Similarly, in a primitive society, the expressive function of an
economic transaction may be integral to it, a recognition of the
asymmetrical relations between uncle and son, for example, or
between king and vassal. The language in which such relations
are expressed may be mythical and symbolic, and the social
reality that individuals have to find coherent and meaningful
may not express motivational patterns that can be reduced to
general assumptions about utility maximization.

Polanyi's argument calls for structural categories which will
distinguish between different empirical economic systems and
classify them along his broad developmental continuum. He

abstracts three fundamental and logically exclusive principles on which relationships involving the transfer of social and material goods can be based. They are in effect three ideal types—a given empirical system may incorporate elements of all three. Each comprises a set of attributes, norms governing expectations and behaviour, which are stable enough to be described in structural terms. Each, it is claimed, has distinctive functional consequences and entails different constraints for the actors, and qualitatively different options. Criteria of rationality that dominate at one point will not do so at another. He describes the three ideal principles of economic relationships as 'reciprocity', 'redistribution' and 'exchange'. Each principle has its structural correlate, a type of social organization that generalizes the basic features of a range of instances. These he identifies as, respectively, 'symmetry', 'centricity' and 'market'.[21]

A classical example of reciprocity in economic transactions is Malinowski's analysis of the complex trade ring among the islands of the western Pacific, which was much later reconsidered by Singh Uberoi.[22] In terms of the case studies we have considered, economic relations among the Nuer consist of transactions between individuals which reflect their different degrees of proximity within the segmentary structure. They reflect that latent structure and are determined by norms of reciprocity. But the economic skeleton of the hierarchical structure of Rwanda is a redistributive one. The ideological fiction was that the kingdom belonged to the mwami. Good emanated from him, and the hierarchy of officials was concerned with the business of collecting directly in the form of tax, absorbing its percentage, and then redistributing the balance. Zazzau also was organized to make massive economic extractions in the interests of the court and central bureaucracy, redistributing to maintain this structure of domination through the institutions of client and vassal. In its feudal relations with Sokoto, Zazzau was part of a larger system of centralizing tributary states. Market systems, finally, can vary widely in their complexity and scope, but they are necessarily most highly developed in industrialized societies.

There is some association between variations along this continuum and differences in environment or ecology. The rationale of reciprocity under conditions of extreme material deprivation is obvious. But the effect of environment on the emergence of more complex structures is much more indirect and uncertain than Montesquieu would lead us to suppose. In his study of Dahomey, Polanyi is careful to say only that the forms of human settlement and, hence, of state structure, are 'not unaffected' by the basic environmental factors.[23]

Polanyi's macroscopic categories block out a number of provisional distinctions between different types of structure. They also embody provisional and undeveloped normative judgments on the actual societies the ideal types help us to identify. The judgments may be sweeping, but he recognizes that economic relationships are one aspect of the total structure of social relations, and that the analysis of economic behaviour forces the observer to consider and introduce his own judgments on the behaviour of particular groups and the quality of life in the society. Partly as a result of the controversy Polanyi provoked, subsequent studies have confined themselves less to narrow disciplinary perspectives, and have become increasingly sensitive to the relevance of kinship structures and other aspects of social organization to relations of production and systems of exchange.[24]

But he assumes that the continuum of ideal types represents an historically descending scale of normative integration and maturity, and this is romantic in a weak sense of that frayed word. It is too easy to throw doubt on his system of generalization by taking some of their implications and setting them against evidence that has been assessed in a more sharply focused frame of reference. There is reason to suspect that the path of social and economic change he sees in history is neither logical nor necessary. Societies which are by any standards intensely traditional can, under certain conditions, absorb economic structures that are entirely of the world of markets, wages and impersonal norms of productivity, without apparently threatening the positive reciprocity of their customary relations.[25] Furthermore, in recent years historians have been able to show that market systems of considerable scope have much longer histories than had been assumed, and it has been suggested that the distinction between market and non-market exchange systems is much less useful, at least for West Africa, than a distinction between long-distance and short-distance trade. Whilst the relative level of development of a market system is not easy to gauge, the latter distinction makes it possible to ask quite specific questions about the factors that encourage or inhibit the development of either geographically extended or local exchange.[26] Polanyi's broad identification of structural type and normative system can be challenged on other grounds. A sense of the whole, of a moral community, may characterize some societies that are highly evolved and in no sense primitive in terms of social organization. This would seem to be true of the traditional jajmani system in India, at least as described by the French anthropologist Dumont. The positive reciprocity of the village finds a universalistic justification in religious beliefs, and is encapsulated within the centrist economic order of the state.[27]

> An economic phenomenon presupposes an individual subject: here on the contrary everything is directed to the whole, to the 'village community' if one likes, but then as part and parcel of a necessary order. This view of an ordered whole in which each is assigned his place, is fundamentally religious. Within this overall view are located the various functions and specializations which seem to be very unequally religious in themselves.

But the theoretical generalizations can also be broken down by a conceptual analysis which looks much more closely at possible connections between observed economic behaviour and its normative content. Sahlins has pointed out that within any one primitive society, let alone between them, there will be different forms of reciprocity. It is pointless to distinguish these formally in order to quantify their incidence for 'objective' and scientific comparisons, because the differences are differences of moral content, both to the individuals involved and to the observer. The differences can be identified conceptually, but they can hardly be subjected to comparative quantification. At one extreme, we can observe what he calls generalized reciprocity, the ideal type of which would be the 'pure gift' described by Malinowski. Pure gifts certainly involve counter obligations, but Sahlins points out that 'the counter is not stipulated by time quantity, or quality; the expectation of reciprocity is indefinite. It usually works out that the time and worth of reciprocation are not alone conditional on what was given by the donor, but also upon what he will need and when'.[28] The prestations to be described by Alavi come near to this end of the continuum. At the other extreme, different both formally and ethically, we can observe what he calls negative reciprocity, which is frankly impersonal and exploitative. Further differentiating at this extreme, 'one of the most sociable forms, leaning toward balance, is haggling conducted in the spirit of "what the traffic will bear". From this, negative reciprocity ranges through various degrees of cunning, guile, stealth, and violence to the finesse of a well-conducted horse raid. ' The normative contrasts outlined here, within the traditional system of reciprocal exchange, are at least as stark as Polanyi's, and since their distribution is not random, they too have their structural correlates. Different forms of reciprocity emerge in the expectations that define different types of role relationship. Sahlins suggests a generally inverse relationship with kinship distance, so that one would expect for a number of reasons that negative reciprocity would characterize transactions between remoter segments among the Nuer, but that there would be a much less utilitarian accounting in gift-giving within the more immediate face-to-face groups in a residential unit.

Polanyi's market economy is also overgeneralized and its normative evaluation undeveloped. Richard Titmuss, in a comparative analysis of the provision of blood for medical purposes, has expressed a social philosophy very close to Polanyi's, and he is as aware of a common tradition of social inquiry. [29]

> Customs and practices of non-economic giving—unilateral and multilateral social transfers—thus may tell us much, as Marcel Mauss so sensitively demonstrated in his book The Gift, about the texture of personal and group relationships in different cultures past and present. We are reminded, whenever we think about the meaning of customs in historical civilizations, of how much we have lost, whatever we may have otherwise gained, by the substitution of large-scale economic systems for systems in which exchange of goods and services was not an impersonal but a moral transaction, bringing about and maintaining personal relationships between individuals and groups.

But the assessment of relations between economy and society is intricate and complex in his empirical analysis. His comparison relates to the bearing of market forces on the transfer of a specific social good, blood, and he is comparing two market economies, the United States of America and the United Kingdom. His conclusion is that market relations determine the supply of blood in the United States, with consequences that are bad. The system is rationalized in one sense; there is a structure of determinate relations between supply and demand of blood under different circumstances, a price system within which various constraints and inducements are created for donors, entrepreneurs and users. The working of this system can be predicted in terms of price theory. But the system is substantively irrational in two related senses. Market inducements encourage practices (such as over-giving, the use of old blood and inadequate screening of donors, with the consequent risk of actually transmitting hepatitis) which defeat the social purposes of these programmes. They also deny people an opportunity, good in itself, to give. In the United Kingdom, potential donors at least

have this area of free choice. A substantively rational management of this resource has ramifications, functional connections
with other types of relationship.[30]

> private market systems in the United States and other coun-
> tries not only deprive men of their freedom to choose to give
> or not to give but by so doing escalate other coercive forces
> in the social system which lead to the denial of other free-
> doms (and maybe life itself) to other men who biologically
> are in no position to choose—the young and the old, the sick,
> the excluded and the inept as well as the sellers of blood.

Titmuss is not suggesting that this system in operation is an
adequate general moral indicator. The point is that there is one
area which, within a market economy, can provide the opportunity
for an act of reciprocity that is more completely unconditional
even than the 'pure gift' described by Malinowski.[31]

> Unlike gift exchanges in primitive societies, there is in the
> free gift of blood to unnamed strangers no contract of custom,
> no legal bond, no functional determinism, no situations of
> discriminatory power, domination, constraint or compulsion,
> no sense of shame or guilt, no gratitude imperative and no
> need for the penitence of a Chrysostom.

The evaluation of a system of social relations cannot be simply
spun out of clichés about market man or noble savage.

The limitations and merits of Polanyi's conceptualization are not
difficult to identify. His ideal types embody a general theory
about types of structure which is explicitly normative, but at
the same time offers criteria for distinguishing between different empirical systems. The propositions of the general theory
are difficult to put to a direct test. They are definitions rather
than descriptions, and they characterize relationships at a level
of considerable generality. We can, however, ask if the ideal
types assimilate the structures construed in particular empirical situations, relating them coherently together and generating
new and consequential problems. By these standards Riggs has
developed better ideal types than Polanyi, narrower in scope,
easier to interpret operationally, and illuminating complexities.
Polanyi's encounters with empirical evidence rather more
rapidly expose the weaknesses of an overgeneralized argument
about structures. He also shows signs of a weakness to which
typological thinking is peculiarly prone, of insinuating simplistic
assumptions about the development through time of a complex
structure of relations.[32]

IV

The monographic literature on economic and social change seems
to place severe restrictions on comparative theory of any great
generality. Abstractions of any scope seem to be defeated by
two related empirical constraints. Firstly, the complexity and
diversity of the economies of primitive and transitional systems,
and, second, the variety of ways in which these have engaged
historically with larger, colonial and international economic
systems. Unquestionably there are general trends. Market
systems begin to develop, for example, as conditions encourage
institutions which provide credit and the possibility of saving.[33]
However, markets do not emerge from uniform systems of
reciprocal or redistributive exchange. Many primitive economies are multi-centric. Thus the Siane had three main categories of goods, which circulated in independent spheres and
expressed different social values. Subsistence goods were distributed to maintain a 'standard of life', but this standard had
different forms for each accepted social position. The transfer
of valuables, such as axes, expressed fluctuations in power and
increments in informal social rankings. Whilst a final category
of luxuries provided insurance against excessive rigidity by
catering to the whims and preferences of individuals.[34] Similar
economic spheres are characteristic of economies having long-
standing connections with outside markets. Bailey describes
three systems in Highland Orissa: a peasant system for food
and crafts, a commercial system that connected the village with
the world outside, and another, consisting of the economic activities of the government agencies.[35]

The relative importance of such economic spheres, the extent
to which they are used in local competition for power and
prestige, their modification by the intrusion of wider economic
systems, provide the material for a variety of local histories.
In some situations, as we have seen with northern Nigeria, new
connections with the outside world lead to the development of
a market system, but under circumstances in which existing
élites take the initiative, make use of their political dominance
and control existing structures of authority and of customary
deference. In its formal aspect the traditional structure might
then remain much the same as it had been, but with widening
disparities between groups, the decline of mutual obligations
between strata—asymmetrically disposed though these might
have been—and the development of a new nexus of orientations in
response to a transformed system of incentives. Elsewhere,
an exchange sector, controlled by the norms of the market, is

insulated, at least for a time, from a pattern of economic life that reflects relations of power and authority in the corporate ownership of property by clans, lineages and residential groups.[36] There are groups such as the Tiv, in which the normative content of the traditional economic system has been inevitably destroyed, whilst the nature of the traditional system clearly determines the form that structural changes take. The Tiv had a subsistence sphere for foodstuffs; a prestige sphere for slaves, cattle, certain kinds of cloth (tugudu), medicine and magic, in which brass rods were the special currency; and, finally, there was a sphere concerned with the exchanging of wards and wives. There was a specialized overlap between them since the ultimate form of maximization was to convert goods in the food or prestige sphere into credit at the level above it. When the money economy was introduced, the Tiv appear to have clung to their old preferences; wives and children continued to be the ideal form of investment. However, with the new money economy it was easy for the enterprising to make a good thing out of selling subsistence goods to outside markets. Since the number of women available remained more or less constant, their price was inflated. Subsistence goods drained into the export market, and there were other untoward consequences for the social order. Once initiated, the conclusion to this internally contradictory dynamic was foregone.[37]

But this line of argument need not lead us to confine ourselves to the particularistic monograph and a narrow context of inquiry. The sense of groping, of partial and unevenly integrated success, which emerges from our consideration of attempts to develop theory by social scientists, does hint at the form a satisfying explanation of social change might take, one that plays the levels of theoretical analysis off against each other within a specific historical context, and achieves a distinctive generality and comparative power. At this point formal description will convey less than an example, even a modestly limited one.[38]

> Indonesia [Geertz has argued] may—looking at her geographical and cultural diversity, one is tempted to say necessarily will—develop in fits and starts rather than continuously, and in an uneven and disjointed rather than a systematic and coordinated manner.... In the sort of jammed and disorganized situation of Indonesia today, no genuine growing point is so small or so peripheral as to be irrelevant.

He compares two such growing points, Modjokuto, a market town in eastern central Java, and Tabanan, in south-western Bali, which still retains a much more traditional pattern of social organization. Both are involved in a changing regional economy, which is in some respects exceedingly old, and this introduces a number of exogenous determinants into their respective situations. He describes the historical structure of each town, the situation of different groups in relation to the structures of power and authority. And he shows how systematic tensions develop and determine the logical evolution of these relations.

The key to the development of the market economy in Modjokuto, specifically away from a bazaar-type economy to one organized by firms, is a Reformist Muslim class of traders, proto-typical Weberian Puritans in their work ethic, abstemiousness and righteousness. Their socially marginal status relative to both peasants and landowners provides them with the opportunity to pursue a disesteemed form of activity in an attempt to improve their status in a rapidly changing society. The traditional social organization out of which they are emerging can be described in terms of functionally related segments, peasants, gentlemen and traders, culturally divided and with the former two much more solidly justified in terms of Javanese ideology than the latter. The market itself, as an arena for economic rationality in the behaviour of the individual entrepreneur, is very highly developed. There are ancient customs regulating the conduct of trade, but 'commercial activities are not here entangled in an awkward and complicated fabric of social prejudices and obligations which inhibit rational calculation, egoistic behaviour, or technical proficiency.' The bazaar economy is insulated from relations of authority and status, reflects the political and cultural subordination of an energetic group, and has reached in its internal working a state of baroque overdevelopment. Role differentiation within the market is minute, a functional response to the sheer number of potential entrepreneurs.

Historical generalizations about economic development are of some importance in the analysis, but as benchmarks rather than grounds for prediction. Geertz refers to Henri Pirenne's observation that it was export trade in medieval Europe that led to the development of a merchant class, and there is some general similarity between the merchants of Modjokuto and the European bourgeoisie. The bazaar traders were beginning to emerge as a distinct economic class rather than continuing as the useful itinerant pedlars they had traditionally been. But Geertz is not prepared to see the historical parallels as precise ones. For one thing, an even more marginal Chinese community, culturally at any rate expatriate and not so likely to be assimilated, controls substantial economic resources and has access

to external finance. Indigenous resources are very limited.
Needs and demands are expanding. For reasons such as these
the British industrial revolution provides a weak historical
model. So the emergence of an economic bourgeoisie is pro-
blematical in a number of senses. It is complicated by a degree
of ethnic and economic pluralism, but it is also not certain that
the economic base for it is sufficient under contemporary circumstances.

However, the major constraint in Geertz's view lies in the
retailing and distributive organization of this market system,
which is a product of the wider structural position of the group
which dominates it. In its own terms the market system is
highly rationalized. There is a sliding price system (which
places a premium on the bargaining skills of buyer and seller,
rather than on competition between sellers), a credit system
which ties small traders to larger, a fractionation of risks and,
consequently, of profits. This elaboration of the commercial
system has the incidental effect of reducing the number of un-
employed, so there is a widespread commitment to it. But potential for economic development within such a system is objectively
limited. It is not easy, for example, even on a joint investment,
for a concern to establish dependable relations with distributors,
and, through them, to develop a relatively predictable clientele.
A major structural constraint is the absence of incentives
extending beyond immediate economic transactions to modify
an overcomplicated process of exchange which does not have
cumulative effects on sustained growth.

The chronic disorganization of the process of economic growth
and development that this entails is not necessarily reduced by
the development of vertical divisions round nationalist political
parties, alirans, which in some respects reflect the urban
homogenization of recent years.

The salience of different elements in the social structure is
very different in Tabanan. Here too we have a fitfully expanding
economy, but the economically progressive group consists of
the politically displaced indigenous aristocracy. The revolution
has removed them from the arena of national political competition, or drastically altered their position in it. But they are left
with other resources, transferable assets and a local cultural
ascendancy. With their own rhetoric or ideology of moral
excellence, corresponding in function but not in content with
the prayerful diligence of the reform Muslims, operating as
aristocrats born to lead, they have developed a number of concerns, such as transport companies, or the type-recapping

monopoly of the Lord of Krambitan. They have responded shrewdly to their situation, through local branches of nationalist parties, securing contracts and franchises, in a deliberate attempt to reconstitute their local eminence on an economic and industrial base rather than the traditional political one. But they are pursuing this course in an attempt to retain a traditional social structure of paternalism and dependence. The aristocrats have become an administrative and civil service élite, effectively adapting the locally traditional habits of collective work to the requirements of modern industrial organization, and strengthening their prescriptive rights to organize local labour and retain the perquisites of their status.

Geertz concludes his study by making half a dozen sociological generalizations that could serve as points of departure for other comparisons. The first three, for instance, refer to the fact that in both cases the economic innovators come from relatively well-defined and homogeneous groups, locally rooted, with a status in a wider field of relations which is undergoing change. The conclusions are consistent with other observations of the entrepreneur or leader as in some sense a marginal or interstitial figure, a link between strata, who is constrained to make his way by playing off one set of relationships against another.[39] Such generalizations summarize a characteristic possibility under favourable circumstances, describe a modal structural process, but it is confusing to think of them as law-like statements of however provisional a kind.

We can distinguish a number of aspects to the theoretical content of Geertz's account. Dominating the whole analysis is a highly generalized model of a developing economy, which we are left, quite reasonably, to infer. He is matching the empirical realities against a broad picture of a society that has developed forms of purposive organization which can be depended on to improve the quality of life in the society as a whole. Where Polanyi committed himself to an explicit general model of economic 'success', Geertz invokes a generalized possibility for a particular society. He also avoids introducing schematic moral evaluations. He draws out a comparison between the 'success' of Japan and the stagnation of Indonesia, since they have in the past been comparable in many relevant respects. But he emphasizes that it is not his point that the Indonesian peasantry suffer now, or that the Japanese peasantry did not suffer during the intensive commercialization of agriculture after the 1860s, but that, from our historical perspective, the Indonesian peasant has suffered to achieve so little. Development in the widest sense would now involve a greatly increased

ability to control involvement in the international economy, a
revolutionary degree of social involvement and a corresponding
exploitation of resources and productive capacity. The prospects
are slim.

In gross terms, economists, geographers and demographers can
specify those broad constraints which are not subject to direct
control. (There are, in fact, substantial reserves of raw materials.) But Geertz's main concern is with the political economy
at a grass roots level. A macro analysis of the economy may be
able to propose alternative paths to development—Indonesia
is notorious for the bulk and sophistication of its paper
plans—but such an analysis presupposes institutions, beliefs,
networks of communication and levels of knowledge that may
or may not exist in reality. The absence or presence of these
factors cannot be simply acknowledged, as in a distillation from
a large-scale comparative analysis, since they are part of an
historical complex at a particular point in time. What he
attempts to do is to identify the complex structures which seem
to confound the efforts of political and administrative élites,
even when, as has arguably been the case since the Sukarno
period, there have been rationally conceived national plans to
put into effect. His analysis develops by identifying the component ethnic and status groups, tracing the economic, political
and administrative aspects of their interactions, and building up
a powermap of their relations along an historical dimension.
He describes a complex of partial, historically open systems,
which intervene on each other and encapsulate each other to
produce critical historical opportunities, which could have been
taken and might have led in the direction of his implicit developmental model.

The most complete, and effectively homeostatic systems he has
to describe are the ecological systems incorporating the
historically dominant processes of production. In his more
ambitious study, Agricultural Involution, he traces the cycles
of two ecosystems, one involving the production of rice and
sugar (sawah agriculture), and another (swidden) which includes
the production of coffee. Each of these is anchored to a functional complex of biological interactions, an energy system
which human intervention can develop. But the parameters of
these ecological systems are socially interpreted. Production
requires the organization of labour, involves the evolution of
systems of land tenure, which will condition all other aspects
of social interaction, and which can be modified by the intervention and dominance of other systems of exploitation, colonial

demand for raw material, particularly sugar, and its dependence on fluctuations of price on the world market.

The historical evolution of the colonial economic system, from its mercantilist to its corporate periods, was associated with developments in the indigenous society which, Geertz argues, cauterized the growing points of a diversified market economy. For example, what Geertz calls the 'culture system' rationalised the production of sugar from the point of view of the Dutch companies by relating tax incentives to a flexible and predictable production of the export crop. The dual economy comprised Western, mechanized processing, and production by an Indonesian labour force of adjustable size. This rationalization of the factors of production was possible largely because the ratio of sugar (export crop) to rice could be varied from year to year, since one could be substituted for another on the same terraces; also because the output of rice rose with labour intensive cultivation; and finally because the traditional pattern of social organization allowed for the indefinite subdivision of rights to land, and the perpetuation of traditional kinship and authority structures. Population expanded on the basis of a more intensively worked subsistence economy. The energy system working in on itself, became superheated as it were, with fatal consequences for any possible additional provision of incentives. Groups able to take advantage of them could not emerge to develop a more diversified, less vulnerable and dependent complex of economic relations. Other opportunities do develop, but the comparison between Modjokuto and Tabanan gives specific force to generalizations about possible complexities. Such development is 'lumpy', contingent on the strength of cultural factors in local subsystems; the social organization of the market system of Modjokuto prevented the development of a credit cycle capable of sustaining substantial growth, and in Tabanan economic development consolidated local power structures. In each case traditional structures adapted, but without raising any positive prospects for development in the sense Geertz gives it.[40]

Particular historical events, even some that were affected by accidents of personality, are of considerable importance in Geertz's historical account. In 1830 a new Governor-General, van den Bosch, arrived, with a plan that was critical in organizing the production of export crops that has been referred to. This was a 'stroke of fiscal genius' which established the 'culture system', 'the remission of the peasant's land taxes in favour of his undertaking to cultivate government-owned export crops on one fifth of his fields or, alternatively, to work sixty six days of his year on government-owned estates or other projects. ' But the introduction of this system by van den Bosch was only possible because of complex preconditions, and it is essential to the analysis to see it as 'only part of a much larger complex of politico-economic policies and institutions'. The history that unfolds is multi-stranded, but Geertz's contribution is to order these strands by distinguishing conceptually between different conditioning systematic processes. He has to draw on work in a range of disciplines in order to do so, and partial models of these functional interdependencies can be proposed with greater confidence in some cases than in others. The micro-ecology of wet rice production, for example, though biologically enormously complex can be described as a stabilizing system in a determinant relationship with its environment. Its product is an input into another system, the international market, and has identifiable consequences for the performance of the Dutch economy. At the local level the rate and direction of change is constrained by the involuted social structure of the villages, the cultural and economic relations between gentry, peasants and entrepreneurs. How these evolving, partial systems of interaction intervene on each other is a matter for informed judgment. This will depend on an assessment of the political, ideological and administrative constraints effective at given points in time. Clearly, the further the analysis moves from the predictable behaviour of the rice terrace, 'a sort of slowly drained, managed pond focused on an edible plant', towards the complex structures of local social subsystems, the more the speculative dimension of the analysis is conditioned by assumptions about patterns of motivation and the extent to which they can be modified, the likely consequences of different paths to development, and their relative feasibilities. Parts of the analysis are supported by intelligibly organized and verifiable evidence. The rest is organized round preferences and expectations, whose validity and realism may be accepted after persuasive argument, but cannot be directly determined by factual demonstration.

But what if we do not share Geertz's complete fabric of assumptions, whether at the level of individual motivation, collective organization or the large structural transformation he sees as essential to social and economic development? It may be easiest to clarify the issues raised by the question of the acceptability of a complex historical explanation by turning to a contrasting illustration. Alavi's work on Pakistan has much in common with the Indonesian study, but his perspective is explicitly anchored in Marxist assumptions about economic

relations and the nature of social change.[41] The contrast is
a significantly representative one, between a synoptic normative
perspective, characteristic of some distinguished work by social
scientists,[42] and an attempt to develop a Marxist tradition which
is neither historicist nor doctrinaire.

V

Contrasts between studies in Marxist and non-Marxist traditions will be drawn out in the next chapter, in the first instance
between Alavi and Geertz, but also introducing other dimensions, which are important in the work of Balandier. But
Marxism, like positivism or functionalism, is a general umbrella
which covers considerable theoretical diversity. It is therefore
as necessary, before considering Alavi's work in detail, to make
some elementary internal distinctions for Marxist theory as it
was in the case of the other grand rubrics.

It is characteristic of contemporary divisions between the social
science disciplines that Marx's own work has been segmented at
their convenience, so that professional economists have tended
to stress weaknesses of logic and conceptual ambiguity in his
abstract economic theory, whilst political scientists and
sociologists have concerned themselves with large categories,
class, alienation and the like, but without paying too much
attention to their basis in an integrated abstract theory of the
economic process. There is some justification for the selective
emphasis, since the fertile insights of the general theory, which
is a normative theory about the characteristics of different
types of social structure and their historical evolution, do not
depend on strict logical derivation from a logically comprehensive abstract argument.

There have been many attempts within the Marxist tradition to
demonstrate that the whole theoretical complex is a 'scientifically' integrated one, that the categories of the abstract economic
analysis have correctly identified the structural realities and
that all the basic functional dependencies in a dynamic economic
process can be specified. But we are not concerned here with
attempts to justify a doctrinal interpretation of Marxist theory,
since academic economists deeply sympathetic with the tradition have shown most persuasively that Marxist abstract theory
shares the predicament of any abstract and logically integrated
theory of social behaviour.[43] There are many difficulties about

the realism of basic assumptions in relation to changing economic realities in the capitalist system. By contrast with traditional economic theory—precisely because, we might say, Marx
shares the anthropologist's sense of economic relations as an
aspect of a specific totality of social interactions—his analytical
categories are rough, and there are many fissures in the logical
cement that binds them together. Rhetoric and logic are sometimes confounded,[44] whilst some assumptions, the constant rate
of exploitation, for instance, are simply not persuasive. The
significance of the abstract theory lies less in any achievement
as a 'scientific' formulation and its superior powers of prediction than in the historical fact that it opened up questions which
conventional economics either could not ask within its own
analytical terms of reference, or could raise only in a supplementary way. Thus Marx, in common with other economists,
failed to discover a law governing the distribution of income.
But the general issue of relative shares, controversially
explored in his theory of wages, is a central issue, and it is
posed in such a way as to lead into an analysis of social
structure and the existing patterns of ideological control and
other sanctions. The political economy is the object of inquiry,
rather than a precondition taken as given for the purposes of
theoretical analysis.

The general normative theory provides an interpretation of
historically evolving social structures which draws on inter-
connected factors important to the abstract theory of economic
exploitation. These include conflict of interest between economic strata, the relations between unemployment and economic
dependence, the relation between employment and technology,
and the dependence of labour's share in capital on its organization and bargaining power. But these and others are the general
categories which can be used in a comprehensive analysis of
the social structure, to lead into the configurations of economic
dependence, to discover latent and emerging conflicts of interest
and to identify the possible points of structural transformation.
They are indicative and cannot be operationally precise, and
since that is the case they cannot be used to support predictive
or historically determinist forms of analysis.

Class, for instance, a category at the heart of the general
normative theory, is operationally ambiguous, though theoretically precise in its most abstract formulation. The implicit
ideal type of the general normative theory requires the observer
to look for indications that social categories exist, or are
emerging, which appear to fit the general definition of class
relations in a given historical setting. In some respects the

description of social structure in class terms is required
simply by an act of definition: there are objective differences
between the relations of different groups to the process of
production. But there are other senses, having to do with collective awareness and organization, which cannot be given such a
positive identification. The normative theory looks for them,
since it seems in class consciousness the only potentially adequate
agent of structural change. But a positivistic identification of
these aspects of social consciousness is out of the question,
though doctrinaire Marxists have frequently not acknowledged
this. The historian E.P. Thompson has reminded his more
scientific and unhistorical fellow Marxists that 'class itself is
not a thing, it is a happening'.[45] It is an emergent category,
which can be finally defined only in relation to other classes
and diachronically, not as a discrete feature of a synchronic
structural analysis. It is within this historical tradition, which
the general normative theory directs, that Alavi and Balandier
are writing. Though many of their particular conclusions could
be arrived at by other routes, the ideal type that is implicit in
their studies is particularly fertile in suggesting interpretations
of empirical regularities, whether overtly economic, or relating
to kinship structures, or even to forms of religious belief.

CHAPTER EIGHT

Theories and explanations

I

This chapter has to be about power. The concept, it is often
pointed out, is both central to the analysis of politics and profoundly elusive. Political scientists attempting to develop formal theories of power have made definitional refinements and
uncovered philosophical and operational problems, and there
are situations where it would be necessary to confront these.[1]
A rigorous operational definition of power might be a possibility
in the sort of situation alluded to in Chapter 3, where game-
theoretical models have valid applications. But in the context of
this discussion we are not looking for a theoretical entity which
can be given a positive identification remotely analogous to
mass or velocity in physics. The underlying theme of this
chapter is that a definition of power is one component of a
general theory, and emerges from interpretations of social behaviour in a specific analysis. The studies that remain to be
considered all have a good deal in common, but there are also
fundamental differences between them, and these are reflected
in their respective interpretations of the dimension of power.

They share the assumption that an adequate analysis of the
political structure cannot depend on a sharply focused investi-
gation of the pursuit and formal transfer of powers within the
institutional structures of elections and legislatures. An analysis in terms of electoral arithmetic, for example, may have a
kind of precision, but it may or may not begin to identify shifts
in the distribution of power in any significant sense. The point
is well made in a study of the elections of 1969 and 1970 in
Kenya and Tanzania. Theories of electoral behaviour focus on
such events as necessarily significant and revealing acts of
political will. But each of these elections can be seen as a side
show, failing to connect with nationally important issues, in
particular the emergence of economic divisions and the impact
of the foreign sector on the economy. A conventional analysis
would fail to identify their wider implications, in Kenya the consolidation of an established political élite, and in Tanzania the

exploitation, by an emerging élite, of official socialist rhetoric
to clothe a localistic pork-barrel politics. The authors argue
that the study of the formal expression of political conflict must
be 'firmly subordinated to a study of the broad political context
which makes the legitimating function of an election important
or marginal, temporary or lasting, rational or irrational, good
or bad'.[2]

Determinist assumptions about the dimension of power do not
belong with this perspective, whether they come in the form of a
mechanistic structural-functional analysis or in the economistic
forms of Marxism, since it has a normative preoccupation with
political choice and recognizes the labile and open-ended nature
of political activity. In the light of their various preferences,
Alavi, Geertz and Balandier show different degrees of optimism
about the societies they study, but none of them assumes a fore-
closed future. They all look for points where political purposes
can develop and objectives can be secured. The convergence of
their theoretical perspectives is indeed striking at a number of
points. It reflects common intellectual traditions, with Geertz
and Balandier owing more to a tradition of historically sensitive functional analysis, and Alavi more to a Marxist historio-
graphy. Substantial theoretical differences remain, however,
which emerge in their historically specific interpretations of
the nature of political power, its bases and modes of articulation. There are differences in prior assumptions about the
structural characteristics they identify as crucial to an analysis
of political change.

II

Alavi's debt to the work of social anthropologists will become
clearer as we proceed, but it would be wrong to make too much
of it. He shares the tradition's sense of the unique integrity of
each particular social system, whilst redefining structure in
terms of a general theory of social change. But other traditions
are of primary importance, elements in the Marxist tradition,
obviously, but also a context of historical evidence and historical
analysis of change in the Indian subcontinent, for which there is
no very substantial parallel in African studies. Some of the
consequences of Pakistan's 'green revolution', to take one example, echo in important respects consequences of the rise of
land prices in the Banaras region between 1795 and 1850. Cohn

analyses the relationship between the two contending groups of entrepreneurs in that situation, the former zamindars and the urban-based purchasers of land, who contrived to split the increased income in such a way as to shore up the zamindars' local political ascendancy, and at the same time to ensure the purchasers of an urban standard of living. He comments:[3]

> In discussion of social mobility and change, we often tend to think consciously or unconsciously in terms of closed systems. This model may be adequate for the study of isolated primitive societies, but not for India in the nineteenth century, or for the Banaras region as a case in point. Hence, unlike a hydraulic pump, the change in one part of the system, that is, the rise of one group or class, did not necessarily mean the concomitant fall of another.

Which is to say that, despite its intrinsic theoretical appeal, the equilibrium model is of doubtful value even as a provisional analytical convenience in the face of the historical record. Seen from the vantage point of a familiarity with Indian history, some of the African studies must appear to be making tendentiously heavy weather of the theoretical models in terms of which they analyse structural stability and structural change. The emergence of new social categories is in no sense a novelty in the Indian context, and historians are accustomed to look behind the idiom of caste which is used to disguise and validate the social mobility of groups where it occurs.

At the same time, the most persuasive historical analysis is consistently preoccupied with the problem of identifying the essential structural characteristics of the society and their penetration by imperial control of the economy, and administrative control by a British civil service. The tendency in more recent work has been to disaggregate the broader structural models of the caste society and to explore what Cohn refers to elsewhere as 'the sociological reality of the situation'. In a passage that is reflected almost word for word in Alavi's approach to contemporary Muslim society in rural Pakistan, he points out that[4]

> the effective social unit in the case of the caste system is not the categorical level but the kinship and face-to-face grouping in the society—the biraderi and jati levels, the endogamous and exogamous group. Hence, what was important to Indians in the late nineteenth century was not the fact that someone was a Brahman, but that he was a particular kind of Brahman belonging to a particular gotra (clan) whose kinship ties were with specific groups.

The implication is that an effective generalized analysis will
have to be constructed out of painstaking work at the grass
roots, which will at one level organize observations into a model
of a local system of relationships, a network of roles expressing
local distributions of power and authority and articulating all
the public aspects of the lives of its members. This is precisely the task of a functional analysis, in the loose methodological sense attempted by social anthropologists.

Alavi is at great pains to dissociate his evaluation from assumptions underlying much work in that tradition, variants of the
organicist model with their reification of role systems and
their tendency to invoke the integrative aspect of cultural norms.
But he is no less anxious to distinguish his position from the
more fashionable contemporary forms of what he calls 'methodological individualism', which, he suggests, in effect invert the
limitations of the ahistorical synchronic model of functionalist
analysis. They stress the potential plasticity of situations in
which individual entrepreneurs or groups pursue their goals,
but at the cost of underestimating the structural constraints of
a given social system.[5] His own presuppositions identify the
latent structure of systematic and constraining patterns of social
interaction in the underlying relations of production. However,
this fundamental speculation about the priority of economic
relations does not dispose of 'non-economic' aspects of social
organization. The functional problem then becomes one of
deciding how they operate as the mediating social form of the
underlying relations of production, with their own distinctive
subjective bases and with consequences which can be broadly
anticipated for the behaviour of different categories of individual.

The analytical problem from this perspective has been very
succinctly described in the correspondence of Engels. He
writes in a letter to Bloch in 1890:[6]

> According to the materialist conception of history, the
> ultimately determining element in history is the production
> and reproduction of real life. More than this neither Marx
> nor I has ever asserted. Hence if somebody twists this into
> saying that the economic element is the only determining one
> he transforms that proposition into a meaningless, abstract,
> senseless phrase. The economic situation is the basis, but
> the various elements of the superstructure—political forms
> of the class struggle and its results, to wit: constitutions estab-
> lished by the victorious class after a successful battle etc,
> juridical forms, and even the reflexes of all these actual
> struggles in the brains of the participants, political, juristic,

philosophical theories, religious views, and their further
development into systems or dogmas—also exercise their
influence upon the course of the historical struggles and in
many cases preponderate in determining their <u>form.</u> There
is an interconnection of all these elements in which, amidst
all the host of accidents ... the economic movement finally
asserts itself as necessary. Otherwise the application of the
theory to any period of history would be easier than the
solution of a simple equation of the first degree.

So Alavi is writing in the context of what one historian has
claimed as a Marxist tradition, as against a Marxist doctrine,
when he identifies the primacy of the latent structure, relations
of production and the social definition of economic behaviour, as
determining the significance of other, analytically distinct,
aspects of social structure and organization.[7]

Certainly this assumption affects causal interpretations to some
extent. Reference was made in the previous chapter to the
alternative causal models which are logical possibilities in
an analysis of the association between innovation in agricultural
practices, economic feasibility and modernizing attitudes. The
literature is full of explanations of differential rates of economic and social change, which are organized round a prior
assumption that innovation or its absence is a consequence of
some independently identifiable psychological state, rational or
irrational, an orientation towards available means and ends,
which is the product of a given quantum of, say, achievement
motivation.[8] Within the assumptions guiding Alavi's inquiry, a
more plausible suspicion would be to see attitudes of caution
and resistance to change as dependent variables. An understanding of the structure of available choices would then be of
primary importance, and the analytical problem would be to
find a rationale for the non-innovative response. So the working assumption gives a sense of direction to the analysis. But
it cannot be allowed to forestall the analysis itself. It may not
be possible to account for non-innovative behaviour as the
result of a rational calculation of economic probabilities, that
is within the scope and perspective of the people concerned.
Other systems of social meaning, religious beliefs for example,
may have an independent effect on response and innovation.[9]
However, the analysis will be centrally concerned with the political economy. Alavi's general model of structural change
pivots on the development and resolution of conflict between
classes, and seeks to indicate the critical historical conjunctures at which political resources might be mobilized to pre-
cipitate a desirable transformation.

A substantial analytical problem, as Lemarchand pointed out for
the Rwandan 'revolution', has to do with what correspondence
actually exists between specific events and the generalized
structural model the theory provides for them. Indeed, this is
the analytical problem. We have to infer the state of development of underlying conflicts, which ultimately, but in indirect
ways, refer back to relations of production. There are two aspects to the problem, and it is in their interpenetration that the
specific difficulties of historical interpretation lie. It is necessary, first, to see the relationships between groups in terms of
material differentiation. But it is also necessary to capture
changing interpretations within the society of relations of power
and authority. The inferential analysis of different forms of
collective 'consciousness' raises the problems encountered by
Evans-Pritchard and Leinhardt in their studies of the Nuer and
the Dinka, of relating beliefs and expressive acts to the existing
principles of social organization, but with the significant difference that these are seen in relation to determinate possibilities of structural innovation.

So, the most immediate methodological reflection of the general
theory is in the way the aggregate economic data relating to the
grass roots situations are organized. An analysis of agricultural
change must start from the internal comparison of different
localities enjoying different ecological conditions. A basic geo-
grapher's distinction in this region is the variation in precipi-
tation, which permits barani (rainfed) cultivation in the northern,
Rawalpindi and Lahore divisions. Within this area there is a
further distinction between the Rawalpindi district, which depends almost entirely on rainfall, and the rest which can also
use canals or wells. Further criteria on which the taxonomy is
elaborated express Alavi's preoccupations. The size of farms
is a critical variable for a series of functional interconnections.
It is associated with levels of 'subsistence' and 'surplus', with
technology and family size (between ten and twelve acres is
the conventional maximum which can be cultivated by one pair
of bullocks and two men), and, in relation to population, it is a
measure of the increasing salience of landless labour. The
taxonomy allows a number of further revealing associations to
emerge. Census data comparing the two barani districts (excluding the urban concentration of Lahore) indicate that the
general level of literacy is substantially higher in the poor
district of Rawalpindi, where there is considerable fragmentation of landholdings and a sizable mobile population with strong
incentives to acquire some education, emigrate and remit some
of their earnings, with significant consequences for the local

economy. Furthermore, technological innovation correlates most strongly with farm size and not with education, which supports an assumption indicated by the general theory, that 'Innovation is a function of economic feasibility and not simply that of education and attitudes towards modernization.' Geertz has a somewhat different emphasis in his account of entrepreneurial motivation.

An analysis of the preliminary classification, which incorporates other data, such as the type and percentage of different crops produced in the different areas, establishes theoretically important distinctions even on a cursory examination but, as Leach pointed out in connection with the data from Ceylon discussed in Chapter 5, fragmentary indices have to be interpreted in terms of the relationships from which they were abstracted. To take one important example, variations in the rate of farm mechanization as between holders of 50-100 acres and the large landlords who hold more than this, make sense in terms of the different utilities of the two groups. It is a rational use of resources for the middle range landowner to evict all sharecroppers and to mechanize intensively. But the large holding needs a dependable supply of manual labour at peak periods, and this is secured by evicting some sharecroppers and keeping the acreage of remaining tenants to a level even below normally accepted standards of subsistence, in order to ensure their dependence on the availability of seasonal work. In this structure what he refers to, without begging historical analogies, as 'capitalist' and 'feudal' relations interpenetrate. There is no reason to suppose that this 'multiplex economy' is a transitional form, since it is in the interests of the politically dominant strata to maintain a structure from which they derive economic advantage and political security.

This analysis of aggregate data, discriminating on ecological grounds between different localities and informed by direct observation of the modal economic relationships, reveals a complex but clear pattern. The evidence shows that the technological inputs of the 'green revolution', subsidies and technical expertise, have been unevenly distributed, with the effect of increasing the relative wealth of a small rural élite and depressing the conditions of the vast majority of the people. Regarded historically, there are grounds for inferring that the regulatory system of taxation and subsidy is a contributory cause to the widening of these disparities. From the point of view of national economic planning, the cyclical effects have been substantively irrational. Increases in expenditure in luxury consumption goods by the well-off are directly related to

increased prices for basic consumer goods, and to pressures
of foreign exchange. Thus the economic disparities are systematically accentuated.

Further to substantiate the abstraction of class, Alavi will have
to interpret other systems of relations, kinship for example,
that existed long before the recent economic developments and
whose economic elements have always involved complex reciprocities across social roles and political hierarchies. Where
a theory of development may see the middling landowner as a
growth point—an innovator with his mechanization and comprehensive rationalization of production, adding to the gross
product—the Marxist perspective also relates him to other
groups and to the national structures of power and authority, as
an element in a more equivocal and uncertain process of differentiation. In this process the participants may come to recognize new criteria of rationality and discover the means to realize them in purposive action, transforming power equations
and structural constraints in the process.

This argument can readily be illustrated from the attention
given to kinship structure in Alavi's analysis of social change in
West Punjab.[10] In this situation, caste structure, though characteristic of Muslim as well as of Hindu societies in the subcontinent, is a relatively unimportant element in normal social
identifications. The idiom of kinship identifies the specific
solidarities and mutual obligations which organize social behaviour, and an analysis that makes its approach through this
aspect of the social system will be sensitive, almost as a
commonplace of professionalism, to the implications carried
in the kinship idiom for political relations between different
groups. We begin, in fact, with a classical analysis of the kinship system. The biraderi is the basic category in the idiom,
but, at the most inclusive level, it is used in two different
senses. First, it refers to the patrilineal descent group, both
as an entity of indefinite size and as an exact genealogy of
some depth which is at least remembered if not recorded.
Second, it is a horizontal category, a fraternal or solidary group,
which may be dispersed over many villages, but which is also
recognized for certain purposes within the village itself (pattis).

The ethnographic account suggests a prototype of reciprocity,
since one behavioural manifestation of the fraternal 'biraderi
of participation' is a ritualized exchange of gifts, which serves
certain economic functions, such as ensuring the recipient
sufficient resources to cope with special demands, over a marriage, circumcision ceremonies and the like, but which also pro-

vides a sensitive and public language which registers solidarity or open conflict. The gifts returned must exceed in value the gifts previously received, even if this means resorting to polite and face-saving fictions where one party is relatively poor. Gifts of equivalent value indicate a squaring of obligations and a settling of accounts. There are elaborations. The prestations (vartan bhanji) are differentiated by a symbolism of food. Pakki vartan (referring to food that is cooked, ripe, firm, or permanent) identifies the full operation of this institution. A weaker form of mutual recognition is expressed in katchi vartan (referring to food that is raw, unripe, weak or temporary). There are other refinements, expressed in the treatment of messengers involved in the ritual exchanges, which indicate the extent of the rift.

Fission and fusion, the systematic pattern of social conflict and reconciliation, has to be described in terms of segments of biraderis. As with the Nuer, antagonism and solidarity must be defined almost exclusively in terms of kinship and face-to-face groups. It is the case that where two major segments of a biraderi split, a third may be divided between them. But this will occur when the third is a weaker branch, in which individual households have links of marriage or dependence with powerful families in either of the two major segments. The expectation is that an individual will align with his patti, whatever his personal relations with individual members of the rival segment. Whatever the occasion for a dispute, there will always be forces working towards a reconciliation. It would be in the interests of a fragmented weaker section, for example, to mediate between the opposing parties. A suitable marriage within the exogamous group constituted by the fractured biraderi might then provide a basis for reconstituting the solidary group and starting afresh the cycle of prestations.

Alavi refers to exact ethnographic accounts of this system, which have given a classical functionalist interpretation of its implications. Vartan bhanji is seen to possess certain economic functions, but this is marginal to its importance in focusing and dramatizing patterns of solidary interdependence and reciprocity within a geographically extended community.

Such an interpretation, however, is not inconsistent with an open-ended historical perspective on politics at a national level. Fission and fusion amongst biraderis are more than likely, in contemporary circumstances, to be the grass-roots dimension of a politics of faction and counter faction which is played out at regional and national levels within and between party organizations. The 'issues' at one level may be ambiguously related to

the 'issues' at another. National politicians may be concerned
with spoils or principles. But they will construct the essential
political support of numbers by whatever means lie to hand. In
a society where, for most people, the immediacies of life are
very local, and local group identifications are deeply rooted
through the economic resources and personal ties of kin, parties
will have to develop their followings by attracting powerful
intermediaries, individuals with dependants tied to them by the
existing categories of social organization. What can be observed
at the local level is the competition between factions, as well-
consolidated groups are drawn into the national orbit by influentials who control them, whilst somewhat less dependent groups
exercise what choice they have in the light of how their leaders
perceive their best interest.

There is a substantial literature on the factional bases of political conflict in peasant societies, and Alavi recognizes its
importance. He is, if anything, even more emphatic than some
of the authors on the intimate relationship between the primordial categories of kin and caste and the specific patterns of
factional conflict in any given historical situation.[11] The structural importance of primordial loyalties to a politics of faction
is undeniable from whatever perspective they are considered.
From the point of view of political leaders in a national arena,
they must represent a constraint that determines strategy and
influences ideology. Whatever the uncertainties and whatever
exceptional resources might be mobilized, their existence
establishes some criteria for purposive political activity. The
same will be true for the middleman, the political entrepreneur
with a potential following to dispose of and a political market
in which to negotiate. For the ordinary person they represent
powerful and complex constraints, social pressures, shared
identifications, a highly selective network of information and
interpretation.[12]

Social anthropologists like Bailey have added a degree of conceptual self-consciousness to the discussion of factional politics,
but the significance of local patterns of conflict to political action at a regional and national level can best be illustrated
here from an historical account. The particular instance, a
study of Gandhi's rise to power, also has the advantage of suggesting a connection between political action and political theory
and its validation, which is relevant to Alavi's analysis. As an
activist, Gandhi had to come to terms with the constraints of the
existing social structure, whilst committing himself to a nationalist theory that presupposed its transformation.

Judith Brown has organized an outstanding historical analysis of
Gandhi's political leadership round a sequence of comparisons
between the different political arenas into which he moved by
chance or his own choice between 1915 and 1922. His entry
into Indian politics was marked by three campaigns in which
he introduced his tactical approach to political protest and resistance, known as 'satyagraha'. There were many important
points of historical difference between the three situations,
Champaran in northern Bihar, Kaira and Ahmedabad in Gujerat.
And whether the allusion to other generalizing, or simplifying,
social sciences is intended or not, the author issues an historian's
caveat by pointing out that the differences between the three
situations[13]

> are a warning not to expect any one pressure for change. Just
> as local power structures varied so did local strains and
> stresses; and in other backward areas these might produce
> people who would not find in Gandhi a leader who could re-
> present their interests, nor even in institutional politics an
> arena where they could forward those interests.

But the changes that did occur are intelligible. Each local campaign was a logical product of the sudden interpenetration of
local and central structures. Gandhi's initiatives and the style
of his leadership activated tensions within and between administrative and grass-roots structures. The implicit demands and
implied threats he directed at provincial and central governments precipitated the intervention of the authorities. A combination of tact and provocation directed at the administration
from Champaran, for example, made it possible to exploit
official uneasiness over peasant distress, and anxieties over
illegality and traditional abuse of influence by indigo planters.
In 1917 the burdens of such traditional oppression were compounded by the side-effects of an economy geared to the war.
Geographical isolation and a limited range of economic production, food and indigo, meant that the general shortage of
rolling stock generated severe local inflation in the prices of
basic imported commodities. In some cases officials inter-
vened to control prices before traders could exploit these
shortages, but administrative action alone could have little influence on the shortage of money and, apparently, even less on
the manipulation of land tenure and tenancy. At the same time
Gandhi was able to articulate effective political action through
local networks of influence which already existed. In Champaran the key to the campaign was an influential local trading
community. In Kaira political activity was organized through a
stratum of wealthy farmers, the patidars.[14]

Gandhi, on a heroic scale, has an obvious correspondence with
the leopard-skin chief of the Nuer[15] in the nature of his relationship to the segmentary structure of political competition. He
maintained, with great astuteness, an elusive and marginal status,
with the long-term purpose of developing a radical structural
transformation of Indian society. He had an alternative, never a
possibility for the leopard-skin chief or the Sanusi of Evans-
Pritchard's later study, which was to accept political identification with one or other of the 'natural' factional groups which he
mobilized from a pluralistic society. A central theme in Brown's
account is the constant pressure on him to do so, to come to
terms more completely with empirical alignments and work on
the possibilities of extending and consolidating them among
ordinary people. A full account of why he was able to resist the
specific gravity, as it were, of an intrinsically factional politics
and to hold out for the more problematic prospect of a broader-
based political organization does not emerge from Brown's
account. For that we would need further insight into the development and organization of an historical personality, which
would take us into theoretical speculations at a very different
level. There is one such attempt in the Freudian analysis by
Erikson, based on evidence relating to much the same period,
which interprets Gandhi's relations with his disciples and
followers, and the ethical imperatives which directed his
involvement in politics.[16] Much of what Erikson says as a
clinician, interpreting documents and interview material in the
context of a general theory of psychological development, throws
light on the historical analysis, and by doing so indicates the
limitations of the scholarly caution which is one of the many
virtues of Brown's account. Working within disciplinary constraints, though these are imaginatively interpreted, her explanations are necessarily partial.

However, she does clarify the distinctive philosophical grounds
for Gandhi's refusal to capitulate to the manifest realities of
political life, and this is relevant to the theoretical perspective
informing Alavi's analysis. Both Gandhian and Marxist perspectives share a healthy respect for the empirical constraints on
political action and the value of a pragmatic, even temporizing,
stance. But neither are content with a mechanical interpretation
of the equation of political power. A descriptive theory of the
dynamics of factional competition is not in itself adequate. Both
make assumptions about immanent possibilities, which well-
directed efforts might bring to a realization. There is an important difference between identifying the typical characteristics
of a factional politics, and, going further, accepting these as a

sufficient configuration of evidence for a general explanatory
model of political conflict and historical change.

A specific consequence of this orientation in Alavi's analysis is
that the classical account of the 'traditional' system of solidary
relationships expressed in the idiom of vartan bhanji must be
reconsidered, as must the implications of a factional politics
relating fission and fusion among biraderis to regional and
national political organization.

Alavi's implicit taxonomy in terms of class-related characteristics suggests an obvious empirical question. Is vartan bhanji
in its full range of connotations a characteristic of all biraderis or only of some, and if the practice is observed to be
unevenly distributed, what are the significant correlates of its
presence or absence? He finds a clear differentiation, which
had not been noticed, or at least had not been interpreted, in the
classical accounts of the institution. The differences are related to economic stratification. But the core of his concept of
class is a certain relationship between groups. The pattern of
intercorrelated characteristics must be interpreted in terms of
patterns of interaction between the different economic strata,
between the independent smallholders and the lower stratum of
sharecroppers and landless labourers, and again between these
two together and the upper stratum of the big landlords. What
is to be observed in these patterns of interaction is the acquisition, consolidation, erosion, dispersion and use of political power
by the different groups, a structural configuration constantly
shifting in response to the activities of its component parts,
in conjunction with forces external to the locality.

The biraderi as a solidary group with a continuing organization
proves to be weakest among sharecroppers and labourers,
leaving aside the kammis or village servants who are too
thinly dispersed among villages to have the numerical basis for
a village patti. The prestations themselves at this level are
relatively unimportant. These groups cannot afford to apply
the rules of endogamy stringently, and the status implications
of failing to do so are hardly severe, since they have little of
status to lose. Furthermore, there is an absence of integrating
institutions such as a panchayat with common law functions and
some ability to represent the biraderi as a group. On the other
hand, it might be pointed out that the accepted role of the big
landlord includes settling disputes among tenants and labourers,
which would be brought to him as a matter of course, and making
political decisions on behalf of the locality dependent on him.
Like the English gentry of former times, the landlord has a de-

gree of legitimate, de facto authority.[17] Tenants form the core of his faction and accept him as their political representative and the natural arbitrator in their disputes.

However, whatever the degree of identification on the one side and obligation or responsibility on the other, the relation of client to patron is one of economic dependence. In a situation of economic and technological change social reciprocities find themselves stretched to the limits, and evidence of more overt forms of exploitation becomes easier to find. We learn, for example, that landlords even engage gangs of thugs (goondas) to control their dependants.

Seen in this light biraderi organization appears to have a more complex function than either the abstract and static model of solidary practices, or the structural analysis of factionalism would allow. For it is in the independent smallholder stratum that the biraderi is most completely realized as a social institution. It may even be the case that among smallholders two panchayats exist in particularly compact biraderis, one, of older men, dealing with marriage exchanges and disputes, and another of energetic younger men who look to the interests of the biraderi in its relations with external administrative and political agents. Thus, for smallholders the biraderi is more than a traditional social process with integrating functions. It is a rational collective response to conditions of great insecurity and even physical risk. As an organized group, they stand some chance of being able to negotiate with factional leaders attempting to build up their local followings. For this reason it is necessary to threaten with severe sanctions, ostracism and isolation individual families which are tempted to break ranks by contracting advantageous marriages outside the endogamous group.

For the big landlord, the value of biraderi organization is very different. Endogamy is important because it consolidates interests and maintains distinctions of status, so the marriage of a daughter outside the biraderi would be very rare. Conversely, bringing women into the endogamous group is regarded as a measure of social ascendancy. A landlord may use his biraderi to consolidate the core of a faction, by activating the ideology where tenants are of the same biraderi. But since he will be oriented towards a large political context of factional competition within the upper stratum, the biraderi as an institution for settling disputes at this level will be weak.

The interpretation which these patterns seem to support is one in which there is a constant tension between vertical and horizontal divisions within the structure. There are increasing differentials in income. There is a pattern of evictions and a growing stratum of dependent sharecroppers, a logical outcome of technological innovation as it has been introduced in this situation. But it would be naïve to expect the inevitable translation of this process of economic polarization into a class-based revolutionary situation. For one thing, the group most capable of concerted action, the smallholder, tends to distinguish its predicament from that of the sharecropper and labourer, even though it is possible to argue, as Alavi does, that the smallholder is in an eroding position and should see his common cause over the longer run with the dispossessed. As a corporate client to an effective politician, the smallholder's biraderi can secure access to the bureaucratic structure of the state, or at least be left unmolested. Much as was the case in Fulani Zazzau, dependence and identification can establish a stake in the existing structure of political conflict. And yet, within a self-perpetuating system of political competition and control, there are tensions and conflicts which could express themselves in a new and widely shared sense of the modalities of power and the legitimacy of authority. The problem is to identify any effective political actors pursuing purposes that might lead in this direction, and the beginnings of a more clearly defined conflict of interests. In general terms, the theory sees a transition from the familiar vertical and segmentary divisions of conflict to a horizontal division as both possible and desirable. The structural foundation of the social system is identified in the common interest of the economically well-to-do, whatever the factional competition they engage in, and in the economic dependence of the majority. Questions about the rationality of the behaviour of those involved are bound to focus on that contradiction, as must the observer's interpretation of the rationality of any substantive change.

Canons of scientific method, in the sense of predictive modelling, are not relevant to an assessment of the validity of theory at this level of generality. The explicit normative orientation of the analysis is obviously a function of a range of uncertain prospects it seeks to identify. The analysis is not disposed of if history in fact delivers more of the same, as it were, only worse. Neither, in such a case, would it be claimed that the theory had a merely heuristic value, organizing an analysis round a limited set of assumptions, which may only have been partially valid, but which did serve to throw light on some aspects of the process of change. On the contrary, the analysis claims to have been directed by the general theory on to funda-

mental realities. Whatever the developments in the long or
short term, a sensitivity to the bases of conflict, both segmentary and in economic stratification, provides a relatively more
complete account of the structural premises out of which any
degree of change will be a logical, if not predictable, outcome.

A critique must proceed indirectly, by considering the density
of the evidence organized by the simplification of the general
model. Does evidence, described at one level of abstraction,
relate coherently to evidence abstracted according to different
criteria? So, for example, the general assumptions of the theory
require that raw economic data be collected and aggregated in
such a way as to discriminate between different social groups
and geographical regions. But is this dimension of the classification used to discriminate other patterns of association from
which relevant functional inferences can be drawn? It is
suggested that in fact the other variable dimensions accumulate
to plot out a network of social predicaments and opportunities
that are systematically distributed. Land tenure, the functions
and organization of the biraderis, margins of economic surplus,
technological innovation, education, physical coercion, are drawn
into a common focus of conflicting but intelligible purposes.
Observed over time, the tendencies clarify the dynamics of an
historically specific system of political and economic power.
Its manifestations, and, plausibly, potential properties seem to
correspond to the configuration of a general model of emerging
class conflict. But this conclusion emerges from a mode of
analysis shaped by a general theory, rather than required by an
abstract law of historical change with a preordained outcome.
The model for the general theory is in Marx's work as a contemporary historian, exploring the structure of control and the
articulation of power in a specific factory system.

The exploration of a broad political context takes us beyond the
formalistic, or disingenuous, constitutional theory of the
regime, which provides for virtual or delegated representation as an approximate form of democracy suitable to an
illiterate peasant society. It articulates social and economic
relations at the grass roots to the central structures which
emerged from the colonial machinery of government. Seen in
this light, Ayub Khan's 'basic democracy' as a structure of
representation expresses a reality of local control by a landlord class engaged in factional alliance and competition
with urban bureaucratic and military élites.

III

The social structure of rural Pakistan cannot be described as simple. And yet, moving to Alavi's study after the complexities of Geertz's Indonesia, there is a relative simplicity to the dynamic system which represents his understanding of the social changes taking place there. This is not achieved by sacrificing the problematic uncertainties of history or by ignoring complicating particulars. Unfortunately, a second-hand and selective summary cannot convey the more tentative aspects of the interpretation. However, though simplicity is a virtue in a theory capable of interpreting a wide range of phenomena, from the point of view of a Marxist interpretation of change, some situations are indeed simpler than others. As with Evans-Pritchard and the Nuer, Alavi may be demonstrating a particular analytical treatment on peculiarly compliant material. It is not so difficult to accept, after all, in the situation he describes, that the traditional idiom of kinship may come to mediate an altered awareness and provide an organizational nucleus for more extended forms of class solidarity. But in Geertz's material, there are ethnic divisions which are integral to the organization of the economy, having deep historical, cultural and religious roots. Complex subsystems of social organization are intricately tied to each other. Whilst it is clear that economic differences were polarizing during the period he studied, it is less evident, on his account, that this polarization will supersede social conflicts that are well established for other reasons, or drain them of their cultural or economically particularistic significance.

And yet the Marxist orientation must be equally valid for both situations. That is the kind of general theory it claims to be. Whatever the unique historical contingencies, whatever the disparate factors operating as causal determinants, explanation within that tradition must claim to make better sense than an alternative based on any other premises. We need now to consider some of these premises in the light of Geertz's analysis. The conclusion must be that, though an empirical analysis under either of the two perspectives might share a good deal of common ground, at the most crucial level the two interpretations cannot be reconciled, and at this stage the appeal must be to assumptions which cannot be subjected to empirical verification or disproof.

For a start, it is clear that the Marxist analysis has no monopoly of awareness of the ultimate priority of economic and technological determinants. Geertz conceives of the societies of Indonesia as historically encapsulated in the workings of a macro-economic system, which has systematically transferred economic resources to satisfy purposes outside the reach of local control. At the grass roots, almost in a literal sense, an ecological system in which man was a dynamic agent established other basic parameters determining the range of economic advantages which different social groups could pursue. The process of agricultural involution which actually took place was one logical unfolding of the complex but loosely textured historical premises he represents in his model of unevenly intersecting systems of relationships. He suggests that there were at least distinguishable points at which political and economic decisions could have been made otherwise. Thus, like Alavi, on the critical issues he is concerned with possibilities rather than probabilities, and certainly not with determined outcomes, and the appropriate form of comparative method, implicit in Alavi's analysis but elaborated in Geertz's comparison with Japan, is the suggestive historical parallel.

In each case, also, cultural systems are seen in economic and political terms. Family organization in Indonesia and the customary details of rights over land are integral to an understanding of the exploitation of the ecological system, above all in wet rice, sawah, cultivation. Geertz shows how the nexus of factors here makes it possible for the rapid growth of population to be absorbed. The response to demographic pressure was to accept the logic of kinship structure in the villages, which provided for an indefinite subdivision of rights, to survive on an increasingly labour intensive process of cultivation, whilst traditional institutions of social control and integration elaborated in desperate complexity.

Geertz conveys the sense of social desperation with great force, and at these points the emotional quality in the analysis is an important clue to the nature of the difference between the two general perspectives we are comparing.[18]

> Thus, although political, economic, and intellectual disorder has reached—at least on a national level—a stage of near catastrophe, ecologically speaking the postwar picture in Indonesia is about the same as before the war, perhaps more so. Most of Java is crowded with post-traditional wet-rice peasant villages: large, dense, vague, dispirited communities —the raw material of a rural, nonindustrialized mass society.

Without pursuing definitional refinements, what he is describing here and elsewhere would be evidence of massive alienation in a Marxist history. Its implications for prospective political movement and change would have to include possibilities which may be thinly disguised by the evidence of a defeatist psychology. But Geertz does not respond to that possibility as a real one. He is not looking for an emergent class category as a creative possibility in anything like a Marxist sense. From several passages it is clear that he expects a disaffiliated peasantry to become integrated to a national political system on inauspicious terms, as the victim and accomplice of some form of totalitarian regime. The problems of adapting to economic and technical change under conditions of extreme demographic stress, particularly over the long term, require the opportune mobilization of resources and rational planning of a comprehensively controlled kind. This will necessarily involve extensive redistribution, but there are no obvious grounds to expect that the co-ordinating rationality necessary for the future can be conjured out of those groups which are suffering most severely at present. It is conceivable that other groups, such as the traders of Modjokuto, will be able to respond to incentives to develop aspects of the market economy, and that governments will underwrite essential capital and organizational resources. But the systems that have evolved at different levels are locked in contradictions. A solution to the problems of demographic growth will depend on the exploitation of a favourable conjuncture of resources and preferences of different groups. And yet there seem to be no grounds for anticipating that a political transformation will provide for the rational use of economic resources.

A full comparison of the two perspectives requires a far more detailed and informed consideration than is possible here of how they would deal with specific historical events and other aspects of change in their respective areas. But perhaps enough has been said to indicate the extent to which they share a common frame of references and the level at which they are clearly committed to alternative intepretations. The underlying normative assumptions in a theory are sometimes spoken of as if they introduce an unresolvable circularity or relativism into the business of systematic analysis: initial assumptions are presumed to determine the outcome of the inquiry in general and the organization and selection of evidence in detail. But the comparison suggests a much more intricate process of feedback and development between theoretical categories and observations. Both studies are historical in the sense that they take an understanding of change to lie in insights into the logical evolution of particular situations, rather than in their correspondence with determining general laws. Both are fully

sensitive to the complementary analytical aspects that identify
a social system in its totality, relations of power and authority,
economic organization with its intended and unintended consequences, culturally specific interpretations of social action
and the intersubjectivities which give specific ecological and
demographic facts their significance. Over most of this they
would presumably be able to agree, accepting the validity of
similar empirical generalizations or special theories about
the economic system, concurring on the rationality of a particular group's response to a given situation, though perhaps
disagreeing on the range of alternatives open to it.

None the less, they are making different emphases and selec-
tions. They do not see the same significance in past events (and
consequently make direct or indirect allusion to different historical parallels). For Geertz the issue is the rational use of
resources, indigenous control, differentiation of production and
organization, to meet explosive social needs. Success is defined as long-term economic viability, a situation demanding
increased differentiation of roles, and quite compatible with a
substantial degree of economic and social stratification. Characteristically, the emerging political formations he refers to
(alirans) are vertical and segmentary, whilst his example of
Japan's historically successful path of development is an equivocal one in a different historical perspective. For Alavi,
success can only mean a transfer of political control, necessarily revolutionary. The issue for him is the substantive
irrationality of the existing political and economic tendency.
The technical aspects of development planning are not assumed
out of existence, but the implication is that they will be defined afresh, in the light of a radically different set of political
and social priorities. The complex constraints of the economic
system are not seen as so absolute or so binding, since he is
committed to a belief in the possibility of economic exploitation generating a creative political alternative and exposing
the metaphysical and the contingent aspects of purposes en-
shrined in the laws of a capitalist economy.

Science, finally, has no methodological grounds for deciding
between these general expectations and their empirically
grounded prescriptions. At the worst, history can provide
evidence of difficulty and failure, and grounds for cynicism or
'realism', but not disproof. On this score Geertz's position is
less exposed than Alavi's. Certainly he assumes a capacity
for innovation that is not distributed like a quota of genetic
endowment, for instance, but as a general capacity for economically rational behaviour that will be realized according

to circumstances. But he communicates an oppressive sense
of the burden of circumstances, the complex inertia of social
institutions—particularly in societies where there is, in Riggs's
sense, both fusion and overlap of social roles—and the extraordinary difficulty of mobilizing appropriate new forms of
organization in order to cope with the impersonal constraints
of the economic system. Recent journalistic reports from
Indonesia describe sectors of economic growth, but also evidence of grave social disorder. A Marxist interpretation of
such a situation would have to come to terms with its traditional
problem of an indefinitely receding horizon of revolutionary
expectations. For Geertz, current events hang together readily
as a logical outcome of the predicament he describes.[19] He
need invoke no unobserved or uncertain potential. 'It is an
infinite advantage in every controversy', wrote David Hume, 'to
defend the negative. If the question be out of the common
experienced course of nature, this circumstance is almost if
not altogether decisive.'[20]

However, Humean scepticism in analytical method provides a
rule of thumb which may have a very uneven relevance to
questions of different scope and generality. Where inferences
are being drawn from data that are essentially statistical in
form, causal or functional hypotheses encouraged by an assessment of the probabilities of joint occurrence, we can read Hume
as saying that a good inference does not go outside the grounds
it establishes in the evidence. Where the questions have to do
with the emergence of new purposes and new forms of social
organization in historically unique circumstances, methodological caution or rigour can come near to discrediting whole
generations of academic activity. Witness the notorious failure
of mainstream political science and sociology to say much
before the event about Viet Nam or ghetto politics in the United
States.

IV

It is this theme that the final illustration is mainly concerned
with. Balandier's monumental comparison of the Fang and
Bakongo peoples of the Gabon-Congo could not have been produced without the evolving tradition of functional analysis.[21]
But his analysis of structural interdependence is pursued in the
context of a general theory of historical change which throws

light on the exploitative nature of the colonial situation and
collective responses to it. His general orientation allows him
to see elements of political innovation in other aspects of
social behaviour, to challenge existing interpretations, and to
offer an interpretation of the dynamics of change that incorporates but goes beyond the purposes of which particular
groups were directly aware.

It would be absurd to attempt a summary, but we can at least
draw on aspects of the analysis particularly as it has a great
deal in common with other studies that have already been considered. It incorporates detailed ethnographic data which are
used in elaborating a functional interpretation of the traditional
societies, the interconnections between land, kinship and marriage, cults, institutions of social control and so forth. It identifies in the organization of roles characteristic patterns of
conflict and fission. Like Turner, Balandier finds it essential
to interpret expressive or symbolic behaviour in terms of the
structural tensions focused on particular social expectations
and to relate these to demographic changes and to economic
and political pressures. In fact, he sets out assumptions about
societal integration which read, out of context, very much like
an admission of the organicist assumptions that have been so
important in the tradition of social anthropology. There is an
essential difference, though, since he is not invoking the abstract properties of equilibrating or homeostatic systems, but
describing the collective response of a group to its dismem-
berment as a social entity. Both Fang and Bakongo were subjected to the rigours of the colonial situation with chilling
completeness. Balandier's assumption is that as fused and
undifferentiated, though structurally complex, societies, both
the negative and the positive response to these pressures would
implicate all aspects of social organization. What he observes
is a ruthless historical process of fragmentation of the traditional social system, but simultaneously adaptation and the
reconstitution of forms of solidarity improvised out of what
remained.

Balandier is attempting an extended history of two very
numerous peoples, but the evidence is organized to justify a
structural analysis rather than a chronology. However, in contrast to Smith, he finds little to be gained in abstracting synchronic models of the social systems. For one thing, both
societies were far from static even before the colonial period,
and, for another, to think of distinct traditional systems as
bounded entities on which the exogenous factors of the colonial
economy and administration impinged would involve a distor-

tion of the historical relationships. The dominant and determining relationship was the colonial one, which is why he refers
always to the 'colonial situation' as the arena which has to be
made intelligible. There were specific and massive demands
made by specific colonial figures, missionaries, civil authorities or employers, on particular groups. Understanding this
fluid system requires a linking of inferential structures that
are constantly modified in the working out of historical interactions and confrontations. It is significant that, like Turner,
who also thinks of the 'social system' as a conceptual rather
than an empirical reality, his method is to fasten on particular
episodes of evident social crisis, though obviously on a larger
canvas, and to probe them for indirect confirmation of his
sense of the modalities of change. The logical constraints on
change cannot in this history be captured in a durable hierarchy
of structural principles. Political purposes were not formally
institutionalized. Indeed, he suggests that what is to be observed is a series of quite effective social improvisations on
old themes.

In his underlying assumptions about historical change, Balandier
is closer to Alavi than to Geertz. That is, not only is the significance of the colonial situation identified with its essentially
exploitative, economic character, but it is assumed that the
genesis of any transformative process must be identified in the
innovative responses of the large social categories most consistently victimized by it. However, whilst this extrapolation
from the tradition of Marxism is essentially analogous to
Alavi's, there are aspects of the situation itself which might be
expected to relate only awkwardly and with difficulty to the
general specifications of this historical model. The relative
'goodness of fit' in the West Punjab situation can hardly be
expected here. A general analogy between class and colonial
exploitation is one thing, but the Fang and Bakongo societies
themselves appear to represent a turmoil of interethnic rivalries, transected by the consequences of geographically acciden-
tal missionary activity, and prone above all to recurrent bouts
of irrational Messianic fervour, in massive religious movements behind charismatic leaders. From the 1920s through to
the 1940s a succession of such movements caused the authorities considerable anxiety, the followers of Simon Kimbangou,
Andre Matswa (Amicalism), and Simon-Pierre Mpadi (Khakism).
Typically these developments emerged from sectarian churches
representing weird blends of biblical fundamentalism. Kimbangou, for example, appeared to the Bakongo people as a
miracle worker, and as a prototype of the Christian Trinity

(*Gounza* in the Kikongo tongue). He was imprisoned and de-
ported but survived, like Matswa, even more effectively as an
idealized object of devotion. The authorities had overlooked
the potency and irrefutability of the myth of the resurrection
and the idea of a chosen people.

The explanatory problem Balandier defines for himself is that
of discovering forms of rationality in these exotic confusions
that fit his general assumptions. This will involve him in
relating social behaviour, as it is interpreted by those involved,
back to a situated analysis of the economic process. On the
face of it any connections will be circuitous.

The outlines of a parti pris Marxist interpretation are predictable, and clearly a cue for assertion and counterassertion
rather than argument, that the conditions of repression and
deprivation deny any other form of political activity, that the
religious movements are in reality movements of political
protest using the only available and intelligible idiom. This,
very crudely, is the argument of the book, but what we need to
illustrate is its development as a cogent analytical proposal. In
brief, it seems reasonable to claim that the analysis subsumes
the valid core of functionalism in the tradition, the sensitivity
to the many-sidedness and interconnectedness of facets of
social behaviour; that its ultimate focus on the social correlates
of economic change provides a compelling theoretical coherence,
but without introducing crude causal arguments; that the comparative analysis of Fang and Bakongo in a common situation is
used to explore the structural characteristics of each society,
and the variations made to account for the course of specific
historical developments.

The basis for Balandier's analysis is the argument that, because of differences between their respective social systems
at the point of entry into the colonial situation, the Bakongo
peoples were able to respond with a greater degree of resilience as a people, and showed a greater capacity for resistance, adaptation and innovation. In no meaningful sense did
these patterns of social organization survive as systems. What
this history describes is the logical evolution of a structure,
the selective use and adaptation of specific elements of social
organization.

So the social anthropology of the Fang presents in the first instance a problem of historical reconstruction. Traditionally
the Fang were expansionist and Balandier is able to relate what
is known of the traditional social structure to their organization as a predatory force in an analysis analogous to Sahlins's

on the segmentary structure of the Nuer. There were certain problems which demanded a functional solution, in particular the necessity to maintain groups sufficiently large for military effectiveness, but not necessarily to control large numbers of groups. The Fang were a diffuse ethnic group, linked through ancestral and kinship ties, but not through any lasting connection with territory or by any centralized organization. The system of social relations was consistent with their expansionary purposes. The kinship group was organized to make collective decisions and regulate work under the authority of the elders. Authority was maintained by means of various institutionalized sanctions, initiation into the seniority system of the smaller kinship group (nd'è bôt), mutual criticism, rules often with supernatural sanctions attached (biki). But the management of internal tensions over wives and agricultural land also depends on reciprocal restraint on the part of the elders. He suggests that the viability of this institution was a function of security needs and economic resources. A breakaway was possible at a certain size, but a rupture might be tempered by awareness of a future need for co-operation.

This sketch at least indicates structural characteristics that were not to be found among the Fang. They had no need to develop hierarchical organizations for purposes of war or taxation. Expansion was an incremental and cellular process of contact and amalgamation. It is also clear that their own political economy depended on the constancy of certain factors, in particular a scarcity of external wealth and, in order to ensure the controlled circulation of wives, more or less closed lineages.

The impact of colonial development on the society was drastic. Quite simply, the main value of the indigenous groups was as a cheap labour force, and the need to develop an infrastructure of roads, for example, meant that it was treated as a reserve of mobile labour. Communities were moved at administrative convenience. Direct and indirect consequences are traced in the detail of Balandier's demographic analysis. The Fang experienced a numerical decline; major health problems developed, increasing levels of sterility, particularly in the Bas-Gabon. There was substantial emigration. These harsh facts were interpreted by the Fang in the light of their perceived social implications. Thus, the disproportion of adult men and women and, even more, the loss of fertility among the women, precipitated crisis, in normal expectations and relationships and in social control. This was inevitable 'in a society in which numbers not only differentiate between and determine the importance of the groups, but are also the basis of personal prominence'. There was both a sudden increase in the importance of women and a male judgment on their failure. There were other reasons for antagonism between men and women, but it seems likely that this was the most important.

It hardly matters at which point one starts with the impact of the colonial situation, since the structure was insufficiently differentiated to insulate the reverberations of change. Thus, as with the Tiv of Nigeria in Bohannan's account, the gradual introduction of a money economy drastically affected not only relations between the sexes, but also the whole basis for traditional authority and the control of generational conflict. Young men, now able to pay for wives by themselves instead of depending for the necessary capital loan on an older member of the group, entered into direct competition. To an extent that was not previously true, women became a commodity, and the marriage payment became a price, which was inflatable as a direct consequence of a local increase in production. Furthermore, in the changing economy, there were more possibilities for an individual to increase his relative wealth. The system of social control based on an age-graded structure of reciprocities could hardly survive such pressure. But at the same time, the capitalization of wives survived as a basic priority, since this was the obvious measure of status and prestige. In terms of market criteria for the rational use of resources this last implication became a serious distortion, since the price inflation was being consumed unproductively in the allocation of wives. Since there was no basis for any substantial accumulation of capital, in farming or commerce, new social formations could not emerge on an economic base, whilst the old were deeply disturbed. There was even evidence, for instance, of women protecting their position by restricting services to their husbands and forming women's organizations.

Other factors, familiar in African ethnography, contributed to the disintegration of relations within and between kinship groups. Religious 'conversion' superimposed lines of competition and conflict. Whatever authority was delegated by the colonial administration to local communities was not vested in the traditional structure, and in any event, its functions were otherwise defined. Such insertions merely provided opportunities for working the system to secure particular advantages.

It is in the light of his analysis of structural disintegration that Balandier turns to the evidence of religious behaviour. The Fang produced an important structural innovation, a religious

cult referred to as <u>Bwiti</u>. 'Villagers who do not belong to the
sect frequently refer to its members as "those who have drunk
<u>iboga</u>", a powerful drink made from the grated bark of a plant
(Tabernanthe Iboga), which produces aphrodisiac effects and
hallucinations, and is drunk for the first time at the initiation
ceremony'. The use of the plant reflects the preoccupation of
the cultists with the acquisition of a new potency, and with the
quality of a ritually directed hallucinatory experience. He
points out that doctrine in any formal sense is of small importance beside the emotional experience which secures entry
to the cult. Colonial authorities have seldom been unaware of
the potential political implications of religious movements, as
bases of organization and as means of mobilizing large numbers in a threat to law and order. More rarely still have they
been in any doubt about the intrinsic unreason represented by
the practices and rituals involved. Having appropriated the
Christian literature of revelation and outlived its appeal, the
European is revolted by the cult's mish-mash of sacred and
profane, fetishistic paraphernalia and embarrassing imitation
of familiar and decent church performance, Anglican or
Catholic.

Balandier, however, attempts to reappraise the irrationality of
the cult by relating its characteristics to other attributes of
the situation and social structure. At one level, he argues that
joining the cult could be subjectively rewarding for individuals. But he also claims that, given the complex constraints
imposed upon the Fang, the cult represented a purposeful collective attempt to reorganize the society as a political and
social entity. It was by no means completely effective, in the
face of more or less direct repression, clan antagonism, rivalries between cult leaders, Christians and initiated. But despite its confusions it needs to be interpreted as an emergent
nationalist response to the colonial situation. It is distinctively
Fang, and weakest in the more ethnically heterogeneous localities. It was behind a degree of regrouping of villages around
tribal affinities and undertakings of common interest. The
emphasis evident in its symbolism, sharpened by official
hostility, is on the solidarity of the cult and its pervasive responsibility for customary patterns of behaviour. It expresses
a total rejection of the alien culture. Within it, energetic individuals most aware of the colonial situation discovered a system
of prestige and authority, a transformation of the traditional
fraternal age groups, together with a proliferation of offices.
This organization was not compromised or stultified like the
more explicitly 'political' attempts, though more rationalistic

elements in the indigenous leadership failed to realize the implications of the diffuse and inarticulate consciousness the cult was developing. For many individuals membership was a form of therapy, a liberation from the imposed rationalization of the authorities, but its idiom, its traditional basis and collective concerns, provided some sort of structural precondition for greater unity and effectiveness, and at different levels participants were aware of this.

However, it remained true that the Fang did not produce any response that could compete really effectively with the direct control imposed by the authorities. The bwiti cult represented an innovation from within the tradition, but that tradition provided organizationally weak models for large-scale co-operation and control during and after the terminal phase of colonialism. The contrast with Bakongo society gives some indication of the structural significance of the historical legacy.

The traditional functional complex of Bakongo society is constructed round three core elements, land belonging to the clan, a kinship system shaped by matrilineal descent, and a sense of a socially organized history focused on ritual connections with the ancestors. Networks organized under a specific complex of these principles were linked to each other through the marriage system. The old kingdom of the Kongo was a centralized state, with hierarchies of chiefs, clans and lineages. To some extent this system of status stratification has been projected into modern times, but more important, perhaps, a strong awareness of the significance of the group is clearly revealed in customary behaviour. It is reflected, for example, in economically inefficient but community-based agricultural practices as well as in the continuing use of sorcery to control individualistic competition. The individual who moved into the urban life of Brazzaville retained his connections with kin and locality, would expect to return, would exercise rights and obligations in that social context.

The comparative significance of the impact of the market economy on the Bakongo is reflected in the development of a potential conflict built into the traditional system of relations. Matrilineage entailed the controlled transmission of property rights through a customary relationship between the son and the mother's brother, which ensured clan control of property. The introduction of individualistic economic criteria is manifestly a threat to this entire complex. It is likely to increase the importance of the connection between father and son, as independently acquired resources are directly transmitted, and to weaken the economic underpinning to the interdependencies between land, lineages and the ancestors. That this form of dis-integration has not occurred to the extent that it might have done is seen as a reflection of the resilience and vitality of the underlying structure of social relations, despite the substantial assaults made on it by external agents. And it is the survival of this extensive and integrating complex of interdependencies that Balandier uses to explain the scope and purpose of the Messianic movements.

The official records bear witness, often with considerable sur-prise and alarm, to the strength and persistence of the move-ments. And Balandier effectively documents the hopeless mutual incomprehension of colonist and native which led to an escalation of repression and resistance. But he also argues for the fundamental coherence of the movements, their ex-pressive meaning for those who participated and their genuinely creative conservatism in adapting the patterns of shared social realities to meet the pressures of the colonial situation. Much of his evidence in this analysis is quite explicit, songs about the leaders, about the past and the struggle with the Whites, or political interpretations of the movements by in-formants. But it is also necessary to interpret symbolism and ritual and to understand the affective organization they con-stitute. This is a familiar problem for the social anthropolo-gist, though the contrast between the associative freedom of the imagery of the movements and, say, the crystallized cosmic myths of Evans-Pritchard's Azande or Nuer, suggests a paral-lel with vers libre and the classical structure of Paradise Lost.

Balandier refers to the baroque mental equipment of Matswa's leading followers, though Matswa himself had lived in Paris and founded the Amicale as a political organization. Books in the possession of Pierre K., a 'delegate' to the administrative authorities, included 'a French grammar, a dictionary, a Dalloz law manual, a couple of parish magazines, a collection of prayers, a compilation called The Book of Atonement in 23 volumes, four pamphlets on magic, an army manual for non-commissioned officers and a selection of speeches by the Governor-General'. But the elements of confusion and down-right illusion embodied in the syncretic beliefs and practices of the followers have to be considered in the light of what was available as a public language and in the light of their conse-quences for social organization. One can reasonably argue that the highly literal use of biblical themes—and the Bible had been an authoritative literary source since early in the 1500s—represented a theological tradition very much more

radical, in the root sense of the word, than its contemporary
European derivations. Certainly it contributed to the mobilization of a total rejection, simultaneously political and cultural, of
the colonial situation and of the imported political and religious
system. Kimbangou, in his apotheosis as Gounza, is identified
by that word not only as a biblical Trinity, but also as the
saviour and liberator of the Kongo ethnic group.

Actual resistance to the colonial regime through the movement
was, generally speaking, indirect. Its significance lies in its
collective nature; an entire community, for example, refuses to
kneel to receive the blessing of the visiting Christian bishop.
Drawing on the continuing coherence of essential aspects of
Bakongo social organization, the movement became progressively
more organized. The organization of Kimbangism became
tighter with each episode of conflict with the authorities in the
1930s, and, with the foundation of the Khakist movement in 1939,
an organizational hierarchy which was capable of controlling
spontaneous mass reactions was set up, on a model borrowed
from the Salvation Army. This development is associated with
an extension of influence by the movement into most aspects of
traditional social life, 'morals, customary law, beliefs and
symbols, attitudes towards power'.

These scrappy indications will have to represent the study,
which is long, imaginative and persuasive. Is it also true, sufficient and conclusive? What would it mean to propose that it
is true, as far as it goes? There is no conclusive answer to
such questions. One can only attempt to arrive at a judgment
on the arguments they provoke.

Balandier is in one sense 'testing' a large historical and sociological generalization.[22]

> Having suggested the widespread nature of such phenomena,
> it is worth recalling that, in comparable situations, heresies
> once served the cause of emancipation ... neither geo-
> graphically nor historically is [Bakongo Messianism] in any
> sense an isolated phenomenon ... situations of the same
> kind, even in societies with very different cultures, produce
> comparable reactions and lead to a very similar use being
> made of cultural material imposed from without.

Clearly he interprets heresies of this kind as a special case
of movements of emancipation, the mobilization of transformative forces out of situations of exploitation. The idiom is related to the degree and form and historical circumstance of the
situation, but the dynamic is more general than that, being a

function of an intrinsic and valuable capacity of social beings, a tendency that can be anticipated within a general type of structural configuration. But he has only tested an assumption in an approximate sense. Bringing the general theory to the evidence, one might say, has given us an insight into the history which one could not have had without it. The bits and pieces hang together. The account of the symbolism of the Messianic movements, their membership, the effectiveness of their organization, their expressed purposes and so on, all encourage one to accept that he has discovered, behind the bizarre surface manifestations, a rational and collective purpose. But his general theory incorporates a specific definition of political action. In the end the persuasiveness of the analysis is a function of a reader's sympathy with that underlying assumption.

His argument also includes, however, a more sharply focused explanation: that of the differences between Fang and Bakongo responses to colonialism. This involves him in identifying and comparing a large number of empirical patterns and variations, which indicate the structural and other constraints. This comparison is fundamental to the general interpretation, since the interpretation of the religious movements depends on the validity of the analysis of the two social systems. At this level, validity is subject to more direct tests. Claims can be shown to be true or false. Fresh evidence can be introduced, and systematic comparisons reshaped, in order to open the evidence up to alternative arguments. Not that a general argument dealing with complex events over a substantial time scale will necessarily be deflated by effective criticisms on particular points—that is a matter of degree and further negotiation, as it were—but cumulative and indirect criticism is the only approach to a particular application of a general theory.

However, the effectiveness of such criticism is not so easy to determine. If the original empirical analysis is rooted in general assumptions, so is the critique. It appeals to its own epistemology and its own criteria of significance. We need to know how much common ground there is and at what point author and critic depart into different universes of discourse.

The issue of theoretical confrontation and empirical test is raised particularly clearly by some of Balandier's critics, and it seems appropriate to conclude on an inconclusive encounter between knowledgeable scholars, working within the same discipline and on very similar material. Mary Douglas, an anthropologist who has made major contributions to our knowledge of this part of Africa, wrote a brief but savage review of

the second French edition of Balandier's work.[23] Compressed
critical comment is always liable to seem unreasonably dismissive, and there are points where she seems to be demonstrably unfair. But fair or unfair, the comment is a highly informed check to the enthusiasm of the unprofessional reader,
inducing the familiar and dispiriting feeling of not knowing
where to turn, which is quite a normal reaction to following the
disputations of the learned. But the virtually unrelieved hostility of the review does allow one to see the range of criteria
against which Balandier is being assessed, and the implications
of conceding different aspects of the case. The general theory
is rejected or, rather, not recognized explicitly; its normative
overtones and large assumptions about the nature of social
change are not conveyed. The validity of the causal and functional inferences developed in the analysis of Fang and Bakongo
social systems is challenged, as is the representative validity
of the data.

The failure to engage with the scope and tone of Balandier's
central themes is a clear enough indication of radical philosophical divergence. Where Balandier sees his material in the
light of a comprehensive theory of social and political change
which invests his historical particulars with a large generality,
the review's references to innovation place the questions in
another context, the problem of effective adaptation by particular groups to an emerging market economy. Normative overtones, essential to Balandier's perspective, evaporate. He relates fluctuations in the market economy to levels of activity
in the movements, but as part of an evaluative and historical
synthesis of the different aspects of change. The review
seems to expect a sharper definition of the determinants of
successful involvement in the changing economy. He sees in
matriliny, with its implications for land rights, a central constraint supporting clan solidarity and commitment to the
community the cultural values of which indirectly support resistance to the colonial situation. But Douglas proposes that
the actual practice of matriliny with virilocality in this society
is a precondition for entrepreneurial adventure by individuals
with access to the large markets.

The critique is appealing to standards of a rigorous comparative methodology which have been discussed in earlier chapters,
a selection of situations that, at whatever level of generality,
are significantly comparable, and as full an identification as is
possible of the relevant attributes and their interconnections.
Douglas's own work on the Lele and the Bushong of the Belgian
Congo is a model for such a comparison. She refuses to specu-

late outside the meticulously deployed evidence of concomitant variations between the two relatively stable and relatively isolated groups.[24] And at this level she provides some substantial points. Balandier generalizes about the Fang, but on the basis of the Fang in Gabon, who constitute only one-seventh of the total Fang population. He draws on Brazzaville when he is talking about Bakongo in modern conditions, on communities across the river when he is talking about tribal organization. The account of demographic change fails to pay adequate attention to immigration and other factors. The contract between Bwiti and Kimbangouism is based on a selective use of detail, and there are no conclusive grounds for accepting its validity. In particular it ignores the geographical isolation of the Fang. Other, unconsidered causal processes may be determining the relative success of the Bakongo in modern urban life.

Whether these objections are as devastating as the tone of the review suggests that they should be must depend on whether one accepts that the problem should be defined in the reviewer's terms. Thus, she claims that there is no good basis in the evidence for supposing that the Fang Bwiti cult is less innovative and successful, more inward looking and negative, than the movements of Bakongo Messianism. But this objection only makes sense if Balandier's identification of the political dimension in religious activity is not accepted, or only in a very qualified form. In fact he makes a more relative contrast than one would suspect from the comments, and supports it with an evaluation of evidence on the forms of organization and awareness in the different situations. Furthermore, he is not attempting to pin down specific determinants, so much as identifying fluid interdependencies that have some coherence over time, but are too complex to be handled in a sharply focused causal analysis. On the other hand, the objections certainly raise doubts about the scope of the generalizations, and the possible significance of other factors. Other causal inferences and functional dependencies might suggest themselves if the data were further disaggregated. The validity of the general argument continues in question until the empirical relations that support it can be consistently interpreted across the internal variations of the data.

CHAPTER NINE

Conclusions

I

A discussion that moves for the most part from one specific
example to another has to accept some obvious risks. The gap
between one stepping-stone and the next may be too wide to
tempt a reader into a confident leap. Submerged foundations
may be uncertain. Alternatively, the route chosen may simply
seem unadventurous, fastidiously avoiding the more turbulent
and interesting passages. Whilst the attempt to do some rough
justice to successive frames of reference is itself likely to
introduce an eclecticism of emphasis. A more respectable
approach, to offer a comprehensive and general discussion of
general themes and issues, has produced some distinguished
contributions.[1] But this alternative has its limitations also. It
presupposes a familiarity with the empirical studies it reflects
upon, inevitably remains at some distance from them and perhaps helps to confirm a tendency to conduct discussions about
the grounds of knowledge in isolation from knowledge about anything in particular. This tendency has unsatisfactory consequences. Philosophical argument for relativism and uncertainty
in social theory can undermine an interest in empirical analysis.
On the other hand it can stimulate an insensitive appetite for
fact, undigested in the case of the mere empiricist, predigested
in the case of the doctrinaire. On these grounds it seemed worth
trying to elicit larger themes, as well as methodological problems in the tension between conceptualization and data, from
a series of specific studies. It remains, finally, to identify these
and draw them together.

Partly on epistemological grounds, because of beliefs about the
nature of theory and explanation, partly, perhaps, for more
dubious reasons having to do with the professionalization of
different disciplines and their credibility as the guardians of
scientific inquiry, the relation between general theory and
particular observation in the social sciences has sometimes
been described along the lines of one interpretation of theoretical

development in the natural sciences. Kuhn's account of revolutions in scientific theory was referred to in Chapter 3 as highly contentious even among philosophers of the natural sciences. We need only take up the application of his interpretation to the development of theory in the social sciences. This is not, it should be added, an application he has made himself.

His account describes the activity of empirical analysis as something taking place within 'normal science'. This means simply that empirical analysis cannot proceed at all unless it can take for granted certain realities it is not concerned with testing. These include absolutely basic assumptions about the configuration of reality—for example, Copernican as against Ptolemaic assumptions about what circles round what in the cosmos—basic laws such as the Newtonian formulations, and the accuracy and suitability of whatever instrumentation is used. After referring to a series of scientific giants from Aristotle to Lyell, he writes:[2]

> Their achievement was sufficiently unprecedented to attract an enduring group of adherents away from competing modes of scientific activity. Simultaneously it was sufficiently open-ended to leave all sorts of problems for the redefined group of practitioners to resolve.

> Achievements that share these two characteristics I shall henceforth refer to as 'paradigms', a term that relates closely to 'normal science'. By choosing it, I mean to suggest that some accepted examples of actual scientific practice—examples which include law, theory, applications and instrumentation together—provide models from which spring particular coherent traditions of scientific research.

A most significant aspect of the paradigm is that it prohibits inquiry within any other conceivable formulation. In a profoundly important sense, Ptolemy and Newton are not talking about the same universe, and their respective positions cannot conceivably be compromised.

In the process of elaborating and internally clarifying a theoretical reconstruction of a field of phenomena, normal science also accumulates unsolved puzzles. These are anomalies which resist the most determined attempts to assimilate them to the paradigm, either through the addition of marginal qualifications to general laws or by locating special factors, extraneous to the system, which affect the predicted regularities. A revolutionary theory in science cannot, therefore, emerge gradually from a systematic exploration of the evidence. As the balance of anomalies increases, the theory which fails to account for them gradually loses its viability.

Science, argues Kuhn, has depended on sudden drastic revisions, when uniquely creative minds have seen a radically different structure in reality, a total redefinition of the problematic field, which declares redundant a generation of painstaking observations and assimilates a backlog of anomalies to a new general model. Scientific development, on this account, is discontinuous, punctuated by a series of 'eureka moments', one might say, after each of which the field in question will never be perceived in the same old way again.

Two themes in Kuhn's account are of importance to his influence on social scientists. The first is the structurally exclusive character of the paradigm, its logical incompatibility with alternative basic assumptions. The second relates the historical evolution of science to the social context in which it is taking place. Thus, the tenacity of a particular paradigm is not simply a function of the explanatory vacuum it can fill. Historians of science can point to theories that have been floated, have sunk and resurfaced, which were as compatible with the known facts as those which became scientifically acceptable. Commitment to a paradigm and to the theorems that specify its implications is a complex social act, which to some degree is the product of chance, and the current distribution of professional influence and power. The social context of science is thus related to an element in the positivist tradition which was touched on earlier, namely conventionalism in theory, the use of a workable and effective formulation of a systematic process, logically exclusive, but having an instrumental rather than a contemplative orientation towards 'reality'. The truth of a theory is therefore a compound of its demonstrable effectiveness and its consensual validation within the profession.

There are interesting and provoking points of correspondence with social science theory. It is true that there are deep logical incompatibilities between paradigmatic theories in the social sciences. Marx and Parsons can be said to inhabit different social universes. At this level, movement from one conceptual universe to another does involve a 'gestalt switch' or a conversion, though, judging from a popular habit among academics of ageing into conservatism, such conversion can be a drawn-out rather than a pauline affair. It is also the case that a basic vision of the nature of social reality impregnates the categories of analysis, which will not find what they do not look for, and can stretch themselves to accommodate recalcitrant evidence. Furthermore, an interpretation of social behaviour, above all an interpretation of social behaviour, is developed by individuals who belong to specific social groups. It is by definition a social construction, and its emphases and preoccupations are a product of historically specific reactions and tensions.

But it is easy to draw unsatisfactory inferences from this correspondence if it is pushed too far. It is important to Kuhn that the paradigm is both complex and inclusive, that it ties general assumptions, definitions and research procedures together in a philosophically satisfactory manner. The alternative is to slip into a false belief that[3]

> There is a natural psychological borderline between theoretical or speculative propositions on the one hand and factual or observational (or basic) propositions on the other. (This, of course, is part of the 'naturalistic approach' to scientific method.)

But how far can one claim that social scientists operate within paradigms in this sense? In political science and sociology, at least, there are no laws which help to articulate a composition of theory and empirical analysis; whatever predictive capacity exists can be explained on a variety of grounds; a limited repertoire of observational techniques is bent to a multitude of theoretical wills; characteristic of work in the social sciences is a propensity for theoretical constructs at the level of broad generalization and theoretical constructs at the level of particular observation to drift apart, or hang together by an act of speculative faith that would be disastrous for a research programme in the natural sciences.

This point has an important bearing on the mutual exclusiveness of paradigms, in the context of social analysis. One interpretation makes the most of a hard-nosed conventionalism in theory. Paradigms are logically incompatible. There are various pragmatic grounds for choosing between them, predictive power, inclusiveness, elegance, compatibility with formal properties of the data. Where none of these considerations seem to be overriding, the value of the paradigm (model, framework, conceptual scheme) is heuristic, which is to say that it serves to clarify and sort out a field of observations. Among political scientists, David Easton has made a sustained argument over several books for a very abstract systems framework, which would be one influential case in point.[4] His description of the political process in terms of inputs of support and demand, 'withinputs', outputs, feedback loops and the rest, makes very little connection with the concern with structure reflected in most of the work that has been discussed here. His theoretical language is that degree more abstract. On the other hand, he does not claim that other frameworks are wrong, rather that they are taking a different slice at reality, closer to the actualities, maybe, but dawdling on the route to general theory.

The alternative interpretation of the mutual exclusiveness of paradigms involves a strong commitment to one paradigm rather than another. In this case the theory, as a fusion of general orientation together with a battery of specific observational concepts, is invested with an integrity and a clarity of contour that demands unqualified acceptance or rejection. But this is an effective formula for a confusion of theory and ideology. Over most of the social sciences, the idea of an advance in theoretical understanding by way of a massive dislodging and reconstitution of a total world view and its attached comprehensive research programme is simply laughable. The constituent social communities of sociology, in the widest sense of the word, have raised frequent cries of eureka, but the echoes have died away. Innovation has passed into history as mere fashion. But this picture of progress might possibly apply to the history of economic theory, which has attained a degree of logical integration and consensual expertise in the measurement and manipulation of data that the other disciplines have not. If it does, it will be necessary to make a special case for some bodies of theory in the social sciences.

Marx himself, in the persuasive rhetoric which inserts his own work into the history of economic thought, provides vigorous support for Kuhnian expectations. He even placed an historical date, 1830, on a point of theoretical crisis. This was a moment of revolutionary significance in a rather more complex sense than would apply to the development of a natural science, since he takes it to represent a social watershed before which a bourgeois economic science had a valid existence, but after which the emergence of class conflict, transforming the stability of the field of economic forces, reduced the residue of that tradition to the level of ideological apologetic. His own analysis was the authentic theoretical quantum jump, which successfully identified the essential structural properties of the new situation. This is a demonstrably tendentious historical claim, and it is not always echoed by Marxist economists. However, with the benefit of a longer hindsight, essentially similar interpretations of the history of economic theory have been put forward, and a theoretical revolution of Kuhnian scope has been located at a later date, around 1871. This historical revision of the

paradigm shift associated with Marxist theory is put forward
by Robinson and Eatwell in a recent introductory text. Another
work deriving from the same general perspective, though placing the theoretical revolution at an earlier date, argues along
similar lines.[5] These claims raise issues of historical fact
which have been taken up by T. W. Hutchison in a devastating
discussion of the two books.[6]

The arguments Hutchison throws cold water on all involve
locating decisive historical watersheds at certain points on the
map of economic theory. But inspection of the terrain itself
reveals that the watersheds are broken up and fold in on each
other to an extent that makes them quite difficult to locate as
a general feature. Thus, he quotes from Dobb's attack on the
abstractions of 'modern' theory, which places 'a theory of distribution entirely within the circle of market relations', and
fails to pay adequate attention to the sociological realities of
the market system. But he can also provide chapters and verse
to show that Walras and other important neo-classical theorists
were well aware of the limitations of Ricardian models, which
Walras explicitly describes as manning one sector only of
theoretical development; Dobb seems to stick to Marx's 1830
watershed. Robinson and Eatwell, who are more roundly
assaulted, propose another at 1871. Their exposition is tailor-
made for a Kuhnian interpretation of theoretical revolution.
It emphasizes the drastic reorganization of established theory,
and it attaches great importance to the sociological significance
of the new consensus in orthodox economics. The triumph of
this particular eureka moment was, indeed, peculiarly ambiguous, since it marked not only the discovery of a fresh perspective on economics (a 'sudden increase in popularity' of individual utility analysis, among other things), but was an ideological
achievement as well. They argue that, in the new political and
ideological climate of the time, classical economic theory
appeared to the establishment 'not so much irrelevant as
dangerous', and it was this that tipped the theoretical balance.

Hutchison's critique indicates the violence such an argument
does to the historical facts. Theoretical changes, for one thing,
were less drastic and more piecemeal than is suggested. For
another, they were being proposed by economists struggling with
the theoretical limitations of their discipline, and no evidence
is provided to show that their conversion was ideologically, or
sociologically, determined, rather than forced on them by the
increasing unreality of assumptions taken for granted by the
mainstream of the profession. There were constant attempts
to expand, adjust and develop the logical apparatus in order to

provide an instrument capable of modelling the behaviour of new economic structures.

The subsequent, Keynesian theoretical revolution is treated differently in the two texts. For Robinson it still represents a substantial theoretical development which clarified rather than fudged inquiry. And there is a significant indication of her essentially Kuhnian interpretation of theoretical advance in the treatment of Pigou, who is shouldered down the Ptolemaic side of this great divide, though Hutchison's critique shows that he straddles it, even anticipating Keynes in some areas, and anticipating the post-war mixed economy.

The argument suggests very strongly that, though there have been major transformations in the history of economic theory, retrospective interpretations of their dramatic impact can be seriously misleading. Certainly, new theories do not emerge because theorists have finally learned from Bacon that 'they must for a while renounce their notions and begin to form an acquaintance with things'.[7] But neither have they leapt into being, fully formed in all essentials. Theoretical developments occur because of conceptual difficulties encountered at a number of different levels, ranging from an increasing emphasis on normative preoccupations which are overlooked in accepted formulations, to new discoveries and realizations about interactions in the field of evidence itself.

II

On one point of overriding importance the philosophers of the natural and the social sciences must agree. They cannot revert to the view that self-evident facts can be expected to speak for themselves, if they are given a chance to do so by the application of an orderly and neutral methodology, that facts can be aggregated, classified and compared until the interlacings of structure and latent structure become apparent to a detached observer. But the primacy of theory has to be asserted in a volatile context in the social sciences. The observer is in a special epistemological predicament, because of the diversity and constant modification of social realities, and the constant modification of what is brought to their interpretation through the normative component of explanatory theories. So alternative insights offered by different explanations in the social sciences can be alternative in a number of senses, and complement or contradict one another at different levels. Balandier and Douglas—in her review of his work—talk past each other, so to speak. Though the specific objections raised in the review have a brisk methodological air to them, one senses that the hostility is directed not merely at the selection and conceptualization of the empirical evidence, but more diffusely and fundamentally at a general theoretical language, its way of interpreting the systematic properties of social change, its orientation towards the behaviour of historical actors, and its speculative interpretation of their rationality in given circumstances. In the case of the aggregative cross-national comparisons, it was suggested, assumptions from a general social theory impregnate the use, or misuse, of methods of logical comparison and analysis. An analysis of specific historical structures will constantly have to appeal against the generalized conclusions of the statistical comparisons, their interpretation of specific observations and their implications for an understanding of change. At another level, formal theories in economics may be rooted in incompatible pictures of what the realities are and what problems call for explanation.

But theoretical disagreement, like political conflict, is a matter of indefinite gradations. There exist, or should exist, areas of constructive argument which result in shifts not only at the level level of specific perceptions but also at more abstract levels of conceptualization. There is a temptation to introduce the fashionable slogan of interdisciplinarity at this point, but interdisciplinarity needs to be invoked with caution. An excellent red rag with which to provoke the departmentally entrenched, it has acquired diffusely optimistic connotations. These may survive closer inspection in some fields, but in the social sciences they do not. It may be less misleading to speak of the convergence, or partial convergence, of insights, with productive interdisciplinary work as a special case.

But the general ideal of convergence is itself too bland and comfortable. Both the psychologist and the historian have important things to say about Gandhi's role in Indian politics, but the accounts of Erikson and Brown stand awkwardly side by side, each being firmly (or cautiously) rooted in a disciplinary tradition. It is one thing to concede that they throw light on different aspects of a complex reality, but another to relate them to each other in an enlarged perspective. Such perspectives can be blended with unsatisfactory results, by collapsing one level of explanation into another and producing an account that is reductionist rather than a reinterpretation of interdependencies in an historical process.[8] The issue was raised in the discus-

sion of problems created for economic analysis by modifications
in analytically distinct systems of interaction such as customary
relations. Rather more clearly here than at some other possible
interdisciplinary meeting-points, a convergence of disciplinary
perspectives involves an encounter between qualitatively
different types of theory. Normative criteria are introduced
in different ways and with different implications. General and
abstract formulations are qualified in order to preserve the
instrumental power of a theory where cultural factors impose
distinctive patterns on economic relations. Similarly, the
introduction of an historical dimension into interpretations of
structure and structural change by social anthropologists led
to new and distinctive conceptualizations. The content of
theoretical abstractions was modified, theoretical expectations
changed, the evidence construed in different terms.

Effective convergence is a theoretical encounter in a specific
field of evidence. In an approximate sense, disciplinary divisions correspond to the more gross distinctions between
theoretical positions and intellectual traditions. But the distinctions exist within disciplines too. We have been concerned
with attempts to negotiate some of these distinctions at different
levels, attempts to develop enlarged perspectives without sacrificing what has been secured on a more limited basis.

III

Theoretical convergence may be represented in conceptual
innovation, a fusion of elements that creates a new perspective
from which to approach familiar material: for example, the
introduction of mechanical models into economics, economic
models into electoral analysis and cybernetic models into
decision-making. We have touched on the issue of analogical
validity which each of these raises. The use of statistical
models generates essentially similar epistemological as well
as technical problems. These may well be further exposed by
recent attempts to introduce entirely new forms of mathematics
in the analysis of social behaviour. Claims for a non-quantita-
tive, topological interpretation of structural change, particularly
sudden and discontinuous change, assail the 'Cartesian' assumptions behind accepted quantitative methods in the social
sciences and their intrinsically distorted representation of
social reality.[9] Certainly social scientists are more rather than

less sensitive to the intrinsic limitations of statistical analysis than they have been in the past.

Related problems emerge with the other aspect of convergence which has concerned this discussion, the counterpoint between generalizing comparative explanations and narrower and more penetrating historical analysis. Putnam's study has suggested that broad generalizations emerging from a methodologically sensitive comparative analysis can upset readily invoked assumptions, discover new questions and provide a frame of reference for further work at quite different levels of abstraction. But one set of insights is not subsumed by the other. Rather they play off each other, in easy complementation at some points, but continuing tension at others. There is always a speculative jump between classified observations and the abstract processes they are taken to represent.[10] There is always a degree of uncertainty about the bearing of a general, comparative configuration on the particular situation. The tension between Riggs's logical elaboration of a general theory and the historical insights Smith derives from his series of models of the evolving political and administrative structures of Zazzau is representative. One study engages with the other because both have significant general assumptions in common. We are left with the problem of interpreting the absence of any explanatory closure.

None the less, it has been the argument of this book that types and levels of analysis which are not readily integrated, and are incomplete even in combination can be imaginatively and constructively exploited to develop more inclusive and at the same time more penetrating interpretations of questions of great importance. Anxieties about 'the distance still to go to the goal of verified theories and general propositions', which were alluded to in the opening pages, seem to be misplaced. The constructive contribution of the social scientist is recognized in terms other than these. The identification of partial systems, through formal theories, empirical generalization and causal analysis, will all be necessary to him, depending on the nature of his evidence and the scope of his inquiry. But the substantive questions are concerned with the context in which these are exploited. They direct attention to the normative component of a general theory, its basic assumptions, the development of its logical implications and its penetration of a body of material.

It is, finally, the material, the specific historical interactions, that hold our attention. Explanation consists of a complex engagement with that material, at levels that relate and work back on each other, to develop an interpretation of its structure and the logic of its development. One's response to such work must be correspondingly complex. Geertz, Alavi and Balandier all exploit and combine analytical approaches that have been independently developed. By doing so within the context of explicit general theories, they reconstitute problematic fields, extend them and integrate perspectives on their dynamic aspects which had not been so connected before. What this leaves us with is not an explanatory theory that can be incorporated in an anonymous corpus of knowledge. In each case it is a mediated encounter with reality, a further convergence of insights connecting a particular vantage point to specific historical events.

Notes

1 EQUILIBRIUM AND HISTORICAL CHANGE

1   For example, Downs has considered voting behaviour in party systems as if the choices involved were very similar to the consumer choices with which economists are concerned. On this assumption, he has attempted to develop a theory with the generality and predictive rigour that is the norm for theory among economists. A. Downs, An Economic Theory of Democracy, Harper & Row, 1957. The validity of the analogy, and the limitations of this kind of theory in the context of political behaviour have been explored by D. Stokes, 'Spatial models of party competition', in Campbell et al., Elections and the Political Order, Wiley, 1966, and in B. Barry, Sociologists, Economists and Democracy, Collier-Macmillan, 1970. See also A. Ryan, The Philosophy of the Social Sciences, Macmillan, 1970, pp. 93-7.

2   This theme has been explored for the social anthropologists in M. Gluckman, Closed Systems and Open Minds; the Limits of Naivety in Social Anthropology, Oliver & Boyd, 1964.

3   Barry, op. cit., p. 182.

4   John G. Gunnell, 'The idea of the conceptual framework: a philosophical critique', Journal of Comparative Administration, 1, no. 2, 1970.

5   Hans Meyer, Die Burundi, quoted in R. Lemarchand, Rwanda and Burundi, Pall Mall, 1970, p. 42.

6   J. J. Maquet, The Premise of Inequality in Rwanda, Oxford University Press, 1961, and 'The problem of Tutsi domination', in Ottenberg (ed.), Cultures and Societies of Africa, Random House, 1960.

7   See Gwyn A. Williams, 'The concept of egemonia in the thought of Antonio Gramsci; some notes on interpretation', Journal of the History of Ideas, 21, no. 4, October-December, 1960.

8   For a detailed discussion, see the Introduction to I. M. Lewis (ed.), History and Social Anthropology, ASA Monographs 7, Tavistock, 1968, and a discussion of the 'fallacy of the ethnographic present' in M. G. Smith, 'History and social anthropology', Journal of the Royal Anthropological Institute, 92, 1962, pp. 73-85.

9   E. R. Leach, Political Systems of Highland Burma, Bell, 1964, p. 9. Maquet derives the ideas from Durkheim's social theory.

10 Quoted in Lemarchand, op. cit., p. 164.

11   Ibid.
12   The forgotten factor of the history of pre-conquest African socie-
     ties has only recently begun to receive serious attention. See, for
     example, Leonard Thompson (ed.), African Societies in Southern
     Africa; Historical Studies, Heinemann, 1969. Ernest Gellner dis-
     cusses the place of historical time in functionalist explanation in
     'Time and theory in social anthropology', ch. 6 of Cause and Mean-
     ing in the Social Sciences, Routledge & Kegan Paul, 1973.
13   Jan Vansina, Oral Tradition; a Study in Historical Methodology,
     Routledge & Kegan Paul, 1961. He points out that in Burundi,
     in many respects a twin society to Rwanda, the monarchy was
     prejudiced against history—it revealed too much of the seamy
     side of their progress to power.
14   A. R. Radcliffe-Brown, Structure and Function in Primitive Society,
     Cohen & West, 1952, ch. 10.
15   Sir James Frazer, The Golden Bough, Macmillan, 1922.
16   Montesquieu, The Spirit of the Laws, Book XIX, 4.
17   Raymond Aron, Main Currents in Sociological Thought, 1, Penguin,
     1968, p. 46.
18   Montesquieu, op. cit., Book XIX, 1.
19   Hugh Stretton, The Political Sciences, Routledge & Kegan Paul,
     1970, p. 52.
20   The distinction between structure and organization is a very dif-
     ficult one to make within the limits of a brief definition. It is a
     most important distinction none the less. See, in particular,
     Raymond Firth, Essays on Social Organization and Values, Athlone
     Press, 1964, ch. 2.
21   J. Maquet, Power and Society in Africa, Weidenfeld & Nicolson,
     1971, ch. 6, 'Repetitive and dynamic models'.
22   Making allowances for the traditional sexual imagery he employs,
     Machiavelli's discussion of fortuna is far from archaic and indeed
     is very relevant to a theme that will recur in the following pages.
     He conceived the effective political actor as a positive and in-
     novative figure, demonstrating his virtù within the general con-
     straints, necessità, of his situation, and in defiance of the unpredict-
     able acts of his competitors and of God. 'I certainly think that it
     is better to be impetuous than cautious, for fortune is a woman, and
     it is necessary, if you wish to master her, to conquer her by force;
     and it can be seen that she lets herself be overcome by these
     rather than by those who proceed coldly.' The Prince, ch. XXV.
23   There is a particularly useful general discussion for our purposes
     in J. H. M. Beattie, 'Understanding and explanation in social
     anthropology', British Journal of Sociology, 10, 1959, pp. 45-59; re-
     printed in Manners and Kaplan (eds), Theory in Anthropology,
     Routledge & Kegan Paul, 1968.

2   VERSIONS OF STRUCTURE

1   'Particularly in the case of Turner's contributions, this reviewer

was never quite sure whether he was reading an analysis of minutely tabulated notions that made sense to the Ndembu or speculations of a Freudian, post-Freudian, humanistic, and literary sort.' Agehenanda Bharati, 'Anthropological approaches to the study of religion: ritual and belief systems', in B.T. Siegel (ed.), Biennial Review of Anthropology, Stanford, 1961. But see also the review by Monica Wilson, Man, March, 1959.

2   See, for example: Leach on Gluckman in E.R. Leach, Political Systems of Highland Burma, Bell, Introductory Note to 1964 reprint; Gluckman on Bohannan, Politics, Law and Ritual in Tribal Society, 1967, pp. 185 ff., M. Spiro, 'Sorcery, evil spirits and functional analysis: a rejoinder', American Anthropologist, 63, 1961, pp. 820-4.

3   'The tradition of conducting fieldwork, usually in more or less isolated and "exotic" communities, and the theoretical perspectives that stem from it, would probably count for many people as one of the major contributions of social anthropology to social science. Against this tradition, it is not surprising that preparation for fieldwork has come to be seen as an essential part of the training of students in the subject, and fieldwork itself as a unique and necessary experience, amounting to a kind of rite de passage by which the novice is transformed into the rounded anthropologist and initiated into the ranks of the profession.' A.L. Epstein (ed.), The Craft of Social Anthropology, Tavistock, 1967, p. vii.

4   See, for example, Leach's modified version of his 1959 Malinowski Lecture, 'Rethinking Anthropology', published with other essays under that title, London School of Economics Monographs on Social Anthropology, Athlone Press, 1966.

5   See Hanna Pitkin, The Concept of Representation, University of California Press, 1967.

6   Thus, the development of empirical methods out of a positivist tradition over the past few decades is seen simultaneously as necessary and as epistemologically tainted. This unease is reflected, for example, in M. Surkin and A. Wolfe, An End to Political Science: the Caucus Papers, Basic Books, 1970.

7   Max Gluckman, Closed Systems and Open Minds, Oliver & Boyd, 1964, ch. 7, 'Modes and consequences of limiting a field of study'.

8   For an outstanding example see Clifford Geertz, Agricultural Involution: the Process of Ecological Change in Indonesia, University of California Press, 1963. This is at once anthropology, economic history, and a substantive reflection on certain of the causes of human misery.

9   R. Frankenburg, 'British community studies: problems of synthesis', in M. Banton (ed.), The Social Anthropology of Complex Societies, ASA Monographs 4, Tavistock, 1966.

10   See A. Cicourel, Method and Measurement in Sociology, Free Press, 1964, ch. 2, 'Theory and method in field research', and ch. 3, 'Interviewing'; and, for the problems of the fieldworking anthropologist, E. Ardener (ed.), Social Anthropology and Language, ASA Monographs 10, Tavistock, 1971, Introductory Essay.

11   Sheldon Wolin, Politics and Vision, Continuity and Innovation in

Western Political Thought, Little, Brown & Co., 1960. 'Each
theorist has viewed the problem from a different perspective, a
particular angle of vision. This suggests that political philosophy
constitutes a form of "seeing" political phenomena and that the way
in which phenomena will be visualized depends in large measure on
where the viewer "stands". There are two distinct but related
senses of "vision"... both of them have played an important part
in political theory. Vision is commonly used to mean an act of
perception.... In this sense "vision" is a descriptive report about
an object or an event. But "vision" is also used in another sense,
as when one talks about an aesthetic vision or a religious vision.
In this second meaning, it is the imaginative, not the descriptive,
element that is uppermost.' (p. 17.)

12   Even in the hands of an anthropologist. 'All this has represented a
kind of dissection of the anatomy of a society, viewing the kinship
links as part of the skeletal structure giving the society its
form.... Explanation of the recognition of the crude fact of the
connection of persons through sex union and birth involves tracing
out a series of relationships through the whole fabric of social
life.' Raymond Firth, We, the Tikopia, Allen & Unwin, 1936, p. 80.

13   'At the close of the Parliament of 1566 [Elizabeth I] warned the
House of Commons not to meddle further with the question of the
succession and asked rhetorically: "Who is so simple that doubts
whether a prince that is head of all the body may not command the
feet not to stray when they would slip?"' S. Beer, British Politics
in the Collectivist Age, Knopf, 1965, p. 5. As Beer points out,
modern British Tories have been known to invoke the organic
and hierarchical society of Tudor political theory by quoting
Ulysses' famous degree speech in Troilus and Cressida. But in the
dramatic context, of course, the metaphor is highly tendentious.
Ulysses is not the mouthpiece of a disembodied Shakespearean
philosophy.

14   E. Durkheim, The Rules of Sociological Method, Free Press, 1964,
p. 49. and, Montesquieu and Rousseau, University of Michigan Press,
1965. Other latent images have been no less important in the social
sciences. For example, the pluralism of political scientists such
as David Truman in the 1950s, with its assumption of an equilibrium between interacting groups, has mechanistic undertones,
with roots in Newtonian imagery used by political economists in
the eighteenth century and later.

15   Montesqueiu, The Spirit of the Laws, Book XVI, 2.

16   Radcliffe-Brown, Structure and Function in Primitive Society,
Cohen & West, 1952, ch. 3, 'The study of kinship systems'.

17   Ibid., p. 54

18   Ibid., ch. 4, 'On Joking Relationships'.

19   M. Fortes, Time and Social Structure, Athlone Press, 1970, p. 272.

20   See Leach, Rethinking Anthropology, ch. 2, 'Jinghpaw kinship
terminology'.

21   E. E. Evans-Pritchard, The Nuer, Oxford University Press, 1940;
Marshall D. Sahlins, 'The segmentary lineage: an organization of

predatory expansion', American Anthropologist, 63, no. 2, 1961.

22   Mary Douglas, Purity and Danger, an Analysis of Concepts of Pollution and Taboo, Routledge & Kegan Paul, 1966, p. 143.

23   E. E. Evans-Pritchard, Nuer Religion, Oxford University Press, 1956.

24   Ibid., pp. 179-80.

25   See E. Ardener (ed.), Social Anthropology and Language, ASA Monographs 10, Tavistock, 1971, Introductory Essay; and Jean Piaget, Structuralism, Routledge & Kegan Paul, 1968, ch. 5, 'Linguistic structuralism'.

26   F. Pocock, Social Anthropology, Sheed & Ward, 1961, p. 75.

27   E. E. Evans-Pritchard, Witchcraft, Oracles and Magic among the Azande, Oxford University Press, 1937.

28   Pocock, op. cit., p. 73.

29   Montesquieu, The Spirit of the Laws, Book XVI.

30   Sahlins, op. cit., p. 339.

31   Ibid., p. 333.

32   Evans-Pritchard, The Nuer, p. 124.

33   Ibid., p. 161.

34   G. Leinhardt, Divinity and Experience: the Religion of the Dinka, Oxford University Press, 1961, p. 135. Leinhardt, to round out an academic lineage, was a pupil of Evans-Pritchard's.

35   Ibid., p. 161.

36   For an extended and historically specific analysis of the functional dependence between a particular segmentary (but not segmentary lineage) system and relations with other societies, see J. A. Barnes's study of the Fort Jameson Ngoni, Politics in a Changing Society, Oxford University Press, 1954.

37   V. W. Turner, Schism and Continuity in an African Society, Manchester University Press, 1957.

38   Ibid., p. 222.

39   Ibid., p. 291.

40   Aristotle, Politics, Book VIII, ch. 6.

41   Leach, Rethinking Anthropology, p. 4.

42   Leach, Political Systems of Highland Burma, p. 4.

43   Morris Freilich, 'Towards a model of social structure', Journal of the Royal Anthropological Institute, 94, 1964.

44   M. G. Smith, 'On segmentary lineage systems', Journal of the Royal Anthropological Institute, 84-6, 1954-6.

3   SCIENTIFIC INQUIRY

1   M. Gluckman, 'The utility of the equilibrium model in the study of social change', American Anthropologist, 70, no. 2, April, 1968.

2   J. Van Velsen, 'The extended case method and situational analysis', in A. L. Epstein (ed.), The Craft of Social Anthropology, Tavistock, 1967

3   M. Gluckman, Custom and Conflict in Africa, Blackwell, 1955, pp. 1-25.

4   Thomas Kuhn, The Structure of Scientific Revolutions, 1962, but see the revised and extended second edition, University of Chicago Press, 1970.

5   Imre Lakatos and Alan Musgrave (eds), Criticism and the Growth of Knowledge, Cambridge University Press, 1970. In this volume, Kuhn, who is given the first and last word, is confronted by seven of his critics.

6   See the lectures reprinted in A. C. Crombie (ed.), Turning Points in Physics, Amsterdam, 1959.

7   Morton Beckner, 'Explanation in biological science', in S. Morgenbesser (ed.), Philosophy of Science Today, Basic Books, 1967. But see M. Ruse, The Philosophy of Biology, Hutchinson, 1973.

8   See, for example, Othmar F. Anderle, 'A plea for theoretical history', History and Theory, 4, 1965.

9   For an analysis of the positivist traditions see Leszek Kolakowski, Positivist Philosophy, Penguin, 1972.

10 The word is used by F. H. Knight, 'Social science', Ethics, 51, no. 2, January 1941; reprinted in On the History and Method of Economics, University of Chicago Press, 1956. In this article Knight warns his colleagues of a position which theorists in a positive social science are liable to fall into, 'an inference, characteristically drawn by the "best minds" of our race, that since natural objects are not like men, men must be like natural objects'.

11 Ernest Gellner, 'Concepts and society', in D. Emmet and A. MacIntyre (eds), Sociological Theory and Philosophical Analysis, Macmillan, 1970.

12 M. Friedman, Essays in Positive Economics, University of Chicago Press, 1953, pt. 1, 'The methodology of positive economics', p. 35.

13 Kolakowski, op. cit., p. 15.

14 A vigorous nominalist account of language appears in Thomas Hobbes, The Leviathan, ch. 4, 'Of speech'. He develops the argument that 'The manner how speech serveth to the remembrance of the consequence of cause and effects, consisteth in the imposing of "names", and the "connection" of them.'

15 Kolakowski, op. cit., ch. 6, 'Conventionalism: destruction of the concept of fact', p. 159.

16 Ibid., p. 145.

17 As Hobbes recognized, when he listed the 'special uses' of speech, the third of which is 'to make known to others our wills and purposes, that we may have the mutual help of one another'.

18 Robert Lekachman, The Age of Keynes, Penguin, 1969, p. 109.

19 Ibid., 'Precaution, foresight, calculation, improvement, independence, enterprise, pride and avarice', p. 79.

20 Robert Heilbroner, Between Capitalism and Socialism, Vintage Books, 1970, p. 13. He also refers to increasing uncertainty about

the linkages between economic change and political attitude and action, an important point that will be taken up in subsequent discussion. 'As a result of these and still other changes in the economic view of things, the very search for a "political economics"—that is, for a theory of social evolution in which a core of economic dynamics would be systematically related to social and political change (which in turn would feed back on the economic process)—has been virtually abandoned. '

21   Stephen Toulmin points out that the distinction has to be observed from the very beginning of science. The Babylonians were even ahead of the Greeks in their ability to make accurate predictions, essentially as economists might from 'time-series', of celestial motions. Yet, while '[the] Babylonians acquired great forecasting-power... they conspicuously lacked understanding. To discover that events of a certain kind are predictable—even to develop effective techniques for forecasting them—is evidently quite different from having an adequate theory about them, through which they can be understood. ' Forecasting and Understanding: an Inquiry into the Aims of Science, Harper, 1963, p. 30.

22   'The economist is not much of an economic man when it comes to borrowing from other sciences. Generally speaking, if, in the pursuit of the world of commodities he stumbles into the world of men, he prefers to make up his own psychology on the spot rather than borrow from the psychologists. ... The core of the economist's interest is not human behaviour as such but the behaviour function which relates his economic quantities, his prices, and his quantities of commodity produced, consumed, or exchanged. ' Kenneth E. Boulding, The Skills of the Economist, Howard Allen, 1958, p. 28.

23   The authors of an occasional paper on cost-benefit analysis point out that 'cost-benefit analysis would not provide the administrator with a means of relieving himself of critically important decisions. In fact decision makers might well beware of experts who "helpfully" simplify their job by making implicit decisions in the course of their analysis: these may include some which later turn out to be wholly unrealistic or unacceptable... The advantages of cost-benefit analysis lie not in making decision making simpler, but in the possibilities for the systematic examination of each part of a problem in hand, for putting diverse decisions on a par, and for following the logical consequences of a synoptic view. In short, it is a means of organizing thought, not a means of avoiding it. ' H. G. Walsh and Alan Williams, Current Issues in Cost-Benefit Analysis, CAS Occasional Papers, 11, HMSO, 1969.

24   See notes 1 and 2, ch. 1. Also W. Riker, The Theory of Political Coalitions, Yale University Press, 1962; J. M. Buchanan and G. Tullock, The Calculus of Consent, University of Michigan Press, 1962; M. Leiserson, 'Factions and coalitions in one-party Japan: an interpretation based on the theory of games', American Political Science Review, September, 1968; R. Axelrod, Conflict of Interest: a Theory of Divergent Goals with Applications to Politics, Markham, 1970.

25   For an entertaining account of such inbred institutional behaviour, which loses nothing from not being formalized in game-theoretical terms, see Nathan Leites, The Game of Politics in France, Stanford, 1959.

26   For a non-technical account by a leading taxonomist of the problem of classification in biology, see Robert R. Sokal, 'Numerical Taxonomy', Scientific American, December, 1966.

27   Biological classification was, of course, very substantially developed by Aristotle, who assumed a unitary scientific method. There is no novelty in drawing out correspondences between the biological and social sciences.

28   For an extended and penetrating development of this logic in making inferential classifications, with reference to the evidence that surveys are able to collect, see Paul F. Lazarsfeld, 'Latent structure analysis', in Sigmund Koch (ed.), Psychology: a Study of a Science, McGraw-Hill, 1959, vol. 3, pp. 476-543.

29   On the assumptions behind measures of two variable relationships, see Hayward R. Alker, Jr, Mathematics and Politics, Macmillan, 1965, ch. 4. This book is an interesting attempt to provoke students of politics into a rigorous use of statistical methods. The author observes that 'as taught to political scientists, mathematics often lacks the intellectual excitement of the original discoveries that have so closely linked much of the mathematical imagination with the social and natural world. Mathematical drudgery or a parochial approach to politics too often obscures the relevance of mathematics to the moral and empirical problems of political analysis. ' (p. 3).

30   Aristotle, Historia Animalium, Book IV, 535.

31   Nicholas Jardine and Robin Sibson, Mathematical Taxonomy, Wiley, 1972, p. 25.

32   L. A. S. Johnson, 'Rainbow's end: the quest for an optimal taxonomy', Systematic Zoology, 19, September, 1970.

33   A. Cicourel points out, however, that 'such data are usually viewed as basic social facts which stand by themselves', and reminds social scientists of the theoretical problem of seeing them in relational terms. Method and Measurement in Sociology, Free Press, 1964, ch. 5, 'The demographic method'.

34   David L. Hull, 'Contemporary Systematic Philosophies', Annual Review of Ecology and Systematics, 1, 1970, p. 33.

35   Johnson, op. cit., p. 299.

36   Jardine and Sibson, op. cit., p. 26.

37   K. A. Wittfogel, Oriental Despotism: a comparative study of total power, New Haven, 1957.

38   E. Leach, 'Hydraulic society in Ceylon', Past and Present, no. 15, April, 1959.

39   Ibid., p. 13. Clifford Geertz quotes the same passage in a discussion of the gradual and incremental refinement of such agricultural systems, Agricultural Involution: the Process of Ecological Change in Indonesia, University of California Press, 1963, p. 35.

40   Rethinking Anthropology, London School of Economics Monographs on Social Anthropology, Athlone Press, 1966, p. 6.

4 STATISTICAL MODELS AND SOCIAL STRUCTURES

1   G. Kalton, Introduction to Statistical Ideas for Social Scientists,
    Chapman & Hall, 1967, is compact and simple. Robert Weiss,
    Statistics in Social Research, Wiley, 1968, is a more extended cover-
    age of much the same ground, including some theoretical discus-
    sion of the relationships between statistical association and causal
    analysis. K. Hope, Elementary Statistics; a Workbook, Pergamon,
    1967, makes analysis of variance clear to the layman, and intro-
    duces factor analytic techniques. Both are taken up at a more
    advanced level in his Methods of Multivariate Analysis, University
    of London, 1968. Non-mathematicians may stall at the matrix
    algebra through which he approaches multivariate analysis, and
    would probably find the geometrical approach of Dennis Child
    easier to follow, in The Essentials of Factor Analysis, Holt,
    Rinehart & Winston, 1970.
2   See Ronald A. Cooper, 'Statistical models of economic relation-
    ships', Civil Service College Occasional Papers, 16, HMSO, 1971.
3   Frederick Harbison et al., Quantitative Analysis of Modernization
    and Development, Princeton University, 1970.
4   Subsequent chapters contain a correlation and regression analysis
    in one time period, and another for four time periods, a graphical
    analysis, a discussion of an index of human resource development,
    and a chapter that relates the key variable of education to the
    rate of economic growth. It is a virtue in studies such as this that
    statistical procedures are varied to complement each other. This
    at least provides a check on purely statistical artefacts.
5   Irma Adelman and Cynthia Taft Morris, Society, Politics and
    Economic Development: a Quantitative Approach, Johns Hopkins,
    1967.
6   There is some discussion of political survey evidence in Graeme
    C. Moodie and Gerald Studdert-Kennedy, Opinions, Publics and
    Pressure Groups, Allen & Unwin, 1970, chs 2 and 3, and pp. 97-104.
7   This is acknowledged by one biologist, who even finds it convenient
    to illustrate a point about the methods with an example involving
    individuals and psychological test scores, Mark Williamson,
    'Principal component analysis and analysis of variance', Int. J.
    Math. Educ. Sci. Technol., 3, 1972, p. 36.
8   Adelman and Morris, op. cit., p. 172.
9   Ibid., p. 150.
10 H. J. Butcher, Human Intelligence, its Nature and Assessment,
    Methuen, 1968.
11 See, for example, J. G. Grumm, 'A factor analysis of legislative
    behaviour', Midwest Journal of Political Science, 7, 1963.
12 One psychologist has turned his techniques to the organization of
    evidence that is particularly confusing in quantity, in a highly
    structured situation, namely, voting in the United Nations. He uses
    'spherical mapping', a version of factor analysis, as a basis for
    interferences about motives, coalitions, etc. K. Hope 'Complete
    analysis: a method of interpreting multivariate data', Journal of

the Market Research Society, 11, 3, 1969. For an attempt to explore and interpret entirely subjective data in a narrowly focused situation by means of a combination of factor analysis (principal component) and two taxonomic cluster analyses, see Michael Davenport and Gerald Studdert-Kennedy, 'The balance of Roger de Piles: a statistical analysis', Journal of Aesthetics and Art Criticism, Summer, 1974; or a more technical report in the Journal of the Royal Statistical Society, (C), November, 1972.

13 Elementary Statistics, p. 72.

14 Williamson, op. cit., p. 35. Psychologists would find another comparison of statistical methods more natural. See Lee C. Crombach, 'The two disciplines of scientific psychology', American Psychologist, 12, 1957, which relates different methodological techniques to contrasting theoretical assumptions.

15 We are avoiding the controversial questions over 'rotating' factors, which do introduce external criteria to this type of analysis.

16 See the analysis of variance in village India by one of the authors whose ambitious cross-national comparisons were criticized earlier, I. Adelman and G. Dalton, 'Developing village India: a statistical analysis', G. Dalton (ed.), Studies in Economic Anthropology, American Anthropological Association, 1971.

5 CAUSES AND STRUCTURE

1 E. Leach, Rethinking Anthropology, London School of Economics Monographs on Social Anthropology, Athlone Press, 1966, p. 12.

2 For a short account of some definitional heavy weather see W. G. Runciman, Social Science and Political Theory, Cambridge University Press, 1965, ch. 2.

3 See in particular Mario Bunge's vividly written Causality: the Place of the Causal Principle in Modern Science, Harvard University Press, 1959.

4 M. E. Spiro's 'Religion: problems of definition and explanation', in M. Banton (ed.), Anthropological Approaches to the Study of Religion, ASA Monographs 3, Tavistock, 1963.

5 H. M. Blalock, Causal Inferences in Nonexperimental Research, University of North Carolina, 1964, p. 38.

6 Bunge, op. cit., p. 91.

7 F. Waisman, 'The decline and fall of causality', in Crombie (ed.), Turning Points in Physics, Amsterdam, 1959, p. 100.

8 Bunge, op. cit., p. 97.

9 Robert D. Putnam, 'Toward explaining military intervention in Latin American politics', World Politics, 20, 1967.

10 This does not mean that 89 per cent of the variability on one index can be predicted in the linear model of the relationship from our knowledge of variability on the other. We get an indication of the quality of the 'prediction' that can be made in either direction from the square of the correlation coefficient, r^2.

11 Putnam, op. cit., p. 97.

12 H. D. Forbes and E. Tufte, 'A note of caution in causal modelling', American Political Science Review, 62, December, 1968.

13 Edward R. Tufte, 'Improving data analysis in political science', World Politics, 21, 1969.

14 Adam Przeworski and Henry Teune, The Logic of Comparative Social Inquiry, Wiley, 1970, p. 30.

15 There are confusions of terminology in this literature, e.g. the more general 'determinants', and 'cause' as it is used in Blalock's exposition. For an instance of causal path analysis here, see Marion R. Just, 'Causal models of voter rationality, Great Britain 1959 and 1963', Political Studies, 21 March, 1973.

16 E. R. Leach, 'An anthropologist's reflections on a social survey', Ceylon Journal of History and Social Studies, 1, no. 1, 1958. This is a review article of a socio-economic study of fifty-eight villages in one region in Ceylon, N. K. Sarkar and S. J. Tambiah, The Disintegrating Village, Colombo, 1957.

17 Leach, 'An anthropologist's reflections', p. 79

18 Ibid.

19 Alasdair MacIntyre, Against the Self Images of the Age, Schocken, 1971. Ch. 18, 'The antecedents of action'.

20 Peter Winch, The Idea of a Social Science, Routledge & Kegan Paul, 1958. There is an extract from this book in Rationality, Bryan R. Wilson (ed.), Blackwell, 1970. There have been several rejoinders. See in particular Ernest Gellner, 'The entry of the philosophers', ch. 5 in Cause and Meaning in the Social Sciences, Routledge & Kegan Paul, 1973.

21 Edwin Ardener, 'The new anthropology and its critics', Man, 6, 1971.

22 See Manning Nash, Primitive and Peasant Economic Systems, Chandler, 1966.

23 H. Leibenstein, 'What can we expect from a theory of development', Kyklos, 19, 1966.

24 For an introduction to this body of literature, see R. W. Fogel, 'The new economic history', Economic History Review, 19, December, 1966.

25 R. W. Fogel, Railroads and American Economic Growth, Johns Hopkins, 1964.

26 T. S. Eliot, 'Burnt Norton', Four Quartets, Faber & Faber, 1944.

27 There are illuminating comments on indeterminacy in physics in Waisman's essay, op. cit.

28 M. Gluckman, 'The tribal area in South and Central Africa', in L. Kuper and M. G. Smith (ed.), Pluralism in Africa, University of California Press, 1969, p. 405.

29 Arthur Marwick, The Nature of History, Macmillan, 1970, p. 106.

30 For example, see Gordon Leff, History and Social Theory, Merlin, 1969, who describes the social science orientation in terms of a strong commitment to the discovery of laws, general and covering. But see in particular The Political Sciences, Routledge & Kegan Paul, 1969, by the historian Hugh Stretton, for an illuminating, if loaded, analysis of the work of some social scientists, together with

the review article by Colin Leys, 'Social science, natural science, and history', Journal of Commonwealth Political Studies, 9, no. 1, March, 1971.

31   Ibid., p. 60.
32   W. B. Gallie, Philosophy and Historical Understanding, Schocken, 1964.
33   Rolf Gruner, 'Mandelbaum on historical narrative; a discussion', History and Theory, 8, 1969.
34   R. Ely, 'Mandelbaum on historical narrative; a discussion', History and Theory, 8, 1969.
35   R. Dray, 'Mandelbaum on historical narrative: a discussion', History and Theory, 8, 1969.
36   Frederick A. Olafson, 'Narrative history and the concept of action', History and Theory, 9, 1970.
37   Leff, op. cit., ch. 5, 'Evaluation', and Stretton, op. cit., passim.
38   This is the theme of Gunnell's article. See ch. 1, note 4.
39   For a critical analysis of Weber's theory, see Martin Albrow, Bureaucracy, Macmillan, 1970, chs. 2 and 3.
40   On the categories of Representation and Participation, see Hanna F. Pitkin, The Concept of Representation, University of California Press, 1967; and Carole Pateman, Participation and Democratic Theory, Cambridge University Press, 1970.
41   Fred W. Riggs, Administration in Developing Countries: the Theory of Prismatic Society, Houghton Mifflin, 1964.
42   Fred W. Riggs, Thailand: the Modernization of a Bureaucratic Policy, East-West Center Press, 1966.
43   See A. K. Arora, 'Pre-empted future? Notes on theories of political development', Behavioural Sciences and Community Development, 2, no. 2, September, 1968.

6   RATIONALITY AND STRUCTURE

1   For psychologists, for example, it focuses a critical distinction between human and animal behaviour. See Jonathan Bennett, Rationality, Routledge & Kegan Paul, 1964.
2   E. g. Lukes, Gellner and Beattie in Wilson (ed.), Rationality, Blackwell, 1970.
3   Stephen Lukes, 'Some problems about rationality', in Wilson (ed.), op. cit., ch. 9.
4   Alasdair MacIntyre, Against the Self Images of the Age, Schocken, 1971, ch. 21, 'Rationality and the explanation of action'.
5   In the course of introducing a number of his papers on the sociology of language, Basil Bernstein records that towards the end of the 1950s 'I was very fortunate to meet and enjoy a continuous relation-ship with Dr. Mary Douglas, now Professor of Social Anthropology at University College, London. As a result, the work on family structures, sociolinguistic codes and their wider institutional relationships became focused upon the idea of the variable strength of boundaries and their relationships to the structuring and

realizing of experience. Full circle, apparently back to Durkheim, but if one remembers that power relationships are expressed through boundary relationships, then the Marx, Durkheim, Meadian matrix may well be able to deal with change.' Class, Codes and Control, Routledge & Kegan Paul, 1971, p. 17. The issues extend far beyond the expressive use of imagery in ritual and religion.

6   J. H. M. Beattie, 'On understanding ritual', in Wilson (ed.), op. cit., p. 58.

7   Herbert A. Simon, Administrative Behaviour; a Study of Decision-making Processes in Administrative Organization, Free Press, 1957. Ch. 4, 'Rationality in administrative behaviour'.

8   Ibid., p. 67.

9   For an example, see T. Lowi's analysis of the organizational independence of the American Atomic Energy Commission, in The End of Liberalism, Norton, 1969, pp. 170-4.

10 Simon, op. cit., p. 68.

11 Ibid., p. 77.

12 Anthony Giddens, Capitalism and Modern Social Theory, Cambridge University Press, 1971.

13 There is a substantial literature on the difficulties of answering such questions systematically. See Socialization: the Approach from Social Anthropology, Philip Mayer (ed.), ASA Monographs 8, Tavistock, 1970. It is hard enough establishing the case for cause and effect relationships between particular learning experiences and subsequent behaviour in an inward-looking group such as the Red Xhosa studied by the Mayers (op, cit., p. 159). But socialization studies in more loosely textured societies often make very tenuous connections. See the discussion in W. H. Sewel, 'Social class and childhood personality', Sociometry, 24, 1961.

14 R. L. Kahn et al., Organizational Stress, Wiley, 1964.

15 P. Bohannan, Justice and Judgment among the Tiv, Oxford University Press, 1957, p. 69.

16 M. Gluckman, 'The judicial process among the Barotse', in Bohannan (ed.), Law and Warfare, Natural History Press, 1967.

17 M. Gluckman, Politics, Law and Ritual in Tribal Society, Blackwell, 1967, p. 256.

18 See the methodological paper by J. A. Barnes, 'Networks and political process', in M. Swartz, Local Level Politics, University of London Press, 1967.

19 Burton Benedict, 'Sociological characteristics of small territories', in M. Banton (ed.), The Social Anthropology of Complex Societies, ASA Monographs 4, Tavistock, 1966, p. 25.

20 R. Needham (trans. and ed.), Primitive Classification, E. Durkheim and M. Mauss, Cohen & West, 1963, Introduction, p. xvi.

21 E. Leach, Political Systems of Highland Burma, London School of Economics, 1954, ch. 9, 'Myth as a justification for faction and social change'.

22 Ibid., pp. 203-4.

23 For an example from a different field, John C. Wahlke et al., The Legislative System, Wiley, 1962. The authors draw heavily on

earlier studies, including work by anthropologists, in their
theoretical discussion. But their methods fail to identify roles
in terms of relationships or to relate these to the rationality of
specific sets of legislative choices.

24   E. Gellner, Cause and Meaning in the Social Sciences, Routledge &
Kegan Paul, 1973.

25   L. Fallers, Bantu Bureaucracy, University of Chicago Press, 1965,
or the brief report, 'The predicament of the modern African chief;
an instance from Uganda', American Anthropologist, 57, April,
1955.

26   M. G. Smith, Government in Zazzau, 1800-1950, Oxford University
Press, 1960.

27   M. G. Smith, 'A structural approach to the study of political
change', Mimeo, UCLA, Fall, 1967.

28   Government in Zazzau, p. 322.

29   F. Barth, 'On the study of social change', American Anthropologist,
69, no. 6, December, 1967.

30   M. Levy, 'Patterns (structures) of modernization and political
development', American Academy of Political Science, Annals
35-8, March, 1965.

31   C. S. Whitaker, 'A dysrhythmic process of political change', World
Politics, 19, 1966-7.

32   Andrew Dunsire, Administration: the Word and the Science, Martin
Robertson, 1973, p. 138. This book deals very thoroughly with the
notion of rationality as it has been used by organization theorists.

33   A. G. Frank, Sociology of Development and Underdevelopment of
Sociology, Catalyst, 1971.

34   Raymond Apthorpe, 'Development studies and social planning',
Journal of Development Studies, 6, no. 4, July, 1970.

35   Colin Leys, Politicians and Policies; an Essay on Politics in
Acholi, Uganda 1962-65, East Africa Publishing House, 1967, p. 51.

36   Riggs is a fertile inventor of jargon, quite rightly believing that
many athletic arguments run themselves into the ground simply
by using old names for new and distinctive facts. 'Sala' is his
term for the system of structurally compromised bureaucratic
roles in prismatic society.

37   R. M. Solow, Growth Theory: an Exposition, Oxford University
Press, 1970, p. 105.

38   Nelson Kasfir, 'Prismatic theory and African administration',
World Politics, 21, 1968-9.

39   Fred W. Riggs, Administration in Developing Countries: the Theory
of Prismatic Society, Houghton Mifflin, 1964, pp. 323-5.

7   LEVELS OF THEORY

1   T. W Hutchison, The Significance of Basic Postulates of Economic
Theory, Kelly, 1938 and 1960, ch. 2, 'The propositions of pure theory'.

2   Ernest Nagel, 'Assumptions in economic theory', and comment by
H. Simon and P. Samuelson, American Economic Review, 53, 2, May,

1963 (Papers and Proceedings). For Friedman see p. 225, note 12.

3   A. K. Sen, Choice of Techniques, Kelly, 1968, ch. 4, 'Some doses of realism'.

4   Hutchison, op. cit., pp. 40-6.

5   Sen, op. cit., p. 47.

6   For one consolidated survey of such empirical theory, see the generalizations organized by P. Bauer and B. Yamey, in The Economics of Under-developed Countries, Cambridge University Press, 1957.

7   A. Lowe, On Economic Knowledge, Harper & Row, 1965, p. 5.

8   He refers to S. Schoeffler, The Failures of Economics; a Diagnostic Study, Cambridge, Mass., 1955.

9   For a non-technical account of relevant techniques see Wassily W. Leontief, 'Input-output economics', Scientific American, October, 1951.

10 For a brief review of such attacks on the instrumental logic of economic theory by an economist who is neither dismissive nor unduly defensive, see Assar Lindbeck, The Political Economy of the New Left: an Outsider's View, Harper & Row, 1972.

11 See, for example, D. C. McClelland, The Achieving Society, Van Nostrand-Reinhold, 1961, and E. E. Hagen, On the Theory of Social Change, Homewood, Dorsey, 1962.

12 L. Pospisil, 'The Kapauku individualistic money economy', in LeClair and Schneider (eds), Economic Anthropology, Holt, Rinehart & Winston, 1968.

13 R. F. Salisbury, From Stone to Steel, Cambridge University Press, 1962.

14 A. Johnson, 'Security and risk taking among poor peasants; a Brazilian case', and C. Wharton, 'Risk, uncertainty, and the subsistence farmer; technological innovation and resistance to change in the context of survival' in G. Dalton (ed.), Studies in Economic Anthropology, American Anthropological Association, 1971. George M. Foster, 'Peasant society and the image of limited good', American Anthropologist, 67, 1965.

15 S. Epstein, Capitalism, Primitive and Modern, Manchester University Press, 1968.

16 See L. Joy's analysis of data collected by Barth in Darfur, a mountain massif about 500 miles northwest of the territory of the Nuer. He translates data on particular transactions into a more precise language, in the form of a matrix of a kind used in the analysis of a firm's production possibilities, or in connection with a general equilibrium model of production and exchange. 'An economic homologue of Barth's presentation of economic spheres in Darfur', in Raymond Firth (ed.), Themes in Economic Anthropology, ASA Monographs 6, Tavistock, 1967.

17 'Aristotle discovers the economy', in Karl Polanyi et al., Trade and Market in the Early Empires, Free Press, 1957. Polanyi's romanticization of the organically integrated social structure emerges strongly in his later work, Dahomey and the Slave Trade,

University of Washington, 1966. See Chapter 5, and his discussion
of the gbe, a kinship institution providing mutual aid.

18   Trade and Market, p. 256.
19   Lowe, op. cit., ch. 8, 'Post-classical pure economics', and Ronald
     Frankenburg, 'Economic anthropology', in Raymond Firth (ed.),
     op. cit.
20   Trade and Market, p. 79.
21   'The economy as instituted process', Trade and Market, ch. XIII.
22   B. Malinowski, Argonauts of the Western Pacific, Routledge &
     Kegan Paul, 1922. J. Singh Uberoi, Politics of the Kula Ring,
     Manchester University Press, 1962.
23   Polanyi, Dahomey and the Slave Trade, p. 116. In this case, the Gap
     of Benin created peculiarly benevolent conditions. Air currents
     from the Sudan are deflected southward by the Toto-Atakora chain
     of mountains; there are moderate rains, and the harmattan serves
     as a trade wind. The climatic advantage was the basis for a local
     surplus of food, supporting the slave rush, and the bureaucracy
     and military administration of a port of trade. The most that can
     be said is that in the absence of certain preconditions it will not
     be possible for particular structures to develop.
24   See Part 1 of LeClair and Schneider (eds), op. cit.
25   M. Nash, Machine Age Mayas, University of Chicago Press, 1967.
     Nash contrasts the community of Cantel in Guatemala with the
     representative African situation in which money wages and in-
     dustrial work have entailed the separation of the wage worker
     from his village and its sanctions and social controls. But see
     also W. Watson, Tribal Cohesion in a Money Economy, Manchester
     University Press, 1958, which qualifies the generalization as it
     applies to Africa.
26   A. G. Hopkins, An Economic History of West Africa, Longmans,
     1973, ch. 2, 'The domestic economy: structure and function'.
27   L. Dumont, Homo Hierarchicus: the Caste System and its Implica-
     tions, Weidenfeld & Nicolson, 1970, p. 107.
28   Marshall D. Sahlins, 'On the sociology of primitive exchange', in
     M. Banton (ed.), The Relevance of Models for Social Anthropology,
     ASA Monographs 1, Tavistock, 1965.
29   Richard M. Titmuss, The Gift Relationship, Allen & Unwin, 1970.
     Reprinted by Penguin, 1973.
30   Ibid., p. 239.
31   Ibid.
32   Gellner refers to the 'vicious kind of abstraction' which was the
     serious methodological weakness of the evolutionists in the early
     days of anthropology. 'It amounted to a tendency to seek causal
     connections at too high a level. Evolutionism was concerned with
     the Great Path.' Cause and Meaning in the Social Services,
     Routledge & Kegan Paul, 1973, p. 115. A similar point could be
     made about the implicit assumptions about historical change in
     many typological theories.
33   See the papers in R. Firth and B. S. Yamey (eds), Capital, Saving and
     Credit in Peasant Societies, Allen & Unwin, 1964.

34   Salisbury, op. cit., p. 171.

35   F. G. Bailey, ch. 6, in Firth and Yamey (eds), op. cit.

36   Simon and Phoebe Ottenberg, 'Afikpo markets 1900-1960', and Claude Meillassoux, 'Social and economic factors affecting markets in Guro Land', in P. Bohannan and G. E. Dalton (eds), Markets in Africa, Northwestern University Press, 1962.

37   Paul Bohannan, 'Some principles of exchange and investment among the Tiv', in LeClair and Schneider (eds), op. cit.

38   Clifford Geertz, Peddlers and Princes, University of Chicago Press, 1963.

39   See Peter Marris and Anthony Somerset, African Businessmen, Routledge & Kegan Paul, 1971 and Peter Marris, 'The social barriers to African entrepreneurship', Journal of Development Studies, 5, no. 1, October, 1968.

40   Balandier comments on his analysis of the impact of a modern economy on the Bakongo peoples; '[Ces remarques] montrent la complexité des inter-relations et les contradictions qui se renforcent, ou naissent, au cours du procès de développement économique et de modernisation. Elles suggèrent la force d'inertie de·certains modèles de rapport sociaux et de comporte-ments (veritable armature du système traditionnel) et, à l'inverse, la plasticité d'institutions que se trouvent formellement maintenues mais changent de contenue et de fonction. ' G. Balandier, Struc-tures sociales traditionelles et changements économiques, Re-publications Paulet, May, 1968.

41   Hamza Alavi, 'The rural elite and agricultural development in Pakistan', in Rural Development in Bangladesh and Pakistan, Michigan State University Press (forthcoming). Studies with a comparable perspective are: Colin Leys, 'Politics in Kenya: the development of peasant society', British Journal of Political Science, 1, 1970; in the context of urbanization, the papers collected in R. Sandbrook and R. Cohen (eds), Towards an African Working Class; Studies in Class Formation and Action, Toronto University Press, 1974.

42   For a general expression of this orientation see the essays by J. Barrington Moore, Jr in Reflections on the Causes of Human Misery, Allen Lane, 1973.

43   See in particular Joan Robinson, An Essay on Marxian Economics, Macmillan, 1942.

44   'I hope that it will become clear... that no point of substance in Marx's argument depends upon the labour theory of value. Voltaire remarked that it is possible to kill a flock of sheep by witchcraft if you give them plenty of arsenic at the same time. The sheep, in this figure, may well stand for the complacent apologists of capitalism; Marx's penetrating insight and bitter hatred of oppres-sion supply the arsenic, while the labour theory of value provides the incantations.'[1] Ibid., p. 27.

45   E. P. Thompson, 'The peculiarities of the English', in R. Miliband and J. Saville (eds), Socialist Register, Merlin, 1965.

8   THEORIES AND EXPLANATIONS

1   W. Riker, 'Some ambiguities in the notion of power', American Political Science Review, June, 1964.

2   Goran Hyden and Colin Leys, 'Elections and politics in single-party systems: the case of Kenya and Tanzania', British Journal of Political Science, 2, 1972. They severely criticize the general theory in terms of which some political scientists have explained the empirical generalizations of the aggregate and survey studies of elections. Particularly offensive to their demand for a broad contextual analysis is the reduction of the political system to a destructured systems model of the type proposed in bulky contributions by David Easton. This reduces the political process to the most abstract elements of a homeostatic system (inputs, outputs, feedbacks, environmental factors, etc.). Voting finds itself explained as an input of 'support', validating the continuation of the system, since the surveys demonstrate the relative insignificance of an informed and 'rational demand' function in recent elections. For a compact but uncritical summary of Easton's general theory, see Morton R. Davies and Vaughan A. Lewis, Models of Political Systems, Macmillan, 1971, ch. 5, 'David Easton's Analysis',

3   Bernard S. Cohn, 'Structural change in rural society', in R. Frykenberg (ed.), Land Control and Social Structure in Indian History, University of Wisconsin, 1969.

4   Bernard S. Cohn, 'Recruitment of elites in British India', in Plotnicov and A. Tuden (eds), Essays in Comparative Social Stratification, Pittsburgh, 1970.

5   Hamza Alavi, 'Peasant classes and primordial loyalties', Journal of Peasant Studies, 1, no. 1, October, 1973. This particular confrontation in contemporary social theory crops up in very different areas: in critiques of phenomenological approaches to the sociology of deviance, for instance.

6   Engles to Joseph Bloch, September 21-2, 1890. Quoted in Lewis P. Feuer (ed.), Marx and Engels, Basic Writings on Politics and Philosophy, Doubleday, 1959, p. 397.

7   E. P. Thompson, 'An open letter to Leszek Kolakowski', in R. Miliband and J. Saville (eds), Socialist Register, Merlin, 1974.

8   Self-confirming prior assumptions in this area have been analysed by Caroline Hutton and Robin Cohen, 'African peasants and resistance to change: a reconsideration of sociological approaches', A. Barnet, D. Booth, I. Oxaal (eds), Beyond the Sociology of Development, Routledge & Kegan Paul, 1975

9   Writing in another context, and bristling at what he sees as doctrinaire and unhistorical interpretations of the basic assumptions, the Marxist historian Genovese observes that: 'there is no excuse for identifying the economic origins of a social class with the developing nature of that class, which necessarily embraces the full range of its human experience in its manifold political, social, economic and cultural manifestations. That the economic interest of a particular class will necessarily prove more important

to its specific behaviour than, say, its religious values, is an
ahistorical and therefore unMarxian assumption. Since those
values are conditioned only originally and broadly by the economy,
and since they develop according to their own inner logic and
in conflict with other such values, as well as according to social
changes, an economic interpretation of religion can at best serve
as a first approximation and might even prove largely useless.'
E. Genovese, 'Marxian interpretations of the slave south', ch. 15
of In Red and Black, Vintage Books, 1972.

10   'Kinship in West Punjab villages', Contributions to Indian Sociology,
T. N. Maden (ed.), New Series, 6, Delhi, 1972.

11   He cites among others, Ralph W. Nicholas, 'Factions—a comparative
analysis', in M. Banton (ed.), Political Systems and the Distribution
of Power, ASA Monographs 2, Tavistock, 1965; F. G. Bailey,
Stratagems and Spoils, Oxford University Press, 1969. He refers
also to Geertz's discussion of alirans, the factions developed in
Javanese politics. See 'Peasant classes and primordial loyalties',
op. cit.

12   The structural importance of inertia, ignorance and confusion in
the relations between leaders engaged in forming coalitions within
the political institutions and their dependent followings is made
very clear by T. V. Sathyamurthy, 'The Dravida Munnetra Kashagam
in the politics of Tamil Nadu; 1949-1971', Mimeo Paper presented
at the Centre of South Asian Studies, School of Oriental and
African Studies, University of London, January, 1974.

13   J. M. Brown, Gandhi's Rise to Power, Cambridge University Press,
1972, p. 122.

14   'To trace the progress of the Patidars is to uncover one of the
success stories of modernizing India; they were unfailing oppor-
tunists, a group who responded eagerly to every change in their
environment. ... Whereas in the early nineteenth century they
were locally ranked as Sudras, they now stood with the Vanias
in ritual status, and reinforced their economic success with those
signs of ritual purity, like the prohibition of widow marriages,
essential to a caste claiming high status.' Ibid., p. 88.

15   Or, more aptly perhaps, to the Sanusi of Cyrenaica, also studied
by Evans-Pritchard. Part of a world-wide religious movement,
not connected with the lineage segments of Bedouin society,
lodges of the order were established at various geographically
significant locations throughout Cyrenaica, and the Sanusi came
to provide the focus and organization for resistance against the
Turks and Italians. In this study Evans-Pritchard fuses an
historical account and a structural analysis of change. The Sanusi
of Cyrenaica, Oxford University Press, 1949.

16   Erik Erikson, Gandhi's Truth, Faber, 1970.

17   In Hindu society the philosophy of the Varnas provides an elaborate
justification for an organic hierarchy which cannot be dismissed
out of hand as a colossal monument to false consciousness. J. H.
Hutton, Caste in India, Cambridge University Press, 1946; Dumont,
op. cit., but also see the controversy with Dumont in Contributions

to Indian Sociology, T. N. Maden (ed.), New Series, 5, Delhi, 1971.
E. Leach takes a position similar to Dumont in Aspects of Caste
in South India, Ceylon and North-west Pakistan, Cambridge University Press, 1960.

18 Agricultural Involution, University of California, 1970, p. 129.
19 For an interpretation of the attempted communist coup of 1965
by a political scientist writing in the tradition of Parsonian functionalism, see Chalmers Johnson, Revolutionary Change, University
of London Press, 1968, p. 159. This book is a particularly lucid
and interesting development of structural-functional theory, another,
mutually incompatible, frame of reference, though with important
intellectual antecedents in common.
20 David Hume, 'On the Immortality of the Soul', Essay 1X, Essays,
Moral, Political and Literary, 1742.
21 Georges Balandier, The Sociology of Black Africa: Social Dynamics
in Central Africa, Deutsch, 1970. (Originally, Sociologie actuelle
de l'Afrique noire, 1955.)
22 Ibid., p. 472.
23 Mary Douglas, 'Sociologie actuelle de l'Afrique noire, by Georges
Balandier, 1963', Man, 65, 1965.
24 Mary Douglas, 'The Lele—Resistance to Change', in Markets in
Africa, P. Bohannan and G. Dalton (eds), Evanston, 1962.

9   CONCLUSIONS

1 For example, three sharply contrasted general essays: W. G.
Runciman, Social Science and Political Theory, Cambridge University Press, 1962; E. J. Meehan, Explanation in Social Science: a
System Paradigm, Dorsey, 1968; Alan Ryan, The Philosophy of the
Social Sciences, Macmillan, 1970.
2 The Structure of Scientific Revolutions, University of Chicago
Press, 1962, p. 10 (Italics added.)
3 I. Lakatos, 'Falsification and the methodology of scientific research
programmes', in I. Lakatos and A. Musgrave, Criticism and the
Growth of Knowledge, Cambridge University Press, 1970, p. 97.
4 Chapter 8, note 2.
5 J. Robinson and J. Eatwell, An Introduction to Modern Economics,
McGraw-Hill, 1973. M. H. Dobb, Theories of Value and Distribution
since Adam Smith, Cambridge University Press, 1973.
6 T. W. Hutchison, 'The Cambridge version of the history of economics', Occasional Paper No. 19, University of Birmingham, Economics Department, 1974.
7 Francis Bacon, Novum Organum, Book 1, 36.
8 See, for example, R. C. Tucker, Stalin as Revolutionary 1879-1929:
a Study in History and Personality, Norton, 1973.
9 M. Thompson raises the issues in Rubbish: the Implications of
Considering the Unconsidered, Paladin (forthcoming). He includes
an analysis of the complex cycle of prestations involving pig-

giving in the New Guinea Highlands. In this a topological model is used to explain relationships between the level of credit and the pig cycle. It takes account of aspects of credit which are not narrowly economic, and both predicts, in an approximate sense, and accounts for, the sudden collapses of credit that occur in the pig cycle. A non-technical account of the geometry he draws on appears in 'The geometry of catastrophe', by G. Zeeman, Times Literary Supplement, 10 December, 1971. An important paper, which indicates its relevance to biology and suggests other applications, is R. Thom, 'Topological models in biology', Topology, 8, 1969.

10   Thus, recent comparative studies by organization theorists, using correlational and factor analytic techniques, challenge and in one sense test weathered assumptions in the literature. They throw doubt on some normative and empirical claims in Weberian theory. But the links between abstract structural concepts and the specific data collected for statistical analysis are necessarily provisional and speculative. See the series of studies by the team working with D. S. Pugh, 'A conceptual scheme for organization analysis', Administrative Science Quarterly, 8, 1963; 'An approach to the study of bureaucracy', Sociology, 1, 1967; 'Dimensions of organization structure', ASQ, 13, 1968; 'The context of organization structure', and 'An empirical taxonomy of organization structure', ASQ, 14, 1969.

Index